ALSO BY PATRICIA WELLS

Patricia Wells' Trattoria
Simply French
Bistro Cooking
The Food Lover's Guide to France
The Food Lover's Guide to Paris

Patricia Wells at Home in Provence

RECIPES INSPIRED BY HER FARMHOUSE IN FRANCE

Patricia Wells

PHOTOGRAPHS BY ROBERT FRÉSON

SCRIBNER

SCRIBNER
1230 Avenue of the Americas
New York, NY 10020

SCRIBNER and design are
trademarks of Simon & Schuster Inc.

Designed by Margery Cantor
Set in Adobe Garamond and Poetica

Clos Chanteduc label and oak tree linoleum cut by Melanie Reim

Manufactured in the United States of America
1   3   5   7   9   10   8   6   4   2

Library of Congress Cataloging-in-Publication Data
Wells, Patricia.
Patricia Wells at home in Provence : recipes inspired by her farmhouse
in France / Patricia Wells ; photographs by Robert Fréson.
p.   cm.
Includes index.
1. Cookery, French—Provençal style. 2. Cookery—France—Provence. I. Title.
TX719.2.P75W45   1996
641.59449—dc20   96-9371
CIP

ISBN 0-684-81569-9

For my editor Maria Guarnaschelli:
With respect and gratitude
for her immense talents,
true friendship,
and certain touch of genius.

ACKNOWLEDGMENTS

IN ESSENCE, THIS BOOK FORMS A SCRAPBOOK OF THE PLEASURABLE YEARS WE HAVE spent in Provence. The days and nights have been greatly enhanced by the presence of friends, family, neighbors, and merchants who have shared our table and helped create a joyous background for life.

I am most grateful to our friends Rita and Yale Kramer, who discovered Chanteduc for us, and to Maggie and Al Shapiro who for more than ten years have helped turn many ordinary days into extraordinary fêtes. Thank you Johanne Killeen and George Germon, Devon Fredericks and Eli Zabar, Sheila and Julian More, for always being willing to shop, cook, and "faire la fête" at the drop of hat.

Winemakers have played a large role in our lives, beginning with our very own patient and dedicated winemaker, Daniel Combe, and his wife, Chantal. Many restaurateurs have helped expand our knowledge of the region and enhance our enjoyment at the Provençal table: Special thanks to Tina and Guy Julien of La Beaugravière in Mondragon, and to Mireille and Jean-Louis Pons of Le Bistrot du Paradou in Le Paradou.

But most of all, to those who were always present in spirit, our friends in Vaison-la-Romaine. Special thanks to Colette and Jean-Claude Viviani and Colette and Jean-Claude Tricart, who have been with us every step of the way. To our merchant friends: Roland Henny, butcher par excellence, Josiane and Christian Deal of Lou Canestou, Josiane and Corine Meliani of Les Gourmandines, Giuseppino and Serre Giacomo of La Maison des Pâtes Fraîches, Eliane and Aymar Berenger of the Poissonnerie des Voconces, Hervé Poron, our truffle maven from Plantin in Puymeras, and Laurence and Jean-Marc Avias, who have shared much of their knowledge of Provençal lore.

I feel particularly honored and humbled to have had the good fortune to work with photographer Robert Fréson, and thank him not only for his stunning photographs but his friendship as well. Thank you also to his assistant, Vicki Moriarity, who enlivened every photo session.

I want to thank my able assistant, Alexandra Guarnaschelli, for her careful editing and invaluable recipe testing, and to Judy Jones for all her careful recipe attention.

At Scribner, I am most grateful to Carolyn Reidy for her support, Pat Eisemann for her publicity ideas, Susan Moldow, Roz Lippel, Olga Leonardo, fantastic designers Margery Cantor and Jenny Dossin, and John Fontana for the beautiful cover.

My greatest respect and admiration go to my editor, Maria Guarnaschelli, who steered me through yet another opus. And of course, to my dear husband Walter Newton Wells: His talents as all-purpose handyman are second only to his ability to keep us on that golden path to true happiness.

CONTENTS

INTRODUCTION   11

1. PALATE OPENERS & APPETIZERS   19

2. SALADS   53

3. SOUPS   79

4. VEGETABLES   105

5. PASTA   145

6. BREAD   165

7. FISH & SHELLFISH   195

8. POULTRY & GAME   221

9. MEAT   249

10. DESSERTS   275

11. PANTRY   311

INDEX   339

Patricia in her ochre-toned kitchen.

INTRODUCTION

A HOUSE, TRANSFORM ONE'S LIFE? I WOULDN'T HAVE BELIEVED IT. BUT almost from the day we first saw Chanteduc—our eighteenth-century farmhouse in northern Provence—our future was altered forever. Ever since the wooded ten acres on top of a stony hill in Vaison-la-Romaine became ours in 1984, my husband, Walter, and I have looked differently at the world.

Chanteduc—a tumble-down *mas* whose name poetically translates as "song of the owl"—turned what was to have been a Paris interlude into a permanent sejour in France. And what was to have been a weekend house became a home, a lifestyle, an obsession, an extension of our very personalities.

Almost before we'd unpacked our bags in Provence, we had more French friends than we had made in all our time in Paris. Within a year, we could no longer even remember life before Provence. For us, it symbolized all the essential elements of happiness we sought in life—friends, family, food, and feasts. It opened our eyes, our ears, our sensibilities to the rituals of French daily life in the countryside. Before, we had only read about this life, and finally we were witnesses, participants; we were making it happen. Was it just the sun, or did this place have a magic way of magnifying ordinary pleasures?

Before long, we could not go to town for a morsel of goat cheese or a sack of nails without the errand turning into a social event. Conversation is central to a Provençal's life: so there was always talk of the sun (or lack of it); talk of the raging local wind known as the mistral, talk of the tourists (or lack of them); talk of the latest scandal or outrage in faraway Paris.

Weather—be it sunshine, rain, or drought—became a preoccupation, for whatever happened in the sky affected our day, our garden, our crops, and the moods of the farmers and merchants around us. When the half-dozen gnarled old cherry trees in the orchard began to bear fruit, we dropped everything to pick the shiny, purple-red fruits and set about putting that bounty to work, making clafoutis, ice creams, confitures, and homemade liqueurs. The unfurling of every leaf—lettuce, grapes, figs, and irises—became the object of our weekly attention. We eagerly turned our attention to a fledgling vegetable garden, only to find that about all this parched, chalky soil could promise were vegetables that tasted of struggle. The growth of nearly every olive in our small grove of trees was followed throughout the season, though more than once we arrived at harvest time to find the trees picked nearly bare by passersby. Thankfully, the village farmer's market is overflowing with baskets of ripe, uncured olives at Christmas time, so my home-cured olives are generally of mixed origins!

We learned about spotting the property's edible wild mushrooms, but only after years of listening to the neighbors boast of discoveries on our land. An invitation to join us for a hunt, with the promise of a multimushroom feast to follow, was the key to uncovering the secret gardens hidden amid the pines. We also learned about unearthing the rare black truffles that hid beneath the soil of our vines, not far from the rows of scrub oak that enclosed the vineyards, but knew secretly that, most years, the poachers' bounty far exceeded our meager findings.

And sometimes we came closer to certain flora and fauna than one would desire. We've fled wild boar at the compost pile, chased wild pheasant and quail in the vegetable garden, and know more about the night habits of the *loir*—a squirrel-like rodent that loves the proximity of humans and their central heating system—than could fill a book.

We had spent most of our adult lives working in cities like Washington, D.C., New York, and Paris, and now, as country folk, we found that our lives were curiously affected by the phases of the moon, the color of the sky, the moistness of the earth, the presence (or lack of) bees, salamanders, rabbits, or butterflies. Soon, like all the locals, we followed the rhythms of the moon, learning that if we planted parsley just after the new moon, the herb would flourish, and if we picked flowers with the full moon, they would last longer.

From the very beginning, Walter and I did not seem to know that Chanteduc was a place where we could be alone. Each weekend every guest room was filled to overflowing. At table, we were always eight, or ten, or even twenty. The guest list was often unconventional, as we routinely gathered the local mayor, the plumber, winemaker, our banker, and the neighborhood poacher for long festive meals beneath the giant oak tree, with lively games of *boules* along the vineyard path afterward.

We found that friendships flourished and were deepened by those long hours at table together, in a way that a single dinner in the city simply cannot. It was amazing how well total strangers got along under a warm and friendly roof. Soon my habit of cooking simple, two-course meals for Walter and myself was transformed into creating multicourse feasts for the masses.

To many local residents, I am sure that we were exotic, if not downright bizarre. We were those crazy Americans from Paris who zipped down on the fast train nearly every weekend to plant espaliered pear trees, make friends with the local fig tree expert, and wade through the French bureaucracy to take responsibility for the six-acre vineyard, which we christened Clos Chanteduc. For the wine label, we adopted the property's mammoth, life-giving oak tree as our family "crest." Soon we found an organic farmer to tend the vines and transform our six acres of Grenache, Mourvèdre, and Syrah grapes into a peppery, spicy, easygoing red wine with Chanteduc's personality, one that we would be proud to drink every day.

In the village at the bottom of our hill, a cast of characters awaited our discovery: Roland Henny, the genial, ever whistling butcher, who often kidnaps me when I go to town, dragging me upstairs to his "atelier" to jot down a new recipe, or insisting that I drive with him to a catering sight to examine his handiwork; our lively plumber, Jean-Claude Viviani (better known as Vivi), who taught me how to prepare the local baby snails (*petit gris*) and scours the region for kitchen paraphernalia he knows I'll love; Christian and Josiane Deal, our cheese merchants, who have instructed me on the proper way to open a chestnut-leaf-wrapped Banon, and how to select a perfectly ripe Saint-Marcellin. And our own homegrown poacher, Yves Reynaud, who grew up on the property and once presented me with a pair of wild rabbits and two fresh truffles before nine in the morning!

As time went on, I realized that this farm had existed for centuries before us and would thrive for centuries after our deaths. That meant we would affect its existence for thirty, maybe forty years at most. We decided that we had a serious responsibility to maintain its integrity, carry on its strong, life-enhancing qualities.

As I began to ask questions about Chanteduc's past I found some answers in the dusty, faded packet of previous sales agreements that had been passed down from owner to owner, all within the same family. From these fragile, tissuelike pages written in flowery script, these *actes de ventes* told Chanteduc's history for the past 125 years. In 1868, as it was passed on (by sale, not inheritance) from Joseph Reynaud to his children Joseph-Charles-Emmanuel, Pierre-Louis-Charles, and Josephine-Rose-Thérèse, the property was largely planted in gnarled olive trees, the source of the wrinkled black *olives de Nyons,* the main crop in the region. (At that time, extensive fields of vines were all but nonexistent.) Even the sun played a role in the description of property limits then, with eastern boundaries noted as *levant* (rising sun) and western boundaries as *couchant* (setting sun). In 1906, when Joseph and Marie-Marguerite Reynaud passed Chanteduc on to their children, Jean-Joseph and Marie-Elizabeth-Angèle, they held on to lifetime rights to pick olives, gather wood from the forest and water from the wells for their personal use! (We also laugh when we read, that with each sale, the property was described as being in a *"très mauvais état,"* or very bad shape.)

The last farmers on the property—Léon Reynaud and his wife Victorine Josephine Février—took possession of the property in 1944. Olives and apricots were still the favored crops of the region, but several severe freezes in the 1950s killed back the olive trees. The trees would eventually come back from their roots, but would not become productive for years. So, like many other farmers in the region, the Reynauds pulled up the olive trees and replaced them with the Grenache vines that make up the bulk of our crop today. Quickly I realized that there is no more direct way to understand the agricultural heritage of a region than to live it firsthand.

Today, the vestiges of the Reynauds' subsistence farm life remain: the rabbit hutch, the mule stalls, a wine vat, remnants of an earlier bread oven, the pigeonnier, the hay barn, and a tiny stone house used as a blind for hunting wild birds. It cheers me to know that Victorine was famous for her rich gamy stew (*salmi de pigeon*), raised her own goats and trekked down the hill to sell rounds of her tangy fresh goat's cheese—*tomme fraîche*—in the streets of the medieval village.

As we look back now at our twelve years there, we realize that we did not have a master plan but we had a passion, and we had dreams. We nurtured those enthusiasms and visions season by season, visit after visit. As we formed the character of the house, it formed ours. Soon the house became a scrapbook of our life together, of our life in France. It was as though we looked up one day and soon the results of all our polishing, nesting, nurturing, planning, and scheming had turned a paradise into a private universe. I have never believed that a house had a soul or could give off "vibrations," but we quickly found that it was difficult to be unhappy at Chanteduc.

I have always had a love affair with bread, and after touring community wood-fired bread ovens all over France, I was determined to someday tuck a round of sourdough into my own oven. A chance conversation with our young mason, Jean-Claude Tricart, turned that into a reality, and soon our courtyard sported a domed, bricklined oven to which we added a sandstone door that had been discarded from a long-defunct bread oven on the property.

Eventually I realized I had my own living food encyclopedia just beyond the courtyard door. When I needed to know the true life of an olive, the exact shade of a fig leaf, the manner in which apricots inform you that they're ripe (they simply fall from the tree), the time it takes a cherry to go from blossom to ripe fruit (six weeks), I didn't turn to my library, but visited the property in search of the answer. One day I found myself giving friends a tour of the land, pointing out an outbuilding, and explaining, "When this was a working farm. . . ." I stopped myself, realizing, that it *is* a working farm.

And of course, over time, my cooking changed. What a treat and a luxury to always have a house full of guests eager to sample any cuisine I put on the table! Almost every recipe for my last four books was tested and retested here. One season it was food from the French farms, then country bistros. We ate our way through the elegant cuisine of Joël Robuchon and devoured the rustic fare of Italian trattorias. My guests, mostly French, American, and British, quickly learned to anticipate the unexpected, sometimes looking up from their plates wondering what chapter from which book we were on now. The most comical response came the day I was working on *The Food Lover's Guide to France* and served a mix of French fare from Brittany, the Loire, Alsace, and Provence at the same meal. A French guest—looking as though a lightbulb had just gone off in her head—exclaimed, "Now I understand. You're serving us California cuisine!"

Naturally, and unself-consciously, I began to develop a style of cooking that I could call my own. It's a method that clearly reflects my philosophy of cuisine: Keep it fresh, keep it simple, respect the seasons, and allow the integrity of an ingredient to shine through. Follow the elementary rule, "What grows together goes together," meaning the lamb that grazes in fields of wild herbs will naturally taste best enhanced with local rosemary, thyme, and summer savory. The rabbits from the land love wild fennel, so why not put them together? The basil plants that grow between my rows of tomatoes are perfect partners, as are the artichokes and fava beans that grow in symbiotic bliss.

My cuisine is a cuisine of *whole* foods, meaning I prefer to roast a fish whole—head, bones, skin, and all—to extract maximum flavor, to take advantage of the gelatins, the texture, its freshness. Leg of lamb is never boned but simply roasted. Poultry is almost always cooked whole, carefully trussed, so that its character and flavor remain intact. Desserts—most often fruit tarts or cakes—follow the seasons, from the first cherries in late May to the last fig in early October, and on to the final grapes left on the vines in November.

Here, then, is my cuisine, one that's accessible, created for the way we eat and want to live today. By natural evolution, it's mainly a Provençal cuisine, with extra-virgin olive oil as the fat of choice, with menus that follow what is in the market and what is in season. Home-cured olives, homemade aperitif, multigreen salads, homemade breads filled with grains and seeds, bountiful platters of regional goat, sheep, and cow's milk cheeses are present at almost every meal. Quite naturally, they've become my trademark at table, and I hope they, too, will become yours.

PATRICIA WELLS
Chanteduc
April 1996

PATRICIA WELLS AT HOME IN PROVENCE

I often wish that Chanteduc could speak, and tell tales of centuries of the labor, love, storms, renovations, celebrations, and happiness it has witnessed over the centuries.

1

PALATE OPENERS
& APPETIZERS

A T CHANTEDUC, THE APERITIF HOUR SIGNALS the end of the work day, the beginning of the play day. Whether it's a lively session with the mason to work out the design on a new bread oven, a social gathering with the winemaker and his wife, or simply a time to catch up on events with neighbors or visiting guests, the end of the day is synonymous with the cocktail hour, the sunset hour. It's then that bottles of anise-flavored pastis and homemade liqueurs, bowls of home-cured olives, thin slices of local black-olive-stuffed sausages, tapenade, and varied cheese spreads are brought out to the sunset terrace, to begin the evening's relaxation in earnest. The following are some of my favorite palate openers, ranging from the simple Smoked Trout Tartare to the elegant Curried Zucchini Blossoms, food designed to assuage hunger as well as stimulate the appetite for what's to come.

ANNE'S GOAT CHEESE GRATIN

Anne McCrae is a Scottish neighbor in Provence who shares my love of simple, big tastes. She served this luscious gratin one spring evening and explained that she devised the recipe when she and her husband, John, lived in an isolated part of northern Provence, in the Drôme. There were no fresh-produce markets nearby, but thanks to neighboring farmers she always had plenty of fresh goat's milk cheese—known as *tomme*. Her larder was always filled with the meaty black olives from nearby Nyons, and wild herbs were as near as the back door. In summer months Anne prepares the sizzling, fragrant first course with fresh tomatoes, and in the winter months she uses canned tomatoes. That evening she served the gratin in individual gratin dishes, but I suggested it might be easier to make one huge gratin and pass it around. "I used to do that," she countered, "but people got greedy and never left enough for the other guests!" So controlled portions it is! This dish lends itself to endless variations: Think of it simply as a pizza without the crust. Add julienned bits of prosciutto, a bit of cooked sausage, sautéed mushrooms, or marinated artichokes. It's also a convenient dish when you're alone and want something warm and quick. I always add fresh hyssop, for the Provençal herb's pungent, mintlike flavor blends well with the tomato-cheese-olive trinity.

EQUIPMENT: Six shallow 6-inch (15-cm) round gratin dishes or one 10½-inch (27-cm) round baking dish

About 10 ounces (300 g) soft goat cheese or a mix of rindless soft goat and cow or sheep's milk cheese, cubed
2 teaspoons minced fresh hyssop leaves (optional)
2 teaspoons minced fresh rosemary leaves
2 teaspoons minced fresh oregano leaves or a pinch of dried leaf oregano, crushed
1½ to 2 cups (33 to 50 cl) homemade Tomato Sauce (page 325), at room temperature
About 24 best-quality black olives (such as French Nyons), pitted

1. Preheat the broiler.
2. Scatter the cheese on the bottom of the baking dish or dishes. Sprinkle with half of the herbs. Spoon on just enough tomato sauce to evenly coat the cheese. Sprinkle with olives and the remaining herbs.
3. Place the baking dish or dishes under the broiler about 3 inches (8 cm) from the heat. Broil until the cheese is melted and fragrant, and the tomato sauce is sizzling, 2 to 3 minutes.

SIX SERVINGS

WINE SUGGESTION: Think of what you'd normally serve with pizza; a pleasant, vigorous red such as a young French Corbières from the Roussillon, a dry Italian red such as a Barbera d'Alba, an Australian Shiraz, or a California Zinfandel.

SMOKED TROUT TARTARE

Not far from our village in Provence there's a trout farm begun centuries ago in the town of Suze-la-Rousse. The farm smokes its own salmon trout, curing it lightly with the local olive oil. I always have the delicacy on hand and love to serve it plain on rounds of homemade toast topped with nothing but snippets of dill from my garden. I also prepare it "tartare style," that is, hand-chopped bits tossed with crème fraîche and dill. The dish is easy to prepare and requires nothing more than a sharp knife and a clean cutting board. (Do not attempt it in the food processor; even if you are careful, the mixture turns mushy. Hand chopping brings out the quality and flavor of the fish that tends to be masked in the food processor.) Usually, no salt is necessary since the smoking process imparts a pungency of its own.

This makes a great appetizer served either with drinks in the living room or individually plated and served before the first course. Accompany with slices of toasted bread or with *Pompe à l'Huile:* Provençal Olive Oil Brioche (page 167) prepared with added fennel seeds.

> About 4 ounces (125 g) thinly sliced smoked trout or smoked salmon
> 2 tablespoons heavy cream
> 2 tablespoons fresh dill or fennel fronds, snipped with a scissors

1. Trim any unwanted bits and ends from the fish. Lay each slice flat on a cutting board and cut into thin, matchstick-size strips, keeping the strips evenly aligned. Cut crosswise into tiny cubes of fish about the size of the fat end of a pencil. (You want a kind of elegantly chunky, not a mashed, tartare.) Toss with the cream and dill.
2. Serve on chilled salad plates with tiny mounds of dressed herbs or lettuce alongside. If desired, garnish with additional fennel or dill. Or serve atop slices of freshly toasted bread, such as the variation of *Pompe à l'Huile* prepared with added fennel seeds.

ABOUT ONE CUP (25 CL) OR FOUR SERVINGS

WINE SUGGESTIONS: A dry white wine goes nicely with this smoked tartare. Try a fresh and fragrant French Sancerre, an oak-aged California or New Zealand Fumé Blanc, or a California or French Riesling.

HERB-CURED FILET OF BEEF: CARPACCIO

This is a fabulous preparation, ideal for those who love the qualities of a classic carpaccio but look for more herbal flavors in their food. Quite simply, a filet of beef is marinated for forty-eight hours in a mixture of sea salt, tarragon, parsley, basil, and thyme, then sliced very thin, carpaccio-style. The herbs permeate the beef, making for a lively, delicious warm-weather appetizer. Note that the herbs need not be stemmed here since they are used simply to flavor the beef and will not be consumed.

> 8 sprigs of fresh tarragon, rinsed and dried
> 8 sprigs of fresh parsley, rinsed and dried
> 8 sprigs of fresh basil, rinsed and dried
> 10 sprigs of fresh thyme, rinsed and dried
> 1½ tablespoons coarse sea salt
> 1-pound (500-g) filet of beef, rinsed and patted dry

1. On a piece of aluminum foil large enough to wrap the beef, place half the herbs in a single bed. Sprinkle with half the salt. Place the beef on top of the herbs. Add the rest of the herbs and the salt on top of the beef. Wrap securely in the foil and place on a large plate to catch any juices that might run from the beef. Refrigerate for 48 hours.

2. Two hours before serving the beef, transfer to the freezer to firm it up and to make slicing easier. Unwrap the beef. With the tip of a knife, brush aside the herbs and salt. With a very sharp knife or an electric slicer, cut the beef as thinly as possible.

3. Serve as you would any carpaccio, with thin slices overlapping on a chilled salad plate, drizzled with olive oil and plenty of coarsely ground black pepper. For a wholesome salad, drape slices of cured beef over dressed arugula, then drizzle with oil and garnish with Parmesan shavings. (I find that the beef stays perky and fresh for three days more. If any is left over, chop it finely, form into patties, and fry it up as a luxury hamburger.)

TWENTY SERVINGS

🌳 **WINE SUGGESTIONS:** A good choice would be a red Sancerre, a Tavel rosé, or—if you can find a bottle—a Ladoix-Serrigny from northern Burgundy, a wine that marries remarkably well with the flavors of rare or raw meat.

LOU CANESTÉOU'S CHEESE CHIPS

These cheese chips make an ideal appetizer—the richness and the saltiness stimulate the palate, as all good appetizers must. I prepare these with the firm Provençal sheep's milk cheese I buy at our village cheese shop, Lou Canestéou. The earthy, buttery cheese (which resembles sheep's milk cheese from the Basque region of France) melts beautifully and rewards the palate with a tangy richness. You will have greater success if the cheese is grated while cold so that the cheese does not clump up or stick to the bowl.

> 4 ounces (125 g) imported French sheep's milk cheese or Dutch Gouda or Monterey Jack cheese, rind removed

1. Preheat the broiler.
2. With a hand grater, grate the cheese into a small bowl.
3. With your fingers, sprinkle 1 tablespoon of grated cheese into a 2-inch (5-cm) round (metal cookie cutter) onto a cold nonstick baking sheet. Take care to spread the cheese out as thin as possible so that it cooks evenly. Leave enough space between rounds to allow the cheese to spread out as it cooks.
4. Place the baking sheet under the broiler about 3 inches (8 cm) from the heat. Keeping the oven door slightly ajar, watch the cheese very carefully as it bubbles, turns lacy, and browns slightly, 1 to 2 minutes. When the bubbling subsides, the baking sheet can be removed from the oven. If some of the chips are not fully cooked on the edges, rotate the pan and keep them under the heat until they are done. (If making chips in batches, take care that the baking sheet is cooled before preparing the next batch.)
5. Remove the baking sheet from the oven and allow the chips to cool and firm up, 1 to 2 minutes. Using a spatula, carefully transfer the chips to a cooling rack. Serve as appetizers. (The chips can be stored in an airtight container for up to 1 week.)

TWENTY-FIVE TO THIRTY CHIPS

 WINE SUGGESTIONS: The ideal wine here is, of course, a few sips of bubbly pink champagne or try a Clairette de Die from the Drôme.

FACING PHOTOGRAPH: *A selection of local goat and sheep's milk cheese from our fromagerie, Lou Canestéou. Top left box: Square* mascaré, *prepared from a mix of half goat and half sheep's milk and enveloped in dried chestnut leaves; tiny* chèvre au poivre, *pure goat's milk cheese flavored with black peppercorns; the larger* chèvre à la sarriette, *goat's milk cheese flavored with a sprig fresh summer savory; Banon, made with 95 percent goat's milk and 5 percent sheep's milk, wrapped in dried chestnut leaves. To the right is a jar of* chèvre à l'huile, *young goat's milk cheese preserved in olive oil with fresh herbs. Top right box: A selection of local goat's milk cheese flavored with* poivre d'âne, *the Provençal name for peppery summer savory. Middle left box: An assortment of local goat's milk cheese from a farm in nearby Buis-les-Baronnies—one natural and one aged and covered with ash. Middle right box: An assortment of Picodon de Dieulefit, goat's milk cheese ripened with a washing of brine and wine and aged in earthenware pots, giving the cheese a sharp edge. Bottom box: An assortment of goat's milk cheese curds (*chèvre caillé*), draining in antique earthenware molds.*

JR'S SHRIMP WITH BASIL

When I first offered cooking classes at Chanteduc, French chef Joël Robuchon volunteered to inaugurate the school. I would have been a fool to turn him down! He came with an entourage and prepared a feast to remember. I was up at 5 A.M. to fire up the bread oven for his homemade sourdough rolls as well as a guinea hen stuffed with foie gras and set on a bed of potatoes, a recipe worked on together for our book *Simply French.*

The lunch began with sips of cool, bubbly champagne and these delicacies: golden, deep-fried Mediterranean pastry twisted around sea-fresh langoustines and dipped in a vibrant green basil sauce. At home, fresh giant shrimp are a worthy substitute. For a festive and elegant winter touch, the basil leaves wrapped around the shrimp can be replaced by thin slices of fresh black truffles. The truffles do a remarkable job of bringing out the iodine-rich essence of the sea.

> 1 bunch of fresh basil, leaves only, washed and dried
> 1 tablespoon coarse sea salt
> ½ cup (12.5 cl) extra-virgin olive oil
> 2 spring onions, peeled and finely chopped
> Several tablespoons chicken stock (if necessary)
> 12 large shrimp, peeled and deveined
> Fine sea salt and freshly ground white pepper to taste
> About 4 sheets of phyllo dough (cut into twelve 6-inch [15-cm] squares)
> 12 small toothpicks
> 2 quarts (2 l) vegetable oil (peanut or safflower) for deep frying

1. Set aside about 12 leaves of basil for decoration. In a large saucepan, bring 1 quart (1 l) of water to a rolling boil over high heat. Add the coarse sea salt and remaining leaves of basil. Blanch for 2 minutes. Transfer to a fine-mesh sieve and refresh under cold running water to stop further cooking and maintain the rich green color. Drain again. Transfer the leaves to the bowl of a food processor and puree. Set aside.

2. In a medium-size skillet, combine the olive oil and onions, and cook gently over low heat just until softened, 3 to 4 minutes. Add the onions to the basil puree and stir to blend. Set aside. (This can be done several hours in advance.)

3. At serving time, warm the basil puree in the top of a double boiler set over lightly simmering water. If the basil puree is too thick, add a bit of warmed chicken stock to thin it.

4. Season the shrimp with salt and pepper. Place a shrimp at the corner of each square of phyllo. Place a basil leaf on top of the shrimp and roll tightly in the phyllo. Twist the ends in opposite directions to form a bow. Secure by piercing the shrimp in the center of the roll with a toothpick. Repeat for the remaining shrimp. The shrimp should not be rolled in advance.

5. Place the oil in a heavy 3-quart (3-l) saucepan or use a deep-fat fryer. The oil should be at least 2 inches (5 cm) deep. Place a deep-fry thermometer and a wire skimmer in the oil and heat the oil to 320°F (160°C). Add the reserved basil leaves and fry until crisp, 1 to 2 minutes. Remove and transfer to paper towels to drain. Season each side of each leaf with fine sea salt. Set aside.

6. Bring the oil to 375°F (190°C). Fry the shrimp in batches, 3 to 4 at a time, until the pastry is crisp and lightly browned, about 1 minute. Remove and transfer to paper towels to drain.

7. To serve as appetizers, place the shrimp and basil leaves on a large warmed platter. Place the warmed basil puree in a small bowl for dipping. To serve as a first course, place a shrimp on a small, warm plate with a bit of warmed basil puree around it and add a few fried basil leaves for decoration. Serve additional sauce on the side.

TWELVE SERVINGS

 WINE SUGGESTION: Champagne is the ideal accompaniment. For a very festive occasion, try a vintage pink champagne from the house of Billecart-Salmon.

TIP: Ever have a problem with food sticking to the skimmer when you attempt to retrieve fried food? It won't happen if you warm the skimmer as you heat the oil.

CURRIED ZUCCHINI BLOSSOMS

Everyone who has a garden in Provence grows zucchini, and with that versatile green vegetable (which grows from the female portion of the plant) you have the advantage of the showy golden flowers (which sprout from the male portion). The flowers—which grow in Provence from June to early September—are always picked in the early morning while they are still firm and open. At our local farmer's market, farmers sell the home-grown flowers in neat little bundles. One Saturday a farmer offered me a baker's dozen, thirteen. Then he asked if I was superstitious. When I said no, he responded that he was, so he upped the number to fourteen blossoms for the evening's appetizer! The blossoms are extremely delicate and fragile, and should be cooked the day they are picked. Place the stems in a vase of water as soon as possible to keep them fresh and unwilted. If zucchini blossoms are not readily at hand, the same deep-fried delicacies can be prepared with fresh zucchini slices.

This batter—prepared with superfine flour to make sure it is smooth—is lighter than a classic fritter or beignet batter prepared with eggs. The idea was inspired by chef Joël Robuchon, who has a great love for curry powder and its magical ability to stimulate the appetite. The resulting flavor of these deep-fried blossoms is quite haunting, almost a spicy, caramelized, candylike treat. I usually prepare these with guests in the kitchen so they can eat the delicious blossoms as soon as they are cooked.

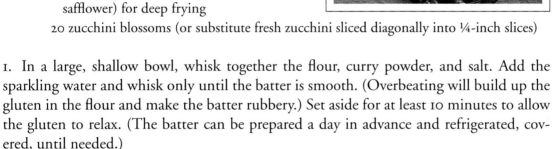

1 cup (140 g) superfine flour, such as Wondra
2 teaspoons curry powder
¼ teaspoon fine sea salt
1 cup (25 cl) sparkling water (club soda or
   mineral water)
2 quarts (2 l) vegetable oil (peanut or
   safflower) for deep frying
20 zucchini blossoms (or substitute fresh zucchini sliced diagonally into ¼-inch slices)

1. In a large, shallow bowl, whisk together the flour, curry powder, and salt. Add the sparkling water and whisk only until the batter is smooth. (Overbeating will build up the gluten in the flour and make the batter rubbery.) Set aside for at least 10 minutes to allow the gluten to relax. (The batter can be prepared a day in advance and refrigerated, covered, until needed.)

2. Place the oil in a heavy 3-quart (3-l) saucepan or use a deep-fat fryer. The oil should be at least 2 inches (5 cm) deep. Place a deep-fry thermometer and a wire skimmer in the oil and heat the oil to 375°F (190°C).

3. With tongs or your fingers, dip each section of the blossom (or zucchini slice) into the batter, rolling the blossoms to coat them evenly. Shake off any excess batter, letting it drip back into the bowl.

4. Carefully lower the blossoms, a few at a time, into the oil. Fry until golden on all sides, turning once, for a total cooking time of about 2 to 3 minutes. Fry only about 6 pieces per batch. (Make sure that the oil returns to 375°F [190°C] before adding each new batch.) With the wire skimmer, lift the blossoms from the oil, drain, and transfer to paper towels.

5. Immediately season each side of each leaf or zucchini slice with sea salt. Serve immediately as an appetizer.

TWENTY APPETIZER SERVINGS

WINE SUGGESTIONS: I enjoy this with champagne (who wouldn't?), a glass of sparkling white Vouvray from the Loire Valley, or a Clairette de Die from the Drôme.

PORQUEROLLES ISLAND TOASTED ALMONDS

One summer while dining on the French Mediterranean island of Porquerolles, we were served a glass of the easygoing local white wine along with a small bowl of these fragrant almonds, toasted with dried and fresh thyme, coarse salt, a touch of olive oil, and a bit of egg white, which helps the thyme cling to the nuts. I instantly added the almonds to my repertoire at Chanteduc, anticipating the day I could make them with a crop from my newly planted almond trees. In the winter time I prepare these just as guests are arriving: The toasted thyme fills the house with a heady aroma that shouts Provence! loud and clear.

4 ounces (125 g) unblanched almonds
2 teaspoons extra-virgin olive oil
1 egg white
1½ teaspoons coarse sea salt
3 teaspoons dried thyme
1 teaspoon fresh thyme, leaves only

1. Preheat the oven to 400°F (200°C; gas mark 6/7).
2. In a large, shallow bowl, combine the almonds, oil, egg white, salt, and dried thyme and toss with your hands to coat the nuts thoroughly. Transfer to a nonstick baking sheet and spread the nuts out in a single layer, so that no two almonds touch. Sprinkle each with fresh thyme leaves.
3. Place in the center of the oven and toast until the nuts are lightly browned and a fragrant aroma of thyme wafts from the oven, about 4 minutes. Remove the baking sheet from the oven. Allow to cool, then break apart any almonds that touch. Remove any excess "crust" formed and discard. The almonds can be stored, well sealed, for up to 2 weeks.

TWELVE APPETIZER SERVINGS

Everything ends this way in France—everything.
Weddings, christenings, duels, burials, swindlings,
diplomatic affairs—everything is a
pretext for a good dinner.

JEAN ANOUILH

SCRUBBED TOAST

So what's the big deal about "scrubbed toast"? Try it and you'll see. This is my favorite version of this Catalan classic, one that depends heavily on superb hearth bread with a thick, appealing crust, truly ripe red tomatoes, and best-quality anchovies. Be sure to begin by rubbing the garlic along the crusty edge to enhance the aroma and flavor.

6 thick slices country bread, preferably homemade
1 plump, fresh garlic clove, peeled and halved
1 large ripe tomato, halved crosswise
12 Salt-Cured Anchovies (page 330) or canned anchovy fillets in olive oil, drained

1. Grill the bread—preferably over an open fire. Alternatively, toast under a broiler or in a toaster. While the bread is still hot, rub one side of each slice with the halved garlic, beginning at the crusty edge and then moving over the rest of the toast. Literally "scrub" the toast with the tomato—cut side toward the bread—rubbing until each slice fully absorbs the tomato juice, and the seeds coat the bread.
2. Place 2 anchovy fillets on each slice and serve immediately. And don't forget the napkins, for at its best the bread should be dripping with the juicy ripeness of tomatoes. Serve as an appetizer or as a quick snack.

SIX SERVINGS

WINE SUGGESTION: This lusty dish calls for your favorite "daily drinking red." Ours is a Côtes du Rhône.

The whole Mediterranean, the sculpture, the palms, the gold beads,
the bearded heroes, the wine, the ideas, the ships, the moonlight,
the winged gorgons, the bronze men, the philosophers—all of it
seems to rise in the sour, pungent taste of these black olives between
the teeth. A taste older than meat, older than wine.
A taste as old as cold water.
LAWRENCE DURRELL

SHEILA & JULIAN'S QUICK FOIE GRAS

Sheila and Julian More are neighbors and good friends in Provence, and we've spent many a happy hour together on their lamp-lit terrace with its panoramic view of the mountains and vineyards that dot their village of Visan. In winter months we move indoors near the fire, where one Christmas night they served an instant version of foie gras cured in salt. The preparation demands much less work than a classic terrine, and the resulting foie gras is uniquely unctuous, smooth, and distinctly elegant. This festive dish should be served as a first course with plenty of freshly grilled toast.

1 fresh duck foie gras (about 1 to 1½ pounds; 500 to 750 g) (see Note)
6 cups (about 1 kg 500 g) coarse salt
Freshly cracked black and white peppercorns to taste
Coarse sea salt to taste (optional)

1. Prepare the foie gras: With a small, sharp knife, gently scrape away any green traces of bile on the exterior of the foie gras. With your hands, separate the 2 lobes. Place the lobes on a large, clean towel. With the knife, scrape off and lift away the clear membrane that covers the outside of the duck liver. Use the point of the knife to guide your fingers into the underside of each lobe in search of the blood vessels that run down the inside. Wherever sinews or vessels are visible, pull gently but firmly to remove them, using your fingers and the point of the knife to go into the foie gras. You may have to poke around a bit to find the vessels, but work slowly and methodically, handling the liver as little as possible. Trim off and discard any visible blood spots or any greenish parts that would turn the foie gras bitter. Slice each lobe lengthwise into equal portions.

2. Pour half of the sea salt into a deep rectangular vessel (such as a roasting pan). Place the pieces of foie gras on the bed of salt side by side in a single layer. Cover with the remaining salt. Set aside at room temperature to cure for 2 hours.

3. Remove the pieces of foie gras from the salt. Gently brush away any excess salt with your fingers. Rinse quickly under cold running water, and pat dry with a clean kitchen towel.

4. To assemble: Place a piece of plastic wrap larger than each piece of foie gras on a flat work surface. Place one of the pieces of foie on the plastic wrap. Using the plastic wrap to help you push, roll the foie up lengthwise, cigar-style, to enclose the foie gras. Gently twist the ends of the plastic to secure and remove any air pockets in the roll. Repeat for the remaining foie gras. Refrigerate until firm, at least 2 hours and up to 6 hours depending on your schedule.

5. To serve: Place the chilled roll of foie gras on a flat work surface. Remove the plastic wrap. With a sharp knife, slice ¾-inch-thick (2 cm) rounds, counting 2 per serving. Place the slices of foie gras on a chilled salad plate and season generously with freshly crushed black and white peppercorns and a fine sprinkling of coarse sea salt, if desired. Serve accompanied by The True Salad Fan's Salad (page 57), a few spoonfuls of Mostarda: Fig & Prune Chutney (page 331), and freshly grilled bread.

EIGHT TO TEN SERVINGS

NOTE: Fresh foie gras can be ordered from D'Artagnan, Inc., 399-419 Saint Paul Avenue, Jersey City, New Jersey 07306. Telephone (201) 792-0748; or fax (201) 792-0113. Ask for Moulard duck foie gras, A prime. The foie gras arrives vacuum-packed in heavy plastic and has about a ten-day shelf life.

Not only are olives and oil omnipresent in Provence, but so are the diverse utensils made from the wood of olive trees: salad tongs, olive picks, salad bowls, and motar and pestles.

Happy is the family which can eat onions together.
They are, for the time being, separate from the world
and have a harmony of aspiration.

CHARLES DUDLEY WARNER

CRUSTLESS ONION QUICHE

This beautifully golden crustless quiche makes a great Sunday night supper in front of the fire, served with a zesty tossed green salad. I've also served it as a sit-down appetizer at a cocktail party, with a glass of chilled white wine.

EQUIPMENT: One 10½-inch (27-cm) round baking dish

Unsalted butter for preparing the tart pan
1 pound (500 g) onions, peeled
3 tablespoons (1½ ounces; 45 g) unsalted butter
1 tablespoon fresh thyme leaves, carefully stemmed
Sea salt and freshly ground black pepper to taste
Freshly grated nutmeg to taste
4 large eggs
¼ cup (60 cl) whole milk
3 tablespoons heavy cream

1. Preheat the oven to 425°F (220°C; gas mark 7/8).
2. Generously butter the bottom and sides of the baking dish. Set aside.
3. Slice the onions in half lengthwise. Place, cut side down, on a cutting board and slice crosswise into very thin slices.
4. In a large unheated skillet, combine the onions, butter, thyme, salt, pepper, and nutmeg. Sweat over moderate heat, covered, until the onions are soft, about 8 minutes. They should not caramelize or turn brown. Taste for seasoning. Set aside.
5. Crack the eggs into a medium-size bowl and whisk just to blend. Whisk in the milk and cream.
6. Transfer the onions to the prepared baking dish, smoothing them out with the back of a spoon. Pour the egg mixture over the onions. Season with additional pepper and nutmeg. Place in the center of the oven and bake until the top is a deep golden brown and the custard is firm, about 30 minutes. To test for doneness, insert the tip of a knife in the center of the quiche. It is done when the knife comes out clean. Do not underbake or the

quiche will be mushy, not firm. Let sit for about 5 minutes to firm up. Serve warm, cut into thin wedges.

EIGHT SERVINGS

 WINE SUGGESTION: I love a light, young Viognier with this, but any good drinkable white will do.

VARIATION: To give the quiche a Provençal accent: Just before baking, arrange eight rinsed and soaked anchovy fillets in a pinwheel on the quiche. Separate the anchovies with a pitted black olive.

∼ **NUTMEG AND DAIRY, A PERFECT MARRIAGE** ∼ Nutmeg is marvelous in savory dishes as well as desserts. A fruit of the *mystica fragrans,* nutmeg is so perky that a touch of it showered on stir-fried spinach or a hearty braised daube imparts a sweet spiciness as well as a whole new layer of flavor. The best marriage, however, is between nutmeg and dairy products. The nutty bite of the nutmeg works magic in cutting through the fat of milk, cream, eggs, and cheese. The highest caliber of nutmeg reputedly grows on the island of Grenada in the southern Caribbean. The flavor of nutmeg is richest when it is grated as you need it. The same heady, perfumed aroma and rich, oily flavor cannot be achieved with nutmeg that is purchased already ground.

HERB CHEESE LYONNAIS

Ever since my first journey to the food-loving city of Lyons nearly twenty-five years ago, this has been a dish I look forward to sampling each time. The French names for the dish include *claqueret* and *cervelle de canut,* which translate as silk worker's brains. The name echoes back to the days when Lyons was a silkmaking capital, and the workers ate this zesty cheese every day at the bistros called *machons.* Generally prepared with a blend of *fromage blanc* (a smooth French version of cottage cheese), shallots, garlic, and herbs (chives are essential), the spread is also animated by a bit of white wine, vinegar, and oil.

2 cups (50 cl) full-fat or low-fat cottage cheese
2 shallots, peeled and minced
1 plump, fresh garlic clove, peeled and minced
3 tablespoons fresh chives, snipped with a scissors
3 tablespoons fresh tarragon leaves, snipped with a scissors
3 tablespoons fresh parsley leaves, snipped with a scissors
½ teaspoon fresh thyme leaves, carefully stemmed
Fine sea salt and freshly ground black pepper to taste
1 tablespoon dry white wine
1 teaspoon best-quality sherry wine vinegar
1 tablespoon extra-virgin olive oil
Mixed fresh herbs, for garnish (optional)

1. Place the cottage cheese in the bowl of a food processor and pulse once, just long enough to break up the cheese curds. Add the shallots, garlic, chives, tarragon, parsley, and thyme, and process very briefly, pulsing only to blend. Season to taste with salt and pepper. Pulse once again to distribute the seasonings.

2. Transfer the mixture to a 6-cup (1.5-l) cheesecloth-lined, perforated mold such as a porcelain *coeur à la crème* mold (or substitute a cheesecloth-lined large sieve) set over a bowl. Cover and refrigerate for at least 24 hours and up to 48 hours.

3. Remove the cheese from the refrigerator. Discard any liquid that has drained from the mold. Transfer the cheese to the bowl of a food processor. Add the wine, vinegar, and oil, and pulse to blend. Taste for seasoning. Transfer to a small bowl. Serve either as a dip with raw vegetables, as part of a cheese course, or as a topping for an open-face sandwich, garnished with additional snipped herbs. (The cheese will stay fresh for up to 2 days if refrigerated. Bring to room temperature to serve.)

ABOUT TWO CUPS (50 CL) CHEESE SPREAD

WINE SUGGESTION: An excellent Beaujolais cru—such as a Fleurie or Moulin à Vent— would be my choice.

⌇ **THE NOBLE SHALLOT** ⌇   The shallot is the most prestigious member of the onion family. Prized by the French for its delicate nature, both cooked and raw, the flavor the shallot adds to any dish falls somewhere between the aggressive tang of the onion and the subtle power of garlic. It is for this reason that this vegetable flavoring has been nobly selected to play a role in such classic French sauces as béarnaise. In recipes where the shallot is to be eaten raw, it is essential that the shallot be chopped as finely as possible. The shallot will release a maximum amount of flavor and be more agreeable to eat in small doses. Finely chopped shallots are also excellent in vinaigrettes or even sprinkled into meat or fish sauces at the last minute to enhance the acidity and flavor of the dish. When buying shallots, avoid any that show signs of sprouting or bruising; they are likely to be tasteless. Be careful to store shallots in a cool place (but not the refrigerator) where they have room to "breathe"; they can spoil easily, and a single bad shallot can spoil a whole bunch.

Patricia returns from the market with flats of colorful primevères, *or primroses.*

What was paradise but a garden full of vegetables
and herbs and pleasures. Nothing there but delights.
WILLIAM LAWSON

TOMATO CLAFOUTIS

Why limit clafoutis—that cloudlike creation of fruits baked with a quick and simple batter—to desserts? This dish, colorful with tomatoes, fragrant with fresh thyme, surrounded by a golden egg-and-cheese batter, is a favorite summertime dish at our house. I have prepared this with both the traditional round and oval (Roma) tomatoes quite satisfactorily. Serve with a light green salad alongside, and you have it made. And need I lecture: Only fresh thyme deserves the honor of this dish.

EQUIPMENT: One 10½-inch (27-cm) round baking dish

2 pounds (1 kg) firm, ripe tomatoes
Fine sea salt to taste
2 large eggs
2 large egg yolks
⅓ cup (8 cl) heavy cream
½ cup (2 ounces; 60 g) freshly grated Parmigiano-Reggiano cheese
2 teaspoons fresh thyme leaves, carefully stemmed

1. Preheat the oven to 375°F (190°C; gas mark 5).
2. Core, peel, and quarter the tomatoes lengthwise. Place the tomatoes, side by side, on a double thickness of paper toweling. Sprinkle generously with fine salt. Cover with another double thickness of paper toweling. Set aside to purge the tomatoes of their liquid for at least 10 minutes and up to 1 hour.
3. In a small bowl, combine the eggs, egg yolks, cream, half of the cheese, and half of the thyme leaves. Season lightly with salt and whisk to blend.
4. Layer the tomatoes on the bottom of the baking dish. Pour the batter over the tomatoes. Sprinkle with the remaining cheese and thyme. Place in the center of the oven and bake until the batter is set and the clafoutis is golden and bubbling, about 30 minutes. Serve warm or at room temperature, cut into wedges.

EIGHT SERVINGS

WINE SUGGESTION: Any daily drinking red is good. My preference is a young Côtes du Rhône.

ROQUEFORT DIP

Half-spread, half-dip, I make this when I'm in the mood for a light cheese that has a bit of the Roquefort drama on the tongue. It can be served as a dip for raw vegetables (celery is the best), as a spread for crackers and sandwiches, or as part of a cheese course. Prepare it at least one day in advance to allow the flavors to mellow.

> 2 cups (50 cl) full-fat or low-fat cottage cheese
> 3 tablespoons fresh chives, snipped with a scissors
> 2½ ounces (75 g) imported French Roquefort cheese, at room temperature, broken
>   into pieces
> Sea salt and freshly ground black pepper to taste

Place the cottage cheese in the bowl of a food processor and pulse just to break up the cheese curds. Add the chives and Roquefort, and process briefly, pulsing once or twice just to blend. Season to taste. Pulse once again to distribute the seasonings. Transfer to a container, cover securely, and refrigerate at least 1 day, to allow the flavors to blend and emerge. Bring to room temperature before serving.

ABOUT TWO CUPS (50 CL) CHEESE

⌁ THE LEGEND OF ROQUEFORT ⌁ The legend of Roquefort cheese tells the story of a young shepherd in the rocky Causses region of south-central France. He left an ordinary lunch of bread and sheep's milk cheese in one of the local limestone caves of the region thinking he would return to it later that day. It was actually several weeks before he retrieved his lunch and discovered an enormous mass of mold. The curious boy tasted the mixture, only to find it was delicious! Ever since, the maturation period of three months to a year takes place in special cool caves in the tiny village of Roquefort-sur-Soulzon. There, limestone cellars eleven stories deep remain an even 45°F (8–9°C), with up to 95 percent humidity, creating a cheese full of character, perfume, and flavor. The prized bluish-green–veined Roquefort is actually the third most popular cheese eaten in France, on the heels of Camembert and goat cheese, or chèvre.

My kitchen is a mystical place, a kind of temple for me.
It is a place where the surfaces seem to have significance, where the sounds
and odors carry the meaning that transfers from the past and bridges to the future.

PEARL BAILEY

MARIE‑CLAUDE'S ARMAGNAC CHÈVRE

Marie-Claude Gracia, owner of La Belle Gasconne in the village of Poudenas in southwestern France, is one of my favorite French chefs. She likes to serve this regional preparation as an appetizer with very thin slices of walnut bread and a glass of champagne. The simple combination of fresh, slightly tangy goat cheese, a touch of sugar, and just a few drops of Armagnac make for a surprising—almost haunting—palate opener.

    1 teaspoon light brown sugar, or to taste
    Several drops of Armagnac or Cognac, or to taste
    4 ounces (125 g) very fresh goat cheese

In a small bowl, combine the sugar and alcohol, stirring to allow the acid in the alcohol to dissolve the sugar. In another small bowl, crush the goat cheese lightly with a fork. Add the sugar-alcohol mixture and crush again to blend. Taste. Gradually add additional sugar and/or alcohol to taste. Transfer to a ramekin and smooth with a spatula. (The spread can be prepared up to 1 day in advance, covered, and refrigerated. Bring to room temperature before serving.) Serve the spread on ultra-thin slices of toasted walnut bread, toasted sourdough bread, or light crackers.

ONE-HALF CUP (12.5 CL) CHEESE SPREAD

Poets have been mysteriously silent on the subject of cheese.

G. K. CHESTERTON

CACHAT: PROVENÇAL CHEESE SPREAD

Cachat is an unbelieveably tasty cheese spread found at most cheese shops in Provence. The cheesemongers prepare it from leftover bits of cheese, just as the Provençal farmers have for centuries. With the help of such modern gadgetry as the food processor, this is one of the quickest ways I know to give a cheese tray a new, vibrant flavor. In principle, you can use bits of leftover cheese of just about any variety. This recipe serves as a simple suggestion of what cheeses to combine. I serve the spread as the cheese course, as part of a cheese course, or as a snack or appetizer, along with Herbed Green Olives (page 49).

> About 1 ounce (30 g) imported French Roquefort cheese, at room temperature
> About 4 ounces (125 g) goat's milk cheese, at room temperature
> About 2 tablespoons heavy cream
> 1 teaspoon eau-de-vie (such as Marc de Provence)

If the cheeses are firm, chop them into small pieces. Place all ingredients in the bowl of a food processor and, using a quick on-and-off motion, lightly blend. Taste for seasoning and adjust if necessary. The mixture should be slightly chunky and not totally smooth. The flavor should be sharp, almost piquant.

ABOUT ONE CUP (25 CL) CHEESE SPREAD

At the Vaison market: a selection of local olives and tapenades—
various spreads prepared with both black and green olives.

TUNA TAPENADE

Each Tuesday our market in the village of Vaison-la-Romaine is filled with olive and tapenade stands, each merchant trying to outdo the other. This recipe was inspired by a green olive tapenade I sampled one morning in July. Explosively tart with the fresh taste of lemon, this tapenade can be spread on toast as an appetizer or used as a dip for raw vegetables, such as carrots or celery; in a pinch it can even be tossed with pasta as a quick last-minute sauce.

> 1 can (6½ ounces; 190 g) tuna packed in olive oil, drained (see Note)
> 4 tablespoons (2 ounces; 60 g) unsalted butter, softened
> 1 cup (150 g) best-quality green olives (such as French Picholine), drained and pitted
> Grated zest (yellow peel) of 1 lemon, blanched and refreshed in cold water
> 2 tablespoons freshly squeezed lemon juice
> 4 tablespoons minced fresh basil leaves

With a fork, flake the tuna in the can and transfer to the bowl of a food processor. Add the remaining ingredients and process only until blended. The mixture should remain slightly coarse. Taste for seasoning. Transfer to a medium-size bowl and serve at room temperature. (The tapenade can be stored, covered and refrigerated, for up to 3 days.)

ONE CUP (25 CL) TAPENADE

NOTE: If the more flavorful tuna packed in olive oil is unavailable, use best-quality white tuna packed in water. Drain the tuna, discarding the water.

RUE DE LÉVIS "CAVIAR"

Simplicity never ceases to surprise. How can three pantry ingredients combine to create a taste and texture so appealing? I call this "spread" of chopped black olives, butter, and coarse sea salt Rue de Lévis Caviar since I first sampled it at a restaurant right off Paris's Rue de Lévis market and the Parc Monceau in the seventeenth arrondissement, Le Bouchon de François Clerc. The restaurant makes its own crusty whole wheat bread and serves this spread in little crocks at the table, in place of traditional butter. One would think that with the saltiness of the olives, the coarse sea salt would turn it too aggressively salty. Surprisingly, the salt adds just the right bit of texture and serves to open the palate for more to come. Try to use the *sel gris de Guerande,* the famed unrefined sea salt from Brittany. Kosher salt or refined sea salt here would be too dominant. Do not attempt this in the food processor: The resulting spread will be an unappetizing gray and much too processed. The caviar is most dazzling (no runny streaks of black in the butter) if the olives are fairly dry, so for best results pit and chop the olives and set them aside to dry on paper towels for a few hours before making the spread.

> 2 ounces (60 g) best-quality black olives (such as French Nyons), well drained
> 4 tablespoons (2 ounces; 60 g) unsalted butter, softened
> ½ teaspoon coarse sea salt, preferably *sel gris* from Brittany

Pit and finely chop the olives. Pat dry with paper towels. Place the butter on a plate and mash with a fork. Sprinkle evenly with the salt and chopped olives. With the fork, care-fully mash to incorporate the olives and salt. To keep the color clear and golden, do not overwork. Transfer to individual crocks or ramekins and smooth with a spatula. Serve as you would butter. This is particularly good with freshly toasted whole wheat or walnut bread. (The spread can be stored, covered and refrigerated, for up to 1 week. Bring to room temperature before serving.)

ABOUT ONE-HALF CUP (12.5 CL) SPREAD

An assortment of Provençal openers, including sausages, homemade bread, and black olives.

ANCHOVY-GARLIC CPISPS

These anchovy-garlic crisps are designed to perk up your appetite but not assault it. This is a pantry appetizer that can be made in a matter of minutes. Chop any leftovers into croutons to toss into salads.

12 Salt-Cured Anchovies (page 330) or 12 canned anchovy fillets in olive oil, drained
½ cup (12.5 cl) whole milk
3 plump, fresh garlic cloves, peeled and minced
4 tablespoons extra-virgin olive oil
4 slices whole wheat bread, crust removed and cut into strips about 1 inch (2.5 cm) wide

1. Preheat the oven to 375°F (190°C; gas mark 5).
2. Rinse the anchovies, discarding any visible bones. Pat them dry and chop finely. Place in a small bowl with the milk. Set aside for 15 minutes. Drain, discarding the milk.
3. In a small skillet, combine the anchovies, garlic, and oil, and cook over moderate heat just until the mixture is well blended and the garlic and anchovies melt into the oil, 2 to 3 minutes.
4. With a pastry brush, brush the strips of bread all over with the anchovy mixture. Place on a nonstick baking sheet and toast until well browned, turning the bread from time to time, about 5 minutes.
5. Remove the baking sheet from the oven and transfer the strips of bread to a rack to cool. The crisps are good warm or at room temperature. They can be stored in an airtight container for up to 1 week.

ABOUT TWENTY APPETIZER SERVINGS

LEMON-FLECKED OLIVES

The rich, meaty tastes of olives and anchovies pair well with the sharp tang of preserved lemons. Here, best-quality anchovy-stuffed olives are tossed with flecks of home-preserved lemons, making for an instant and unusual palate opener. Guests never fail to ask, "What did you add to these olives?"—and then demand the recipe.

3 slices preserved lemon plus 1 tablespoon liquid from the jar of Preserved Lemons (page 319)

1 cup (150 g) best-quality anchovy-stuffed green olives, drained, or substitute French Picholine olives, pitted

Mince the slices of preserved lemon and place them in a small bowl with their liquid. Add the drained olives. Toss to coat the olives with the lemon and liquid. Serve as an appetizer. The olives can be stored, covered securely and refrigerated, up to 1 month.

ONE CUP (150 G) OLIVES

There is no limit to the variety of flavorings added to the green and black olives of Provence: preserved lemon, fresh fronds of fennel, hot pepper, and pickled vegetables.

HARISSA-SEASONED BLACK OLIVES

For those who love the flavor of cumin and cayenne pepper, this olive variation is ideal. I often use these to flavor Anne's Goat Cheese Gratin (page 21) for a pleasant, piquant, change of pace.

> 2 cups (300 g) best-quality black olives (such as French Nyons), unpitted and drained
> 2 tablespoons homemade *Harissa* (page 320), or to taste

In a bowl, combine the olives and *harissa* and toss to blend. Taste for seasoning. Spoon the olives into a jar and shake to blend again. Cover and store, refrigerated, for at least 1 day before sampling and up to 1 month. To serve, bring to room temperature and serve as an appetizer.

TWO CUPS (300 G) OLIVES

ᐅ **ON STORING OLIVES** ᐊ When olives are cured—either with salt, brine, potassium, lye, or ash solution—they are never subjected to high temperatures. Thus they are a cured, not a cooked, product. If you open a jar of olives or have one that has been in the refrigerator for a while, it is possible that a white film has formed on top of the liquid. Not to worry. Simply rinse the olives and store them in water with a dash of salt and vinegar. For even better results, drain the olives, return them to a sterilized jar, and cover them with olive oil. The oil can be recouped later and used as an olive-infused oil to drizzle over fresh salads and pizzas.

ᐅ **BLACK VERSUS GREEN** ᐊ At the earliest stage of maturity, all olives are green, or unripe. As they age and ripen on the tree, they turn from pale green to reddish brown and then to black. Some varieties are better unripe and thus are harvested at the green stage, such as the French Picholine and Spanish Manzanilla varieties. For black olives, French olives from Nice or Nyons or Greek Kalamata varieties are a marvel at full maturity. The darker the olive at harvesting, the higher the oil content, the richer the flavor, the quicker the cure. No matter what the color when harvested, all olives are bitter and inedible and must be subjected to a curing process—with salt, water, brine, oil, potassium, ash, or lye—to render them delicious.

*I know of nothing more appetizing on a very hot day than to sit
in the cool shade of the dining room with drawn Venetian blinds,
a little table laid with black olives, saucisson d'Arles, some fine tomatoes,
a slice of watermelon, and a pyramid of little green figs baked in the sun.
In this light air, in this fortunate countryside, there is no need
to warm oneself with heavy meats or dishes of lentils. The Midi
is essentially a region of carefully prepared little dishes.*

LEON DAUDET

HERBED GREEN OLIVES

These olives are typical of the appetizers served with drinks before a meal in Provence. A bowl of seasoned olives and a few paper-thin slices of sausage are all you need at cocktail time. The herb mixture only serves as a starting point, for seasoning can be adjusted to personal tastes. I particularly like the interplay of fennel and cumin seed.

2 cups (300 g) best-quality green olives (such as French Picholine), drained
2 fresh bay leaves
½ teaspoon fresh thyme leaves, carefully stemmed
½ teaspoon fennel seeds
½ teaspoon cumin seeds
4 plump, fresh garlic cloves, peeled and crushed
1 tablespoon extra-virgin olive oil
1 teaspoon dried leaf oregano

In a bowl, combine the olives, bay leaves, thyme, fennel, cumin, garlic, and oil, and toss to blend. To intensify the flavor of the leaf oregano, rub it between the palms of your hands and let it fall into the olive mixture. Toss once more. Spoon the olive mixture into a jar and shake to blend again. Cover and store, refrigerated, for at least 1 week and up to 1 month, shaking from time to time for even seasoning. Bring to room temperature before serving.

TWO CUPS (300 G) OLIVES

FACING PHOTOGRAPH: *Home-cured and home-seasoned olives and lemon, surrounded by a branch of freshly pickled green olives and fresh thyme, from top: green French Picholine olives seasoned with wild fennel; Chanteduc Black Olives (page 51); green olives seasoned with spicy red peppers; Lemon-Flecked Olives (page 46); Preserved Lemons (page 319); Brine-Cured Black Olives (page 328); and Harissa-Seasoned Black Olives (page 47).*

CHANTEDUC BLACK OLIVES

At Chanteduc we are fortunate to have a grove of about twenty olive trees with a pedigree all their own. Our property falls within the geographic limits of the famed olives of Nyons, the only olives honored with the French AOC, or Appellation d'Origine Contrôlée. The variety of olive is the *tanche,* a plump, purplish black fruit that is traditionally cured rather than pressed for its oil. I always pick the olives around Christmastime, right after the first frost. Once I've cured them—either in brine or in salt—I like to "doctor" them with varied flavors. This is one of many traditional combinations, with a touch of vinegar to balance the acidity, a good hit of garlic to tempt the appetite, and a touch of garden herbs for fragrance and flavor. The flecks of red pepper and oregano make for a simple, appealing appetizer. You can easily adjust it to enliven the cured olives you buy.

2 cups (300 g) best-quality black olives (such as French Nyons), unpitted

4 plump, fresh garlic cloves, peeled and crushed

2 teaspoons best-quality red wine vinegar

½ teaspoon crushed red peppers (hot red pepper flakes), or to taste

1 tablespoon extra-virgin olive oil

½ teaspoon dried leaf oregano

In a bowl, combine the olives, garlic, vinegar, crushed red peppers, and oil and toss to blend. Rub the oregano between the palms of your hands and let it fall into the olive mixture. Toss once more. Spoon the olive mixture into a jar and shake to blend again. Cover and store, refrigerated, for at least 1 day before sampling and up to 1 month. Bring to room temperature before serving as an appetizer.

TWO CUPS (300 G) OLIVES

OREGANO, DRIED VERSUS FRESH Oregano is the only herb that I prefer dried rather than fresh. That's because fresh oregano has little flavor and fragrance. Only in drying does the Mediterranean herb truly come to life, imparting a sharp, intense, very mintlike taste and aroma. Be certain to purchase dried leaf oregano (as opposed to the ground version), and rub the broken leaves between the palms of your hands to release its intensity.

FACING PHOTOGRAPH: *Homegrown Salt-Cured Black* Olives de Nyons *(page 326), begin curing with sea salt, fresh bay leaves, thyme, and garlic, which is added later for flavoring.*

*We first took possession of Chanteduc on a fall day such as this, when the leaves were falling
from the vines growing on the stone walls, the grape harvest was over,
and we were looking forward to the opening of the truffle season.*

2

SALADS

FRESH GREENS MAKE ME SALIVATE. I CAN'T imagine a truly satisfying, complete meal without salad. In fact, in our home, salad often *is* the meal. Which is why I devote a major portion of my vegetable garden to growing all manner of greens, ranging from Swiss chard (*blette*) to pungent leaves of arugula, to mesclun, that colorful Provençal mix of red and green oak-leaf lettuce, arugula, romaine, chervil, curly endive, and trevise. I've learned to put every herb and bit of green to use somewhere, concocting salads of nothing but herbs (all-tarragon or an All-Star Herb Salad mix of parsley, chives, dill, tarragon, and mint) or a flavorful mix of vegetable tops, including carrot, radish, turnip, fennel, celery, and beet tops for The True Salad Fan's Salad. Green beans are a favorite vegetable, and find their way into a variety of salads, as does Belgian endive, a cold-weather standby. Some, like the Cheesemaker's Salad, are there as simple accompaniment, while composed versions such as Saturday Beef Salad honor salad as a meal.

ALL-STAR HERB SALAD

Rather than making herbs part of a green salad, why not make these fresh, flavorful greens *the* salad. The idea comes from Paris chef Alain Passard, who years ago served me an all-tarragon salad at his Left Bank restaurant, Arpège. When tarragon is fresh in the market or your garden overflows with this extraordinarily powerful herb, why not serve it with honor as a salad all on its own? Years later Passard expanded what I called "the tarragon tangle" to a full-scale mixed herb salad—just a few well-dressed bites on a small salad plate—as an accompaniment. The idea really is to mix and match judiciously. Just don't use so many herbs that they lose their personality. Good combinations include parsley, mint, and tarragon. Or consider an all-mint salad to accompany grilled lamb, an all-tarragon salad to accompany grilled chicken, a sage-heavy salad to accompany roast pork. Other herbs that can be added to the following salad mix include a very judicious addition of hyssop, sage, chervil, and marjoram. Just be sure to include leaves only—no cheating—leaving all stems behind!

> 1 teaspoon best-quality sherry wine vinegar
> 1 teaspoon best-quality red wine vinegar
> Fine sea salt to taste
> 1 tablespoon extra-virgin olive oil
> Freshly ground black pepper to taste
> 2 ounces (60 g) fresh flat-leaf parsley leaves, carefully stemmed, rinsed, and dried
> 2 ounces (60 g) fresh chives, rinsed, dried, and minced
> 2 ounces (60 g) fresh dill leaves, carefully stemmed, rinsed, dried, and chopped
> 2 ounces (60 g) fresh tarragon leaves, carefully stemmed, rinsed, dried, and leaves separated
> 2 ounces (60 g) fresh mint, stemmed, rinsed, dried, and leaves separated

In a large, shallow salad bowl, whisk together the vinegars and salt. Whisk in the oil and pepper. Taste for seasoning. Add all the herb leaves and toss to evenly coat the greens with the dressing. Taste for seasoning. Serve in small portions as an accompaniment to roast chicken or grilled or poached fish.

FOUR TO SIX SERVINGS

VARIATION: The dressed salad can also be placed—open-face-sandwich fashion—on top of grilled bread that has been brushed with olive oil.

A varied selection of sage growing outside the pigeonnier, *where the former owner raised pigeons.*

⌁ **GOING WILD WITH HERBS** ⌁ Because herbs are very subjective and each person responds differently to any given combination, here are a few basic guidelines for pairing foods with herbs: Experiment with different combinations until you find the one that suits a mood or dish. For fish dishes, a light toss of fresh basil, dill, or tarragon is excellent. For beef, dill and parsley with a last-minute sprinkling of chives can be a refresher. For lamb, it's amazing what a mixture of dill and mint can do for the flavor of the meat. For vegetables, tarragon and parsley can be a perfect foil for those that have a natural sweetness, such as carrots and tomatoes. For other vegetables that respond more openly to outside flavors, such as the potato, the freedom of choice becomes even broader.

CHANTEDUC WINTER SALAD

In winter months, Belgian endive is a staple in our house. At that time of year, the palate welcomes endive's clean, crispy flavor. This combination of crunchy greens, nutty Parmesan cheese, and a tangy lemon always manages to hit the spot!

2 tablespoons freshly squeezed lemon juice
Fine sea salt to taste
2 tablespoons extra-virgin olive oil
Freshly ground black pepper to taste
4 Belgian endive (about 1 pound; 500 g)
¼ cup (1 ounce; 30 g) freshly grated Parmigiano-Reggiano cheese

1. In a large, shallow salad bowl, whisk together the lemon juice and salt. Whisk in the olive oil and pepper. Taste for seasoning. Set aside.
2. Rinse the endive and pat dry. With a small, sharp knife, remove and discard the core of each endive. Separate each leaf and place in the salad bowl. Toss to coat the leaves evenly. Sprinkle with the cheese and toss again, thoroughly coating the leaves with cheese. Taste for seasoning. Serve immediately on large dinner plates.

FOUR SERVINGS

✌ **BAN THE SALAD PLATE!** ☙ I don't know who ever decided that salads should be served on tiny plates or, worse, in tiny bowls. Composed salads need room to breathe, so why not serve them with majesty on a large dinner plate?

THE TRUE SALAD FAN'S SALAD

The title of this salad is a play on words since in French the word *fane* denotes the tops of root vegetables, such as carrots, radishes, turnips, fennel, celery, and beets. One evening chef Joël Robuchon served us a foie gras with a tiny, bite-size salad of mixed root-vegetable tops. Ever since, I have paired the salad with thin slices of Sheila & Julian's Quick Foie Gras (page 32). The flavors are explosive: The sharp bitterness of the greens helps cut right into the fat of the foie gras, creating an ideal contrast in taste. Since the day chef Robuchon served the salad, my refrigerator has become a repository of ready-to-make salads. And to think as a bona fide salad lover I wasted years tossing those precious tops! This recipe is simply a suggestion. Use as many root tops as you can find. Just be certain to snip the tops into very small, bite-size pieces.

The salad should be served in very small portions as a counterpoint to rich, fatty foods: Try sautéeing rabbit livers or chicken livers quickly in a nonstick pan, then deglaze with a touch of sherry wine vinegar. Serve the livers alongside the salad. For color contrast you can also add very fine juliennes of any of the root vegetables themselves. And remember: only fresh, bright leaves (nothing wilted), and only leaves—no stems allowed!

> 1 quart (100 g) tops of very young root vegetables, preferably a mix of carrot, radish, turnip, fennel, celery, and beet tops
> About 2 tablespoons Double Vinegar Vinaigrette (page 318)
> Sea salt and freshly ground black pepper to taste

Wash the root-vegetable tops and spin dry. Using a scissors, cut the leaves into bite-size pieces. If necessary, wash and spin dry once again. Place in a large salad bowl, add dressing, and toss to evenly coat the greens. Taste for seasoning.

SIX SERVINGS

↭ **PROPER TOOLS FOR TOSSING** ↝ When creating a salad of tiny, bite-size greens such as this, abandon your everyday salad tongs. They're too big and won't properly toss the salad. Instead, use two large serving spoons or soup spoons. They're more compatible with these tiny greens and will do a better job of thoroughly coating the greens with the dressing.

ARUGULA & PARMESAN SALAD

Throughout the winter months, arugula—that wild weed which withstands the cold, the wind, even the occasional snow of Provence—is what saves me. On Saturdays this is our traditional cold-weather lunch: a giant salad of arugula tossed with black olives and cheese and topped with crispy, salty strips of freshly grilled pancetta. In my local market the salty cured pork is sold as *poitrine-roulé,* a delicious black pepper–studded roll of pork breast. If pancetta is not available, substitute a very lean, best-quality bacon. Blanch it for one minute in boiling water, then drain thoroughly. Blanching will remove the smoked flavor from the bacon without cooking it.

2½ ounces (75 g) thinly sliced pancetta
1 tablespoon freshly squeezed lemon juice
Sea salt to taste
3 tablespoons extra-virgin olive oil
Freshly ground black pepper to taste
One 2-ounce (60-g) chunk of Parmigiano-Reggiano cheese
2 bunches (3 ounces; 100 g) stemmed arugula leaves, washed and dried
About 24 best-quality black olives (such as French Nyons), pitted

1. Preheat the broiler.
2. Cover a broiling pan with aluminum foil for easier cleanup. Place the pancetta slices side by side on the foil-covered pan.
3. Place the pan on an oven rack about 3 inches (7.5 cm) from the heat. Broil until the pancetta is golden and sizzling, 2 to 3 minutes. Transfer to a double thickness of paper towels to drain. Break into bite-size pieces. Set aside.
4. In a large, shallow salad bowl, whisk together the lemon juice and salt. Whisk in the oil and pepper. Taste for seasoning. Set aside.
5. Using a vegetable peeler, shave the Parmesan cheese into long thick strips. (If the chunk of cheese becomes too small to peel, grate the remaining cheese and add to the bowl.) Set aside.
6. Add the arugula to the salad bowl and toss to coat each leaf thoroughly. Taste for seasoning. Transfer the salad to 4 large dinner plates. Garnish with pancetta, cheese, olives, and and serve immediately.

FOUR SERVINGS

GRATED BEET SALAD

Rich with garlic and a hint of fresh herbs, this is a colorful summertime salad that hits the spot on a hot day. I love to grow beets, for they're quite forgiving—even in our harsh Provençal soil—and their vibrant red-green tops do wonders for brightening up a potager. Use only the freshest baby beets—or at least the tiniest you can find in the market—which are sweeter and more flavorful than large ones. Serve this as a side dish to cold roast chicken or as part of a buffet.

VINAIGRETTE

- 3 plump, fresh garlic cloves, peeled and minced
- 1 tablespoon imported Dijon mustard
- 1 tablespoon best-quality red wine vinegar
- Fine sea salt to taste
- 3 tablespoons extra-virgin olive oil
- Freshly ground black pepper to taste

- 1 pound (500 g) fresh raw baby beets
- 1 tablespoon mixed fresh herbs such as parsley, tarragon, chervil, and chives, snipped with a scissors

1. In a large, shallow salad bowl, whisk together the garlic, mustard, vinegar, and salt. Whisk in the olive oil and pepper. Taste for seasoning. Set aside.
2. Peel the beets. Grate finely in a salad grater, food mill, or food processor. Transfer to the salad bowl. Toss to coat the beets evenly. Add the herbs and toss again. Serve.

FOUR SERVINGS

ᴗ: **BEETS ARE THE BEST** ᴗ The beet is a vegetable that comes in two parts. Though more commonly used for its violet-red root, the leaves are edible as well (see The True Salad Fan's Salad, page 57). The contrast in textures and tastes between the leaves and the root can provide two excellent components to any dish. In the ancient world, the Greeks and Romans ate only the leaves and used the roots for medicinal purposes. In the eighteenth century, the white or "sugar" beet emerged as a convenient substitute for sugarcane.

When storing fresh beets in the refrigerator, separate the tops from the root before wrapping in plastic. Both ends keep longer this way. When buying, look for uniform color, a lack of blemishes or bruises, and a firm texture.

FACING PHOTOGRAPH: *A local Vaison farmer displays and sells her current harvest of herbs and vegetables.*

People will do almost anything to be healthy. But what people refuse to do
is eat real food. Why? I don't know. They'll do anything
to avoid cooking broccoli or peeling an orange.

CAROLYN BERNALARDI, NUTRITIONIST

RED & GREEN SALAD

For pure, appetizing color appeal, give me fresh green food with flecks of red! Green beans prepared in this manner—in boiling water until crisp-tender and then plunged into ice water to halt the cooking—are ideal with any vibrant, full-flavored dressing. Add the fresh coriander leaves at the last minute: They will add a hint of orange and sage to the sweet-tender flavor of the beans. Since beans vary in size and tenderness, taste as you cook. Once the beans go from tasting "raw" to cooked and tender, remove them from the heat.

DRESSING

1 tablespoon best-quality sherry wine vinegar
Sea salt to taste
3 tablespoons extra-virgin olive oil
2 shallots, minced

1 firm medium-size tomato
Sea salt
1 pound (500 g) young, tender green beans
4 tablespoons fresh coriander leaves, snipped with a scissors, or substitute parsley

1. About 1 hour before serving the salad, prepare the dressing: In a small bowl, whisk together the vinegar and a pinch of salt. Set aside. In another bowl, combine the oil and shallots. Set aside, uncovered, to mellow for about 1 hour. Just before serving, combine the vinegar and oil mixtures, and stir to blend. Taste for seasoning. Set aside.
2. Core, peel, seed, and chop the tomato. Place in a fine-mesh sieve and sprinkle lightly with some of the salt. Set aside to drain.
3. Fill a large pot with 3 quarts (3 l) of water and bring to a boil over high heat.
4. Meanwhile, rinse the beans thoroughly and trim the ends. Cut into 1-inch (2.5-cm) lengths. Set aside.
5. Prepare a large bowl of ice water.
6. When the water has come to a boil, add 2 tablespoons (30 g) of sea salt and the beans.

Boil, uncovered, until the beans are crisp-tender, about 5 minutes. (Cooking time will vary according to the size and tenderness of the beans.) Immediately drain the beans and plunge them into the ice water so they cool down as quickly as possible. (The beans will cool in 1 to 2 minutes. After that, they begin to lose flavor.) Transfer the beans to a colander, drain, and wrap in a thick towel to dry. (The beans can be cooked up to 2 hours in advance. Keep them wrapped in the towel and refrigerate, if desired.)

7. To finish: Combine the vinegar and oil mixtures, and stir to blend; taste for seasoning. Transfer the beans to a bowl, pour the dressing over the beans, and toss to coat evenly. Add the drained tomatoes and coriander, and toss to blend. Taste for seasoning. Serve immediately as a first-course salad or as a side vegetable dish to accompany chicken or grilled fish.

FOUR SERVINGS

ᴠ: **CORIANDER CONFUSION** :ᴠ Coriander provokes a certain amount of confusion since both the seeds and the leaves are used in cooking, but not to achieve the same purpose. What's more, it goes by so many names: cilantro in Spanish, Mexican, and Portuguese cooking; Chinese parsley in Chinese and Japanese cooking; as well as Arab parsley since it is used so freely in Arab cuisine. In South America, one Peruvian tribe is said to so love coriander that their skin gives off the herb's characteristic pungent scent.

The seeds have a milder flavor and are used often in marinades, in pickling, in vinaigrettes, in preparing such French liqueurs as Chartreuse, and in flavoring some cheeses. The seeds also blend well with mushroom dishes and are a component of such seasoning mixtures as curry and *ras el hanout,* a popular Mediterranean spice blend used to flavor couscous, *tagines* (Moroccan stews), and soups. As for the leaves, the strong flavor (a combination of orange and sage) suits them for garnishing salads and soups. I prefer to use coriander leaves sparingly, and always on their own. Blend them with other fresh herbs such as mint, tarragon, and sage—and your palate will experience a taste riot! The leaves hold their flavor and color best when added just before serving.

Because of their specific pungent flavor (detractors say the herb tastes like soap) some cooks prefer to ignore the herb altogether. If that's the case, fresh flat-leaf parsley—its look-alike—is a worthy substitute. Coriander is a very difficult herb to grow in the garden: It bolts and turns to seed as soon as the weather turns warm. Traditionally, coriander leaves are chewed to neutralize the odor of garlic on the breath. Medicinally, coriander acts as a pleasant stimulant.

TARRAGON GREEN BEAN SALAD

When tiny fresh green beans—*haricots verts*—are in the market, I can't get enough of them. Sometimes I'll serve them several nights running, often with a simple grilled salmon or seared swordfish. I prize the combination of freshly picked tarragon, a touch of lemon, a whisper of cream—ingredients that seem delighted to be in the company of crisp, tender green beans.

    1 tablespoon freshly squeezed lemon juice
    Sea salt to taste
    3 shallots, peeled and minced
    3 tablespoons heavy cream
    1 pound (500 g) young, tender green beans
    2 tablespoons coarse sea salt
    4 tablespoons fresh tarragon leaves, snipped with a scissors

1. Fill a large pot with 3 quarts (3 l) of water and bring to a boil over high heat.
2. Meanwhile, in a small bowl, whisk together the lemon juice and a pinch of salt. Whisk in the shallots and cream. Taste for seasoning. Set aside.
3. Rinse the beans and trim both ends. Cut into 1-inch (2.5-cm) lengths.
4. Prepare a large bowl of ice water.
5. When the water has come to a boil, add the coarse sea salt and beans. Boil, uncovered, until the beans are crisp-tender, about 5 minutes. (Cooking time will vary according to the size and tenderness of the beans.) Immediately drain the beans and plunge them into the ice water so they cool down as quickly as possible. (The beans will cool in 1 to 2 minutes. After that, they will begin to lose flavor.) Transfer the beans to a colander, drain, and wrap in a thick towel to dry. (The beans can be cooked up to 2 hours in advance. Keep them wrapped in the towel and refrigerate, if desired.)
6. If the beans are refrigerated, bring them to room temperature before serving. To serve, taste the dressing for seasoning. Transfer the beans to a bowl, pour the dressing over the beans, and toss to coat evenly. Add the minced tarragon and toss to blend. Taste for seasoning. Serve immediately.

FOUR TO SIX SERVINGS

YOGURT GREEN BEAN SALAD

This is a favorite "picnic" recipe, the sort of thing I make when I like to picnic at home. The soothing nature of the yogurt, the gentle sweetness of the beans, and the spiciness of the curry create a harmonious trio. Since the strength of curry powder varies dramatically, add the curry powder to the dressing little by little until the result meets your taste. I like to add a touch of tarragon to this at the end since curry and tarragon are a remarkable pair.

> 3 tablespoons plain, full-fat yogurt
> 1 tablespoon freshly squeezed lemon juice
> Sea salt
> 3 tablespoons heavy cream
> 2 teaspoons curry powder, or to taste
> 1 pound (500 g) young, tender green beans
> 2 tablespoons fresh tarragon leaves, snipped with a scissors (optional)

1. In a small bowl, whisk together the yogurt, lemon juice, salt, and cream. Slowly add the curry powder, stirring well to blend after each addition. Taste for seasoning. Set aside.
2 Fill a large pot with 3 quarts (3 l) of water and bring to a boil over high heat.
3. Meanwhile, rinse the beans and trim both ends. Cut into 1-inch (2.5-cm) lengths.
4. Prepare a large bowl of ice water.
5. When the water has come to a boil, add 2 tablespoons (30 g) of salt and the beans. Boil, uncovered, until the beans are crisp-tender, about 5 minutes. (Cooking time will vary according to the size and tenderness of the beans.) Immediately drain the beans and plunge them into the ice water so they cool down as quickly as possible. (The beans will cool in 1 to 2 minutes. After that, they will begin to lose flavor.) Transfer the beans to a colander, drain, and wrap in a thick towel to dry. (The beans can be cooked up to 2 hours in advance. Keep them wrapped in the towel and refrigerate, if desired.)
6. If the beans are refrigerated, bring them to room temperature before serving. To serve, toss the beans and dressing to coat evenly. Taste for seasoning. Add the minced tarragon and toss to blend. Taste for seasoning. Serve immediately.

FOUR TO SIX SERVINGS

PEAR & WATERCRESS SALAD

Pears and watercress are happy partners: They both add a crunchy quality, while the delicate flavor of the pears tones down the pepperiness of the cress. To bring out their maximum flavor, bring the pears to room temperature. Serve this as part of a cheese and salad course with an assortment of varied blue cheeses, which might include Roquefort, Fourme d'Ambert, and Stilton.

> 1 tablespoon freshly squeezed lemon juice
> Fine sea salt to taste
> 2½ tablespoons extra-virgin olive oil
> Freshly ground black pepper to taste
> 2 firm, ripe Comice or Seckel pears, at room temperature, peeled, cored, and cut into
>   16 lengthwise slices
> 2 cups (50 cl) watercress, cleaned and stemmed

1. About 30 minutes before serving, prepare the dressing and marinate the pears: In a large, shallow salad bowl, combine the lemon juice and salt, and stir to dissolve the salt. Slowly add the olive oil and stir to blend. Season with pepper. Add the sliced pears and gently toss to coat with the dressing. Set aside to marinate for about 30 minutes.
2. At serving time, add the watercress and toss to blend thoroughly. Transfer to large serving plates and serve, if desired, with a blue cheese assortment.

FOUR SERVINGS

WINE SUGGESTION: A fruity, fragrant dry white with good acidity, such as an Alsatian Riesling, will play off the contrast between the sweet pears and the salty blue cheeses.

PARMESAN & CELERY SALAD

One rainy October day in Italy's Piedmont region, chef Caesar Giaccone took a friend and me to Belvedere, a small, bustling trattoria in the village of Serravalle Laghe. The owner, Laura Brusco, served a version of this salad as a welcoming antipasto: fresh diced celery enhanced with a touch of nutty Parmigiano-Reggiano cheese. I like to prepare this with a slightly lemony sauce and serve it quite chilled, making for an ultimately refreshing first course. Thin slices of fresh fennel would be a worthy substitute for the celery. Serve with freshly toasted homemade bread to absorb the flavors.

> 2 tablespoons freshly squeezed lemon juice
>
> Sea salt to taste
>
> 4 tablespoons extra-virgin olive oil
>
> Freshly ground black pepper to taste
>
> 2 cups (50 cl) diced celery hearts with leaves, or substitute thinly sliced fennel with fronds
>
> About 12 shavings of Parmigiano-Reggiano cheese

In a small bowl, whisk together the lemon juice and salt. Whisk in the oil and pepper. Taste for seasoning. Add the celery and toss to coat evenly with the dressing. Cover and refrigerate for a minimum of 2 hours to allow the celery to absorb the flavors of the dressing. Toss occasionally. Place portions of the celery salad in a mound on small salad plates. Sprinkle generously with pepper. Top with shavings of Parmigiano-Reggiano cheese and serve.

FOUR SERVINGS

⌣ **CELERY FOR HANGOVERS** ∾ On festive occasions the Romans would make wreaths of celery leaves and place them on their heads as crowns. The purpose? They believed the headdresses would negate the effects of the potent wine that had been drunk with the meal and hence protect them from hangovers.

SALAD OF ROQUEFORT, WALNUTS, BELGIAN ENDIVE & LAMB'S LETTUCE

This salad is a hearty and colorful variation on the traditional trio of Belgian endive, Roquefort, and walnuts. I sampled it one Sunday at a favored "no-name" restaurant, really a funky sort of bistro situated in an antiques barn in the village of Isle-sur-la-Sorgue in Provence. I like the addition of delicate lamb's lettuce, and the creamy dressing in place of a traditional vinaigrette. And if lamb's lettuce is not available, in this instance fresh watercress leaves would be a worthy substitute.

> 4 ounces (60 g) imported French Roquefort cheese, at room temperature, crumbled
> 2 tablespoons heavy cream
> 3 tablespoons freshly squeezed lemon juice
> Freshly ground black pepper to taste
> 2 Belgian endive (about 8 ounces; 250 g)
> 5 ounces (150 g) lamb's lettuce or watercress
> ½ cup (60 g) whole walnut pieces

1. In a large, shallow salad bowl, whisk together 1 tablespoon (15 g) of the Roquefort, the cream, lemon juice, and pepper. Taste for seasoning. Set aside.
2. Rinse the whole endive and pat dry. With a small, sharp knife, remove and discard the core of each endive. Slice each endive lengthwise into eighths and place in the bowl.
3. Wash the lamb's lettuce or watercress in six to seven changes of water, being sure to eliminate all sand or dirt. Thoroughly spin dry. Break into individual leaves, discarding the stems. Add to the endive in the bowl.
4. Toss to coat the leaves thoroughly with dressing. Sprinkle with the walnuts and remaining cheese. Toss again. Serve immediately on large dinner plates.

FOUR SERVINGS

↶ **THAT GREEN CALLED LAMB'S LETTUCE** ↷ Ever wonder why we call it lamb's lettuce? One day European shepherds observed lambs nibbling greedily at a wild green and wondered at the fuss. The shepherds took a taste, and the rest is history. Lamb's lettuce—which the French call *mâche* and the Provençal call *doucette*—takes kindly to cold, wet weather and is therefore available at the times of year when the selection of other appealing greens may be limited. With its delicate petals, lamb's lettuce grows in little bunches, or "flowers." It has a very subtle flavor, and the French use it to complement strong flavors in a salad. Notably, *mâche* also cuts through the abrasive edge found in chicories, arugula, and endive. To get the best out of lamb's lettuce, trim away any yellow leaves, cut the small stem of soil off the bottom, and wash thoroughly and carefully.

TOUTOUNE'S WINTER SALAD

I think of this salad as a winter vitamin pill—all crunchy, healthy, wholesome. I sampled a version of it one February evening at Chez Toutoune, a longtime favorite Parisian bistro. The white-on-white tone makes one assume there's just a single ingredient, but soon your palate is surprised by the complex mix of flavors, all tangy, perky, and cleansing.

4 Belgian endive (about 1 pound; 500 g), trimmed and cut into matchsticks
2 firm, acidic apples, such as Granny Smith, peeled and cut into matchsticks
4 tablespoons heavy cream
2 tablespoons freshly squeezed lemon juice
Sea salt and freshly ground white pepper to taste

In a large bowl, combine the endive and apples. In a small bowl, whisk together the cream, lemon juice, and seasoning. Taste for seasoning. Toss to coat the fruit and endives thoroughly with the dressing. Serve on large dinner plates.

FOUR SERVINGS

ON ENDIVE Contrary to its bright white and yellow-tinged leaves, Belgian endive grows in the dark in sandy soil. It is a resilient and versatile vegetable. When stored in a plastic bag in the refrigerator, endive will stay crisp for at least a week. If endive has been stored for a few days before actual use, just peel off the first few layers of leaves that may have turned green or brown with time. Incidentally, when buying endive, discoloration of the leaves, especially a green blue, can indicate lack of freshness. In France, endive is revered as a winter vegetable excellent for garnishing meats and game. Even more common are salads that mingle the delicate bitterness with the sweetness and acidity of apples and oranges. Though Belgian endive perhaps holds no superiority over French endive, it is generally cleaner and better trimmed. In northern France endive is called *chicon,* probably a derivative of the word "chicory." If a recipe calls for it cooked, endive is best left whole; otherwise it tends to break up and cook into a puree. For salads and other raw preparations, remove the middle core at the base of the endive to take out excess bitterness that can be unpleasant and overpowering.

FRENCH CAFÉ SALAD

This is an embellished version of a classic French café salad, often a toss of Belgian endive, Roquefort, and walnuts. I've added the pear for a touch of sweetness and smoothness of texture. The fruit also serves as a contrast to the saltiness of the nuts and cheese and the crunch of Belgian endive. The chives add another dimension: a snappy pungency that wakes up the taste buds. It's a great luncheon dish, a meal all on its own, quick and easy to prepare, and applauded by all salad lovers. If Belgian endive is not readily available, substitute romaine lettuce sliced on a diagonal.

> 1 tablespoon freshly squeezed lemon juice
> Fine sea salt to taste
> 4 tablespoons walnut oil or extra-virgin olive oil
> Freshly ground black pepper to taste
> 1 firm ripe Seckel or Comice pear, at room temperature, peeled, cored, and cut into 16 lengthwise slices
> 4 Belgian endive (about 1 pound; 500 g), rinsed, trimmed, and leaves separated but left whole
> 2½ ounces (75 g) imported French Roquefort cheese
> ½ cup (2 ounces; 60 g) walnut halves, toasted and cooled
> 3 tablespoons fresh chives, snipped finely with a scissors

In a large, shallow salad bowl, whisk together the lemon juice and salt. Whisk in the oil and pepper. Taste for seasoning. Add the sliced pears and gently toss to coat thoroughly with the dressing. Add the endive, Roquefort, walnut halves, and chives, and toss until the ingredients are equally distributed and evenly coated with the dressing. Season again with pepper and arrange on individual salad plates.

FOUR SERVINGS

⌁ **A NOTE ABOUT GROWING CHIVES** ⌁ If you grow chives in your windowbox or garden, be sure to snip them regularly. They'll grow back more quickly and evenly. When I know I'll be away for a few weeks, I cut them back all the way, and am assured of fresh, green chives on my return.

DANIEL'S CHICKPEA SALAD

Daniel Combe is our winemaker, and he also keeps us supplied with plenty of home-grown chickpeas, which he raises to feed the family pig (with which he makes extraordinary sausages and pâtés). He knows I am a fan of his earthy, exceptionally tasty beans, and often I'll return home and find a fresh sack of beans at the front gate. This recipe presents a very pure and uncomplicated way of preparing the nutty-flavored beans, and a variation that is as delicious warm in the winter as it is chilled in the summer.

A few rules: Always buy dried chickpeas from a shop that has a good turnover. You're more likely to get ones that are fresher and more flavorful. Be certain to salt them only after they have cooked about halfway through. Adding any acid or minerals—including salt—in the beginning will make for tough chickpeas that will never cook all the way through. If you live in an area with very mineral-rich, hard water, you might want to cook the beans in filtered or distilled water. Some people add a pinch of bicarbonate of soda to offset the hardness, but use this only for the soaking period. Adding to the cooking period would alter the flavor of the beans. And be sure to mince the garlic as finely as possible so that as it cooks it all but melts into the sauce of the chickpeas.

Serve this salad as part of a large summer buffet or as a winter side dish to accompany roast poultry.

1½ cups (8 ounces; 250 g) dried chickpeas (garbanzo beans)
2 tablespoons extra-virgin olive oil
6 plump, fresh garlic cloves, peeled and minced
Bouquet garni: several springs of fresh summer savory, thyme, rosemary, and 1 fresh
    bay leaf, tied in a bundle with household twine
2 to 3 quarts (2 to 3 l) cold water
2 teaspoons fine sea salt, or to taste

VINAIGRETTE
1 tablespoon best-quality red wine vinegar
1 tablespoon best-quality sherry wine vinegar
Sea salt to taste
6 tablespoons extra-virgin olive oil
1 teaspoon fresh or dried savory leaves
Freshly ground black pepper to taste

1. Rinse and drain the chickpeas. Place the beans in a large bowl, add boiling water to cover, and set aside for 1 hour. (The soaking helps the beans reabsorb the water they lost as they were dried.) Drain and rinse the beans, discarding the water. Set aside.
2. In a large, heavy-bottomed pan, combine the olive oil, garlic, and bouquet garni, and stir to coat with the oil. Cook over moderate heat until the garlic is fragrant and soft,

about 2 minutes. Do not let it brown. Add the chickpeas, stir to coat with the oil, and cook for 1 minute more. Add 2 quarts (2 l) of water and stir. Cover, bring to a simmer over moderate heat, and simmer for 1 hour. Season with salt. Continue cooking at a gentle simmer until the beans are tender, about 1 hour more. Stir from time to time to make sure they are not sticking to the bottom of the pan. Add additional water if necessary. (Cooking time will vary according to the freshness of the beans.)

3. While the beans cook, prepare the vinaigrette: In a small bowl, combine the vinegars, season with salt, and whisk to blend. Add the oil and whisk once more. Season with savory leaves and freshly ground black pepper. Set aside.

4. When the beans are tender, remove them from the heat and drain off any remaining liquid in the pan. Remove and discard the bouquet garni. Transfer the beans to a large bowl, and while they are still warm, add the vinaigrette and toss to blend. Taste for seasoning. Serve either warm or at room temperature. The salad can be prepared up to 2 days in advance. Bring to room temperature to serve. Toss again and taste for seasoning before serving.

EIGHT TO TEN SERVINGS

༈ **A SAVORY TIP** ༈ Savory is often called "the bean herb" since its sweet flavor interacts naturally with beans—both fresh and dried—and helps brighten their flavor. But it is also reputed to help combat digestive problems associated with a diet rich in beans and cabbage. In herb gardens, summer savory is a delicate annual while winter savory—*sarriette* in French—is an evergreen perennial. Both have quite a spicy, peppery, almost camphorlike taste, like a blend of strong thyme and oregano. Savory should be used sparingly until the palate becomes accustomed to its potency. *Sarriette* grows wild all over Provence, where it is called *poivre d'âne* ("donkey's pepper") in French and *pèbre d'aï* in the Provençal language. A fresh or dried sprig of the herb is often used to heighten the flavors of the delicate cheeses made from goat's and sheep's milk.

SATURDAY BEEF SALAD

When I make City Steak (page 255) during the week, I always save any leftover meat for this hearty, wintertime salad for Saturday lunch. Chunks of rare beef are tossed with a fiery dressing of horseradish, mustard, and cornichons, along with fresh steamed potatoes.

About 20 small French cornichon pickles, thinly sliced
1 teaspoon imported Dijon mustard, or to taste
2 teaspoons prepared horseradish
Sea salt and freshly ground black pepper to taste
About 8 ounces (250 g) rare-cooked beef, cut into bite-size chunks
1 small red onion, peeled and cut into thin rings
2 tablespoons best-quality red wine vinegar
6 tablespoons extra-virgin olive oil
1½ pounds (750 g) firm, waxy, yellow-fleshed potatoes, such as Yellow Finn
About 12 leaves romaine lettuce, washed, rinsed, and broken into bite-size pieces

1. In a large, shallow salad bowl, combine the pickles, mustard, and horseradish, and stir to blend and evenly coat the pickles. Season with salt and pepper. Add the beef and toss to coat evenly. Set aside.

2. In another large, shallow bowl, combine the onion, vinegar, and salt, and stir to dissolve the salt. Whisk in the oil, season with pepper, and taste for seasoning. Reserve about 2 tablespoons of vinaigrette for the romaine lettuce. Set aside.

3. Scrub the potatoes but do not peel them. Bring 1 quart (1 l) of water to a simmer in the bottom of a steamer. Place the potatoes on the steaming rack. Place the rack over simmering water, cover, and steam until a knife inserted into a potato comes away easily, 20 to 30 minutes.

4. Immediately peel the potatoes. Cut into thin crosswise slices and drop the hot potatoes into the vinaigrette. Toss to blend and evenly coat the potatoes. Taste for seasoning.

5. Combine the potato and beef mixtures, and toss to blend. Set aside at room temperature for at least 1 hour for the flavors to mellow. Before serving, taste for seasoning and then toss the 2 tablespoons of vinaigrette with the lettuce. Place a bed of greens on 4 large salad plates. Place a mound of salad on the greens and serve. (The beef and potato portion of the salad will stay fresh for 2 to 3 days refrigerated in a sealed container.)

FOUR SERVINGS

WINE SUGGESTION: This salad calls out for a fruity young Beaujolais. My favorite is the Beaujolais cru, Saint-Amour.

CHEESEMAKER'S SALAD

Deep in the rugged, misty, and mountainous Auvergne region in central France, one still finds men who live and work in *burons,* tidy two-story gray stone shepherd's huts. Their lives are devoted to the daily ritual of making the rustic, earthy mountain cheese known as Salers. When I visited cheesemaker Raymond Dutrery some years back, we shared slices of his fruity, lactic cheese—so intense it tastes of mountain flowers—and talked of what sort of dishes he prepared in his humble dwelling. When salad time rolled around, Monsieur Dutrery explained that he dressed his greens with fresh cream—always on hand—and he loved the way the cream coated the tender greens. For the salad, he first softened thin rings of shallots in homemade red wine vinegar, tossed them with tender, delicate-flavored greens, then added the cream as a grand finale. The result is a vibrant-flavored, tangy salad that pairs beautifully with a platter of rich mountain cheeses such as the French Cantal or Salers, a farmhouse English cheddar, or a well-aged domestic farm cheddar.

> 2 shallots, peeled and sliced into thin rings
> 1 tablespoon best-quality red wine vinegar
> 1 head mild, delicate-flavored greens, such as butter crunch, oak leaf, or lollo rosso,
>   washed and well rinsed
> Fine sea salt to taste
> 2 to 3 tablespoons heavy cream

In a large, shallow salad bowl, toss the shallots and vinegar to coat the shallots thoroughly. Set aside for at least 15 minutes and up to 4 hours to soften the shallots. At serving time, add the greens, toss to coat with the vinegar and shallots, and season with salt. Add the cream, tablespoon by tablespoon, tossing gently to coat the leaves. Taste for seasoning and serve on large salad plates.

FOUR SERVINGS

SLICED ARTICHOKE & PROSCIUTTO SALAD

Four of my favorite ingredients—artichokes, arugula, prosciutto, and Parmesan—are linked in this terrific salad. With four intense flavors and textures, it is a salad that sings of good health. I sampled a more sophisticated, carefully layered version of this salad one evening at an Italian restaurant in Paris, but prefer this more casual rendition.

1 tablespoon freshly squeezed lemon juice
Sea salt to taste
3 tablespoons extra-virgin olive oil
Freshly ground black pepper to taste
1 fresh artichoke
One 2-ounce (60-g) chunk of Parmigiano-Reggiano cheese
2½ ounces (75 g) thinly sliced prosciutto, cut into matchsticks (see Note)
2 bunches (3 ounces; 100 g) stemmed arugula leaves, washed and dried

1. In a large, shallow salad bowl, whisk together the lemon juice and salt. Whisk in the oil and pepper. Taste for seasoning. Set aside.
2. Prepare the artichoke: Break off the stem of the artichoke as you would break off the tough ends of an asparagus spear, to about 1 inch (2.5 cm) from the base. Carefully trim and discard the stem's fibrous exterior, leaving the edible and highly prized inner, almost-white stem. Cut off the top fourth of the artichoke. Bend back the tough outer green leaves, one at a time, letting them snap off naturally at the base. Continue snapping off leaves until only the central cone of yellow leaves with pale green tips remains. Lightly trim the top cone of leaves to just below the green tips. Trim any dark green areas from the base. Halve the artichoke lengthwise. With a grapefruit spoon or melon baller, scrape out and then discard the hairy choke. Place the artichoke half, cut side down, on a clean work surface. Using a very sharp knife, slice the halved artichoke lengthwise into paper-thin slices. Toss them with the vinaigrette in the salad bowl and taste for seasoning.
3. Using a vegetable peeler, shave the Parmesan cheese into long thin strips directly into the salad bowl. (If the chunk of cheese becomes too small to peel, grate the remaining cheese and add to the bowl.) Toss to blend. Add the prosciutto and toss to blend. Add the arugula and toss to coat the leaves thoroughly. Add several grindings of fresh pepper and taste for seasoning. Serve immediately on large dinner plates.

FOUR SERVINGS

NOTE: When cutting the prosciutto into matchsticks, do this carefully. You may stack the slices, but do this while the prosciutto is cold, and with a very sharp knife.

Fresh artichokes at the Vaison market.

✧ **ARTICHOKE TIP** ✧ Here's advice I've taken from French chefs: The next time you prepare a fresh artichoke, don't cut the stem but break it. Place the artichoke on a cutting board, wrap your hand around the stem, and sharply break it off at the edge of the table. Along with the stem you will remove the tough and fibrous strands that can give an artichoke a chewy, tough texture.

✧ **ON STORING ARTICHOKES** ✧ Not only is an artichoke loaded with vitamins A, B_1, B_2, and C, but it is also equipped with potassium, calcium, phosphorus, and iron. Although it has excellent flavor and health virtues, it is a vegetable that does not keep well; hence, you should prepare them as soon as you bring them home. If you must store them before using, peel off the outer layer of skin from the stem with a vegetable peeler and place them in a stout glass or vase of water. The removal of the outer skin will precipitate the absorption of water and prevent the stems from drying out. After all, the artichoke is a member of the thistle family—so why not treat it like the flower it is?

3

SOUPS

SOUP IS ONE OF THE WORLD'S GREAT COMMUNAL dishes. Nothing can replace the warmth of a steaming soup tureen, placed at the edge of the table, ready to serve a gathering of hungry family and friends. In warm weather, cold soups—such as Chilled Cream of Pea or Cold Tomato with Basil— help perk up appetites diminished by the heat of the sun. In cold weather, a fragrant bowl of Artichoke, Parmesan, & Black Truffle Soup teases the palate as it warms the soul. Main-course soups fit to feed a crowd have become a signature at our farmhouse, where gatherings of fifteen or twenty are common affairs. So year-round, the Provençal aromas of fennel, saffron, anise, and tomato waft from my kitchen, as I concoct another batch of Monkfish Bouillabaisse, a colorful pot of Summer (or Winter) Pistou, or a warming rendition of Maggie's Vegetable Potage.

FACING PHOTOGRAPH: *Patricia checks her indoor bread oven, recently installed in her living room at Chanteduc.*

MONKFISH BOUILLABAISSE WITH AÏOLI

I created this vibrant golden soup one summer afternoon after the local fishmonger, Eliane Berenger, presented me with a plump, glistening monkfish fresh from the Mediterranean. Chunks of mild-flavored, firm-textured monkfish are bathed in a tomato-rich broth punctuated with the sharp, lively flavors of fennel, saffron, garlic, and orange zest. A dab of garlic-rich aïoli adds a crowning touch to this modern bouillabaisse.

2 pounds (1 kg) very fresh monkfish, bone-in, or substitute tilefish, grouper, striped bass, or cod
3 tablespoons extra-virgin olive oil
1 head plump, fresh garlic, cloves separated and peeled
1 teaspoon fennel seeds
Bouquet garni: a generous bunch of flat-leaf parsley, celery leaves, fresh bay leaves, and sprigs of thyme tied in a bundle with household twine
2 teaspoons sea salt, or to taste
2 tablespoons tomato paste
2 tablespoons pastis, or anise liqueur
1 small can (14½ ounces; 400 g) imported whole plum tomatoes in juice
6 plump, ripe tomatoes, peeled and quartered
1½ quarts (1½ l) water
¼ teaspoon cayenne pepper, or to taste (optional)
4 small, firm, fresh fennel bulbs (about 1½ pounds; 750 g), trimmed, quartered lengthwise, and cut into bite-size pieces
A small pinch (about ¼ teaspoon) of saffron threads
Grated zest (orange peel) of 1 orange
3 tablespoons minced fennel fronds or leaves
1 recipe Aïoli (see below)

1. Fillet the fish: With a fillet knife, cut away the thin membrane covering the outside of the fish. Cut along one side of the central bone to remove the fillet. Repeat with the other side. Cut the monkfish fillet at an angle into 3-inch (7.5-cm) *escalopes* (or ask your fishmonger to do this for you). Place the *escalopes* on a large platter, cover, and refrigerate until serving time. Reserve the bone and crack slightly.
2. In a large, heavy-bottomed stockpot, heat the oil over moderate heat until hot. Add the garlic, fennel seeds, bouquet garni, salt, and monkfish bone. Sweat—cook gently without browning—for 8 to 10 minutes. This will create a condensed, flavorful soup base. Add the tomato paste, anise liqueur, canned tomatoes, fresh tomatoes, water, and cayenne pepper, if using. Cover and bring to a boil over high heat. Lower the heat and simmer for 45 minutes. Remove and discard the bouquet garni and monkfish bone. Using an immersion mixer, roughly puree the liquid in the casserole. (Alternatively, pass

(continued on next page)

the liquid through the coarse blade of a food mill and return it to the casserole.) Taste for seasoning. Add the fennel bulbs, cover, and simmer gently until soft, 15 to 20 minutes more. (The dish can be prepared several hours in advance up to this point and reheated when adding the monkfish.)

3. At serving time, bring the liquid to a very gentle simmer to assure that the soup will be thoroughly heated. Add the saffron and monkfish. Lower the heat and cook the fish gently just until tender, 3 to 4 minutes more. Taste for seasoning.

4. To serve, transfer portions of the fish and fennel to warmed shallow soup bowls. Spoon the broth over the fish. Sprinkle with the orange zest and fennel fronds. Pass the aïoli, allowing the guests to swirl a teaspoon or two into their soup. Serve with plenty of toasted homemade bread.

FOUR TO SIX SERVINGS

 WINE SUGGESTION: I enjoy this with an elegant, rich white wine, such as a white Châteauneuf du Pape from Beaucastel.

AÏOLI: GARLIC MAYONNAISE

EQUIPMENT: A mortar and pestle

6 plump, fresh garlic cloves, peeled and minced
½ teaspoon fine sea salt
2 large egg yolks, at room temperature
1 cup (25 cl) extra-virgin olive oil

1. Pour boiling water into a large mortar to warm it; discard the water and dry the mortar. Place the garlic and salt in the mortar and mash together with a pestle to form as smooth a paste as possible. The fresher the garlic, the easier it will be to crush.

2. Add the egg yolks. Stir, pressing slowly and evenly with the pestle, always in the same direction, to thoroughly blend the garlic and yolks. Continue stirring and gradually add just a few drops of the oil. Whisk until thoroughly incorporated. Do not add too much oil in the beginning, or the mixture will not emulsify. As soon as the mixture begins to thicken, add the remaining oil in a slow, steady stream, whisking constantly. Taste for seasoning. Transfer to a bowl and serve immediately. The sauce can be refrigerated, well sealed, for up to 2 days. To serve, bring to room temperature and stir once again.

ABOUT ONE CUP (25 CL) SAUCE

FACING PHOTOGRAPH: *Golden aïoli.*

Noncooks think it's silly to invest two hours' work in two minutes' enjoyment;
but if cooking is evanescent, well, so is the ballet.

JULIA CHILD

SUMMER PISTOU

Our wedding anniversary falls at the end of summer, the time our good friends Rita and Yale Kramer make their annual visit. They usually insist on preparing an anniversary feast, and, inevitably, Yale proudly spends the day chopping and peeling, shelling and simmering, making a memorable version of pistou, a summery vegetable soup. This also happens to be one of my favorite dishes to prepare and serve throughout the season. It's an ideal way to get children who won't eat vegetables to devour them, and after many wasp-troubled meals outdoors, I've learned that wasps don't come near the soup! So hurrah again for pistou.

There are as many recipes for pistou as there are cooks who prepare it, and I am particular about what should go into mine. I insist upon an abundance of carrots for color, a mix of fresh white beans as well as cranberry beans, leeks for a touch of elegance, lots of whole garlic, and plenty of green beans. I like the pasta to be as diminutive as possible so it doesn't overwhelm. My recipe differs from more traditional versions in that rather than tossing all the vegetables into the mix at one time, I sweat some of the vegetables first in oil for better color and depth of flavor. Finally, I love mixing the traditional Gruyère with the untraditional Parmesan, adding yet another layer of flavor to one of summer's greatest dishes. Note that while the soup starts out a brilliant green, the color fades as the vegetables cook. This is why a touch of tomato and carrot are nice, and why a verdant hit of garlic and basil pistou not only thickens the soup but boosts the flavor and color as well.

THE BEANS

    3 tablespoons extra-virgin olive oil

    3 plump, fresh garlic cloves, peeled and minced

    1 pound (500 g) fresh small white (navy) beans in the pod, shelled, or 8 ounces
       (250 g) dried small white beans (see Note)

    1 pound (500 g) fresh cranberry beans in the pod, shelled, or 8 ounces dried
       cranberry beans (see Note)

    Bouquet garni: several fresh bay leaves and several sprigs of summer savory and
       thyme, tied securely with household twine

    Sea salt and freshly ground black pepper to taste

(continued on next page)

Summer Pistou in the making.

THE SOUP

½ cup (12.5 cl) extra-virgin olive oil

2 medium leeks, white and tender green parts only, cut into thin rings

2 medium onions, peeled and coarsely chopped

10 plump, fresh garlic cloves, peeled and quartered lengthwise

4 medium carrots, trimmed, peeled, halved lengthwise, and cut into half-moons

1 pound (500 g) potatoes, peeled and cubed

Bouquet garni: several fresh bay leaves and several sprigs of summer savory and
    thyme, tied securely with household twine

8 ounces (250 g) zucchini, trimmed, halved lengthwise, and cut into half-moons

8 ounces (250 g) tomatoes, peeled, cored, and chopped

8 ounces (250 g) green beans, trimmed and quartered

Sea salt to taste

1 cup (100 g) very small macaroni, such as conchigliette

1 recipe Pistou (page 316)

1 cup (4 ounces; 125 g) freshly grated Parmigiano-Reggiano cheese

1 cup (4 ounces; 125 g) freshly grated imported Gruyère cheese

1. Prepare the beans: In a large, heavy-bottomed saucepan, combine the oil, garlic, and bouquet garni. Stir to coat with oil. Cook over moderate heat until the garlic is fragrant and soft, about 2 minutes. Do not let it brown. Add the beans and stir to coat with oil. Cook for 1 minute more. Add 1 quart (1 l) of water and stir. Cover, bring to a simmer over moderate heat, and simmer 5 minutes for fresh beans, 30 minutes for dried beans. Season lightly with salt. Simmer for 5 minutes more for fresh beans, 30 minutes more for dried beans. Add additional water if necessary. Taste for seasoning.

2. Meanwhile, in a 10-quart (10-l) stockpot, combine the oil, leeks, onions, and garlic over low heat and sweat—cook without coloring—for 2 to 3 minutes, stirring from time to time. Add the carrots, potatoes, and bouquet garni, and soften over moderate heat, stirring regularly for about 10 minutes. This will give a lovely color to the broth and enrich the final flavor of the soup. Remove the bouquet garni from the beans and discard. Add the beans and their cooking liquid to the vegetables in the stockpot. Add the zucchini, tomatoes, and green beans, along with 2 quarts (2 l) of cold water. Simmer gently, uncovered, until the beans are tender, about 20 minutes. (Cooking time will vary according to the freshness of the beans. Add additional water if the soup becomes too thick.) Add the pasta and simmer until the pasta is cooked, about 10 minutes more. Remove and discard the bouquet garni. Stir in about half of the Pistou and half of the cheese.

3. Serve the soup very hot, passing the remaining Pistou as well as the two cheeses to swirl into the soup.

EIGHT TO TEN SERVINGS

WINE SUGGESTION: A Provençal rosé, such as the fine offering from Bandol's Domaine Tempier.

NOTE: If using dried beans, rinse them and pick them over to remove any pebbles. Place the beans in a large bowl, add boiling water to cover, and set aside for 1 hour. Drain the beans, discarding the water. Proceed with the recipe from Step 1.

ROASTED TOMATO SOUP WITH FRESH HERBS

At the end of summer when plum tomatoes are still in abundance in our garden and the days are growing cooler, this flavorful soup is perfect. The process of roasting the tomatoes is the same one used to prepare homemade sun-dried tomatoes, yet the tomatoes are baked in a slightly hotter oven and not nearly as long. What you're looking for is similar to what the French call a *confit,* an intensely flavored, reduced essence of tomato. (Yet unlike the true tomato *confit,* these tomatoes are baked with all their pulp and seeds, making for a less dense, more juicy flavor.) This soup is an ideal gift for anyone who gardens and grows tomatoes.

EQUIPMENT: A food mill

2 pounds (1 kg) fresh plum tomatoes (Roma)
Fine sea salt to taste
4 tablespoons finely chopped fresh herb leaves, such as a mix of summer savory, basil, parsley, and thyme
About 1 quart (1 l) homemade Chicken Stock (page 322) or Potager Stock (page 321)

1. Preheat the oven to 275°F (135°C; gas mark 2).
2. Trim and discard the stem end of the tomatoes. Halve each tomato lengthwise. Arrange the tomatoes, cut side up, on a baking sheet side by side. Sprinkle lightly with salt and about half the herbs.
3. Place in the oven and bake until the tomatoes are nearly dried and shriveled, about 2 hours. Check the tomatoes from time to time. They should still be rather flexible but not at all brittle, and most of their juice should have baked away.
4. Remove the tomatoes from the oven and allow them to cool slightly. Place a food mill (fitted with its coarsest blade) over a large bowl. Transfer the tomatoes to the food mill and puree.
5. Meanwhile, pour the stock into a large stockpot and bring to a boil over high heat. Add the tomatoes and stir to blend. Lower the heat and simmer for about 5 minutes to allow the flavors to mingle. Taste for seasoning. Serve in warmed shallow soup bowls and sprinkle with fresh herbs.

FOUR SERVINGS

CURRIED CAULIFLOWER SOUP

While we were working on our book *Simply French,* chef Joël Robuchon presented me with a series of very complex, multistep soups that were favorites at his restaurant. Since I was never able to duplicate some of them satisfactorily at home, the soup recipes never made it into the book. *Crème de Choufleur,* or cauliflower cream served with a jellied caviar base, has long been one of his most popular dishes. Here I've taken the easiest portion of the recipe—the cauliflower cream—and added an extra dose of curry powder. The result is a haunting golden-hued soup, one that could serve as an elegant first course for a winter's feast or as a homey lunchtime main dish.

> 2 pounds (1 kg) cauliflower, trimmed and rinsed
> Sea salt to taste
> 1 quart (1 l) homemade Chicken Stock (page 322)
> 2 teaspoons curry powder, or to taste
> 1 large egg yolk
> ⅔ cup (16 cl) heavy cream

1. Break the cauliflower into bite-size florets. Bring a large pot of water to a boil over high heat. Add salt and the cauliflower, and blanch for 2 minutes. Drain and refresh under cold running water.

2. In a large saucepan, warm the stock over moderate heat. Taste for seasoning. Add the cauliflower, cover, and simmer until tender, about 20 minutes.

3. Transfer the broth and cauliflower in small batches to the bowl of a food processor. Puree and return to the saucepan. Simmer over moderate heat until reduced to 3 cups (75 cl), about 15 minutes. Season to taste with curry powder.

4. In a large bowl, combine the egg yolk and cream. Whisk to blend.

5. Pour a ladleful of the simmering puree into the bowl with the cream mixture. Whisk vigorously. Return the mixture to the saucepan. Place over low heat and cook, stirring constantly with a wooden spoon, until the mixture thickens to a creamy consistency, 2 to 3 minutes. The mixture should not boil. Taste for seasoning. Transfer to warmed shallow soup bowls. Serve immediately. (The soup can be prepared up to 1 day in advance and reheated. If necessary, thin with warm water or milk. The curry flavor and color will intensify with age.)

SIX SERVINGS

AMAZING SORREL SOUP

While traveling around Germany one summer, I sampled many versions of sorrel soup—a flavor I truly adore—and was astonished and puzzled to find that the soups were all a brilliant, healthy-looking green. One common problem with cooking sorrel is that the herb loses its happy green color, turning sort of a dull military drab when heated. It was chef Dieter Müller who shared his secret: Blend the sorrel with butter, adding it at the end of the cooking time. Even after the soup has been sitting for a while, it remains green. I love this soup hot or cold and have also prepared it with fresh watercress leaves, a worthy substitute.

> 3 ounces (90 g) fresh sorrel leaves, stemmed, thoroughly washed, and spun dry, or substitute watercress
> 3 tablespoons (1½ ounces; 45 g) unsalted butter, at room temperature
> 2 tablespoons extra-virgin olive oil
> ½ small onion, peeled and sliced into thin rounds
> 6 ounces (180 g) starchy potatoes, peeled and diced
> 1 quart (1 l) homemade Chicken Stock (page 322) or Potager Stock (page 321)
> 1 cup (25 cl) heavy cream
> Sea salt and freshly ground white pepper to taste

1. In a food processor, puree the sorrel, pulsing on and off for 30 to 45 seconds. Add the butter and puree. Transfer to a small bowl, cover, and set aside in a cool area of the kitchen. (Do not refrigerate, or the sorrel butter is likely to be too cold to add to the soup at the end.)

2. In a large saucepan, heat the oil until it is hot but not smoking. Add the onion and sweat over low heat until soft, 3 to 4 minutes. Add the potatoes and cook over low heat until golden, 10 to 15 minutes. Remember not to cook over too high a heat, or they will burn instead of coloring a beautiful golden brown.

3. Add the stock and simmer for about 20 minutes or until the potatoes are fully cooked. Stir in the heavy cream. Using an immersion mixer, puree the soup directly in the stockpot. (Alternatively, pass the soup through the coarse blade of a food mill or use a blender. Return it to the stockpot.) The potatoes will give thickness and body to the soup without detracting from the sorrel. Taste for seasoning. Just before serving, whisk the sorrel butter into the hot soup, taking care to mix thoroughly and quickly. Serve in heated soup bowls.

FOUR TO SIX SERVINGS

COLD TOMATO SOUP WITH BASIL

I don't think a day goes by that I don't eat them in a salad, on pasta, in a sauce, or in soup. When I wander through our vegetable garden in Provence, the very fragrance of a tomato plant makes me salivate, bringing back a lifetime's memories of backyard gardens and sturdy tomato plants, staked tepee-style, laden with an abundance of ripe red fruit. Still, we never seem to have our fill of homegrown tomatoes, so the local farmers always end up filling in the gap. This quick, easy, healthy tomato soup is ideal on those days when the farmer's markets and garden are bursting with tomatoes. Note that, for deeper color, the onion is not peeled.

EQUIPMENT: A food mill

2 cloves
1 onion, halved
2 pounds (1 kg) firm, ripe tomatoes, quartered
4 plump, fresh garlic cloves, peeled and quartered
2 teaspoons sea salt
1 stalk celery, minced
1 tablespoon extra-virgin olive oil
2 cups (50 cl) water or Potager Stock (page 321)
1 bunch of fresh thyme
2 bay leaves, preferably fresh
4 tablespoons basil leaves, rinsed, patted dry, and cut into julienne strips
Several tablespoons cream, or a few drops of extra-virgin olive oil,
    for garnish (optional)

Press a clove into each half of the onion and place in a stockpot. Add the tomatoes to the stockpot along with the garlic, salt, celery, oil, water or stock, thyme, and bay leaves. Bring to a boil over high heat, lower the heat, and simmer, uncovered, for 20 minutes. Remove the onions, thyme, and bay leaves, and discard. Pass the soup through the coarse blade of a food mill into a bowl. Taste for seasoning. The soup can be served either hot or cold, sprinkled with fresh basil. For a richer soup, swirl in cream, or olive oil, if desired.

VARIATIONS: Add any of your favorite herbs to the soup as it cooks. At serving time, add any favorite garnish: A *persillade,* or a combination of finely minced garlic and parsley, would heighten the flavor of the soup, hot or cold. For a thicker soup, served hot or cold, reheat the soup and cook a small handful of vermicelli or very fine angel's hair pasta, simmering until the pasta is cooked through.

FOUR TO SIX SERVINGS

CHILLED CREAM OF PEA SOUP

A brilliant green soup with a refreshing touch of mint, this chilled warm-weather soup has the ability to make one feel instantly healthy and revitalized. The secret to maintaining the true green pea color is to blanch the peas and then refresh them in cold water, thus "setting" the chlorophyl. The refreshing ice bath also helps maintain their crisp crunch. The addition of mint to the blanching water is a small "tip" but one that—like so many minor cooking *trucs*—makes the difference between a dish that's flat and one-dimensional and one that is layered with nuanced flavors.

Sea salt to taste

Several sprigs of fresh mint

4 pounds (2 kg) fresh peas in their pods, or about 1½ pounds (750 g) fresh shelled peas

1 cup (25 cl) homemade Chicken Stock (page 322) or Potager Stock (page 321), at room temperature

1 tablespoon sugar

⅔ cup (16 cl) heavy cream

4 tablespoons fresh mint leaves, cut into julienne strips, for garnish

1. Prepare a large bowl of ice water.

2. In a large pot, bring 3 quarts (3 l) of water to a rolling boil. Add 1½ tablespoons sea salt, sprigs of fresh mint, and peas, and blanch just until soft, about 10 minutes. (The peas should be cooked longer than you might normally, since you want them to puree easily.)

3. Immediately drain the peas and plunge them into the ice water so they cool down as quickly as possible. Discard the branches of mint. (The peas will cool in 1 to 2 minutes. If you leave them longer, they will begin to lose flavor.) Drain the peas thoroughly.

4. In the bowl of a food processor, combine the drained peas, stock, and sugar, and puree. Add the cream and mix once again. Pass the soup through the coarse blade of a food mill. The soup should be quite thick—the consistency of split pea soup. Taste for seasoning. Transfer to a bowl and refrigerate for at least 2 hours to chill. To serve, taste for seasoning, transfer to chilled shallow soup bowls, and garnish each bowl with slivers of fresh mint.

FOUR SERVINGS

ARTICHOKE, PARMESAN & BLACK TRUFFLE SOUP

One blustery February evening several years ago I sampled this sublime, sophisticated winter soup at Guy Savoy's restaurant in Paris. Part of a multicourse feast that included perfumed oysters bathed in a jellied cream and a perfectly roasted guinea hen, this ethereal soup combined the nutty flavor of artichokes, the richness of Parmesan, and the fragrance of fresh black truffles. The soup was truly one of the best dishes I had tasted in months. I would almost like to title the dish "clandestine," for its secrets were surreptitiously gathered by my assistant, Alexandra Guarnaschelli, when she worked in Guy Savoy's kitchens as the fish chef. Since this is a home version, the black truffles are optional. I add the fresh black truffles when preparing a festive feast, for artichokes and black truffles enjoy each other's company: Each accentuates the mysterious, earthy flavor of the other. Although I prefer to prepare this with fresh artichokes, I'm aware that many cooks may not be adept at turning out perfect artichoke bottoms. I have tried this recipe with artichokes in a jar and find the flavor too dull; however, frozen artichokes—usually sold in packages labeled artichoke hearts—are a worthy substitute.

EQUIPMENT: A food mill

4 tablespoons extra-virgin olive oil

Sea salt to taste

2 shallots, minced

4 artichokes, 8 baby artichokes (see Note), or two 9-ounce (270-g) packages frozen
    artichoke hearts, thawed

1 cup (25 cl) white wine, preferably a Chardonnay

3 cups (75 cl) homemade Chicken Stock (page 322)

One 2-ounce (60-g) chunk of Parmigiano-Reggiano cheese

1 tablespoon unsalted butter

1 fresh black truffle, thinly sliced (optional)

1. In a large, nonaluminum saucepan, combine 2 tablespoons of oil, a pinch of salt, and the shallots, and stir to blend. Cook over moderate heat until golden, 2 to 3 minutes. Do not let the shallots brown, or they will turn bitter. Add the artichokes and toss to blend. Add the remaining 2 tablespoons of oil and cook, uncovered, until the artichokes are soft and impregnated with oil, about 2 minutes more. Add the wine, pouring it all over the surface of the pan. Adjust the heat to bring the liquid to a gentle simmer and cook, uncovered, until most of the wine—and alcohol—has cooked off, about 7 minutes from the time the liquid comes to a simmer. (The wine not only adds a pleasantly acidic flavor to the soup but will also prevent the artichokes from turning brown.) Add the chicken stock, adjusting the heat to create a gentle simmer. Cover and simmer just until the artichokes are soft

and the flavors have had time to mingle, about 20 minutes more. Taste for seasoning.

2. Place a food mill over a large bowl and puree the soup. (Discard any fibrous bits that remain in the mill.) Return the soup to the saucepan. The soup should be a pleasant golden green and should have the consistency of a slightly runny puree. If the soup appears thin, reduce it slightly over moderate heat. (The soup can be prepared to this point several hours ahead and reheated at serving time.)

3. Using a vegetable peeler, shave the cheese into long, thick strips into a bowl. (If the chunk of cheese becomes too small to shave, grate the remaining cheese and add it to the bowl.) Set aside.

4. To serve, heat the soup and whisk in the butter to add brilliance and to smooth out the texture. Divide the hot soup among 4 heated soup bowls. Place the truffle slices and then the cheese shavings on top of the soup. If done correctly, the shavings should sit delicately on top of the soup, half-melted but still intact. Serve immediately.

FOUR SERVINGS

NOTE: *To trim and prepare artichokes—* Halve a lemon and squeeze the juice into a large bowl of cold water. Add the lemon halves to the water. With your hands, break off the stem from the base. Bend back the tough outer green leaves, one at a time, and snap them off at the base. Continue snapping off leaves until only the central cone of yellow leaves with pale green tips remain. Lightly trim the top cone of leaves to just below the green tips. Trim any dark green areas from the base. Slice the vegetable lengthwise, making it easier to remove the choke. Halve the artichoke lengthwise. With a small spoon or a melon baller, scrape out the hairy choke from each half and discard. Cut each artichoke half into eight even slices. Return each slice to the acidulated water. Repeat for the remaining three artichokes. Set aside.

Fresh black truffles, ready for slicing.

WINTER PISTOU

Like a symphony of winter flavors, colors, and fragrances, this soup plays a warming tune: The squash and carrots add a brilliant tone, the beans an earthy note, while the turnips play percussion, waking the palate like the sound of a cymbal. Anointed with a touch of either summerlike pistou sauce or all-season aïoli, it's the soup I make on Saturdays while puttering about the kitchen with a warming fire nearby.

8 ounces (250 g) dried small white beans

8 ounces (250 g) dried cranberry beans

½ cup (12.5 cl) extra-virgin olive oil

Bouquet garni: several fresh bay leaves and several sprigs of summer savory and thyme, tied securely with household twine

2 medium leeks, white and tender green parts only, cut into thin rings

2 medium onions, peeled and cut into thin half-moons

1 head plump, fresh garlic, peeled and quartered lengthwise

Sea salt to taste

1 pound (500 g) Hubbard or pumpkin squash, seeded, peeled, and diced

4 medium carrots, peeled and cut into thick half-moons

1 pound (500 g) potatoes, peeled and cubed

8 ounces (250 g) turnips or parsnips, peeled and cubed

1 small can (14½ ounces; 400 g) imported whole plum tomatoes in juice

¾ cup (60 g) angel's hair pasta, broken into small pieces

1 recipe Pistou (page 316) or 1 recipe Aïoli (page 314)

1 cup (4 ounces; 125 g) freshly grated imported Gruyère cheese

1. Rinse the white beans and cranberry beans, picking over them to remove any pebbles. Place the beans in a large bowl, add boiling water to cover, and set aside for 1 hour. Drain the beans, discarding the water.

2. In a 10-quart (10-l) stockpot, combine the oil, bouquet garni, leeks, onions, garlic, and 1 teaspoon of salt. Soften over medium heat, stirring regularly for about 10 minutes. Add the drained beans, stir to blend, and cook for 2 minutes more. Add the squash, carrots, potatoes, turnips, and tomatoes; stir to blend, and cook 5 minutes more. Add 5 quarts (5 l) of water, season with salt, and simmer gently, uncovered, until the beans are tender, 1½ to 2 hours. (Cooking time will vary according to the freshness of the beans.) Taste for seasoning. Add the pasta and boil until the pasta is cooked, about 10 minutes more. Taste for seasoning.

3. Serve the soup very hot, passing the Pistou or Aïoli and cheese to blend into the soup.

SIX TO EIGHT SERVINGS

WINE SUGGESTION: A Provençal rosé. My favorite comes from Bandol's Domaine Tempier.

CARAMELIZED FENNEL SOUP

ooking is an art that requires patience, timing, and exactitude; however, mistakes can also bring about fabulous results. Sometimes I get so absorbed in a new recipe or idea that I forget about outside distractions. Other times a quick break from the kitchen can clear my thoughts and help me realize what result I want to produce. I had a straightforward fennel soup in mind, and as my fennel sweated slowly, peacefully, on my stove, I decided to take a trip to the garden for a few herbs. I returned to my stockpot only to discover that the fennel had caramelized in the oil—producing a fragrant, memorable soup, and one that I now make often—on purpose.

> 2 pounds (1 kg) fennel bulbs, trimmed and minced
>
> 6 tablespoons extra-virgin olive oil
>
> Sea salt to taste
>
> Bouquet garni: a generous bunch of fresh rosemary, parsley, bay leaf, and thyme, tied securely with household twine
>
> 1 quart (1 l) Potager Stock (page 321) or homemade Chicken Stock (page 322)

1. In a large, heavy-bottomed stockpot, combine the fennel and oil. Cook, covered, over low heat and sweat for 10 minutes. Coat the pieces of fennel with the oil, stirring from time to time to make sure they are not sticking to the bottom of the stockpot. Be certain that the fennel does not burn, for it would give your soup a bitter flavor.

2. After about 10 minutes, remove the lid and let the fennel continue to cook over a low heat. The pieces should gradually brown and caramelize. Add the bouquet garni and stock, and simmer, covered, for 30 minutes.

3. Remove the bouquet garni and discard. Using an immersion mixer, roughly puree the soup directly in the stockpot. (Alternatively, pass the soup through the coarse blade of a food mill or puree coarsely in batches in a food processor, and return it to the stockpot.) The soup should have a creamy consistency but not be totally smooth. Taste for seasoning. Serve piping hot in warmed shallow soup bowls.

FOUR SERVINGS

TIP: Cleaning fennel of its outer skin is a tough chore but well worth the result. To avoid excess loss, try using a vegetable peeler instead of a knife. The peeler will remove the skin without taking the fennel along with it.

QUICK CHICKEN=LEMON SOUP

As a young bride in the 1960s, I enjoyed making a version of the Greek lemon soup known as *avgolemono* (chicken broth enriched with rice, thickened with egg yolks, and enlivened by a touch of lemon juice). Recently, I revived and revised it, creating a soup that's a relative of the *avgolemono* and Italy's *straciatella*. This soothing, warming soup is a favorite midweek supper dish, one that can be prepared quickly and painlessly. Here the rice and the yolks gently thicken the broth, while the lemon juice brings out the fresh, clean flavors of the poached poultry. Simple as this soup is, it's elegant enough to present to guests when entertaining. Variations are endless: Sometimes I prepare a vegetarian version with potager stock and substitute fresh mushrooms for the chicken. Season at the last minute with your favorite herbs: Tarragon and lemon grass are naturals with both chicken and mushrooms. The soup is also delicious the following day.

1½ quarts (1.5 l) homemade Chicken Stock (page 322) or Potage Stock (page 321)

½ cup (100 g) short-grain white rice

Sea salt to taste

1 skinless, boneless chicken breast, cut into matchsticks

3 tablespoons freshly squeezed lemon juice

3 large egg yolks

½ cup (2 ounces; 60 g) freshly grated Parmigiano-Reggiano cheese

Freshly grated nutmeg to taste

Freshly ground white pepper to taste

Fresh flat-leaf parsley leaves, for garnish

1. In a large stockpot, bring the chicken broth to a boil over high heat. Lower the heat, add the rice and salt, and simmer, covered, for 5 minutes. Add the chicken and simmer for 5 minutes more. Taste for seasoning. (The soup can be prepared to this point several hours in advance.)

2. In a large bowl, combine the lemon juice and egg yolks, and whisk to blend. Add half of the cheese and whisk to blend. Set aside.

3. At serving time, add a ladle of warm (not boiling) soup to the egg mixture and whisk to blend. Pour the mixture back into the stockpot, whisking briskly until well blended. Add a grating of nutmeg and pepper, and taste for seasoning. Serve in warmed shallow soup bowls, garnished with the remaining cheese and parsley.

FOUR SERVINGS

MAGGIE'S VEGETABLE POTAGE

My good friend Maggie Shapiro is a great cook. Every moment I spend in the kitchen with her, I learn some *truc* that she assumes every worldly housewife knows. One rainy September, as our house was bursting at the seams with guests, Maggie took over kitchen duty, with me as her assistant (pen and notebook in hand). Maggie's secret here is to brown all the vegetables slightly first, then add stock, so each element maintains its own character and flavor. The addition of lettuce is a common French custom and one we should all add to our vegetable soup-making repertoire. This is a simple, nonfrivolous, healthy soup—nothing but vegetables, a touch of olive oil, good stock, and a gentle flourish of Parmigiano-Reggiano cheese.

4 tablespoons olive oil
1 leek, white part only, trimmed, scrubbed, and chopped
Sea salt to taste
3 medium carrots, peeled and chopped
2 turnips, peeled and chopped
2 zucchini, peeled and chopped
2 large potatoes, peeled and chopped
A handful of minced cabbage
½ head of lettuce (such as romaine), washed, dried, and coarsely chopped
1 quart (1 l) homemade Chicken Stock (page 322) or Potager Stock (page 321)
One 2-ounce (60-g) chunk of Parmigiano-Reggiano cheese

1. In a large, heavy-duty stockpot, combine the oil, leeks, and 1 teaspoon of salt, and cook until lightly browned, 4 to 5 minutes. Add the carrots, turnips, zucchini, and potatoes in small batches, cooking each vegetable for several minutes before adding the next one. Once all the vegetables are lightly browned, add the cabbage and lettuce, and stir vigorously until wilted. There should be almost no liquid left at this point. Add hot water just to cover the vegetables and simmer, covered, until the carrots and turnips are soft, about 25 minutes. Taste for seasoning. Add the stock and simmer gently, covered, for 30 minutes more. Taste for seasoning.

2. While the soup simmers, prepare the cheese. Using a vegetable peeler, shave long, thick strips of the cheese into a bowl. (If the chunk of cheese becomes too small to shave, grate the remaining cheese and add it to the bowl.) Set aside.

3. Remove the stockpot from the heat. Using an immersion mixer, puree the soup directly in the stockpot. (Alternatively, pass the soup through the coarse blade of a food mill or use a blender. Return it to the stockpot.) Taste for seasoning.

4. To serve, ladle the hot soup into warmed soup bowls and place the cheese shavings on top of the soup. Serve immediately.

EIGHT SERVINGS

A assortment of winter vegetables at the village market.

◡: WHAT'S IN A SOUP? :◡ Originally, *soupe* was the word used to describe the slice of bread used to "sop" up the liquid contents of the cooking pot, or *potage*. In fact, the terms "broth" and "potage" were used until the word "soup" became the fashionable replacement. Soup, as well as *potage,* is essentially water to which any combination of solid ingredients, meats, vegetables, fish, or fruit has been added. Thick soups refer to those that are pureed or strained to give a smooth but thick consistency. Otherwise, a soup is clear, and the ingredients are cooked slowly and served in their broth of cooking juices. Soup originally served the same function as an hors d'oeuvre in the meal. It was a liquid-based dish intended to awaken the palate gently and prepare it for the flavors of the meal. In modern cooking a soup can make a meal in itself, and every country has at least one soup associated with its origins. Examples include Russian borscht, French pot-au-feu and bouillabaisse, and Italian minestrone.

GARLIC FAMILY SOUP

With garlic in such fine abundance year-round in the markets, the garlic family all but takes over my garden much of the year. In the fall I plant shallots and baby onions to enjoy in the springtime. And in summer I plant leeks for the fall. Chives are there for the asking year-round. It's clear that this recipe was born of the need to do something with the vegetable family! Although the final flavor is very creamy, there's not a touch of cream in the dish.

> 6 leeks
> Sea salt to taste
> 3 quarts (3 l) water
> 2 medium onions, peeled
> 6 shallots, peeled and halved lengthwise
> 1 head garlic, cloves peeled and halved lengthwise
> 4 tablespoons extra-virgin olive oil
> Bouquet garni: Several sprigs of fresh parsley and tarragon, several bay leaves and
>   celery leaves, wrapped in the green of a leek and tied with household twine
> 1½ pounds (750 g) potatoes, peeled and cubed
> Fresh minced herb leaves, tarragon, chives, parsley, or chervil for garnish

1. Trim and rinse the leeks, separating the coarse, dark green portion from the white and tender, pale green portions. Chop the white and pale green portions. Set aside.
2. Prepare the leek broth: In a large stockpot, combine the dark green portion of the leeks, a pinch of salt, and the water. Bring to a boil over high heat. Cover, lower the heat to moderate, and simmer for 15 minutes.
3. Meanwhile, slice the onions in half lengthwise. Place each half, cut side down, on a cutting board and cut crosswise into very thin slices.
4. In a heavy-bottomed stockpot, combine the reserved portions of the leeks, onions, shallots, garlic, olive oil, bouquet garni, and salt. Sweat over moderate heat, covered, until the vegetables are soft and tender, about 10 minutes.
5. Strain the leek broth and pour it over the vegetables. Add the cubed potatoes. Cover and bring to a simmer over moderate heat. Cook for 1 hour. Remove and discard the bouquet garni. Using an immersion mixer, puree the soup directly in the stockpot. (Alternatively, pass the soup through the coarse blade of a food mill or use a blender. Return it to the stockpot.) To serve, transfer to warmed, shallow soup bowls and garnish with the fresh herbs.

SIX TO EIGHT SERVINGS

FACING PHOTOGRAPH: *The essential flavors of Provence: Fresh thyme, basil, rosemary, bay leaves, garlic, onions, and shallots.*

From my office window at Chanteduc—I can survey our vineyards as well as Mount Ventoux and the beginning of the Alps to the east.

4

VEGETABLES

GIVE ME VEGETABLES, VEGETABLES, AND more vegetables. as a side dish, as the main course, as a solo player, as part of a symphony of wholesome gifts from the earth. Serve them hot, serve them cold, bathe them in olive oil and garlic, grill them, roast them, braise or sauté them. From my modest garden and the soil of Provence come tender violet artichokes, juicy sun-ripened tomatoes, shiny oval eggplants, anise-flavored bulbs of fennel, buttery white beans or *cocos blancs,* fresh spring peas and late spring fava beans. Preparation can be quick and easy—as in Barcelona Grilled Artichokes or Meaty Grilled Mushrooms—long and slow—as in Pure Tomato Confit or Tender Roasted Shallots—or even an elaborate main-dish vegetarian offering—such as Celery Root Lasagne and Monsieur Henny's Eggplant Gratin. Potatoes take their place of honor in gratins, simply roasted with a sprinkling of salt, smashed with oil and herbs, pureed with olive oil and Parmesan, or simply roasted, as in the favored Fake *Frites.*

BARCELONA GRILLED ARTICHOKES

Artichokes for breakfast? Why not. Especially if you've just finished touring Barcelona's vivid, kinetic covered market and stopped at the Bar Pinochio for a bracing espresso, a breakfast of thinly sliced flattop-grilled artichokes, fresh-from-the-fishmonger's langoustines, and sheerly decadent fried sweets. This artichoke dish is quick and versatile, to be served as an appetizer, a quick vegetarian luncheon dish, or as a particularly complementary accompaniment to roasted or grilled fish.

    1 tablespoon freshly squeezed lemon juice
    Fine sea salt to taste
    3 tablespoons extra-virgin olive oil
    2 plump, fresh garlic cloves, peeled and minced
    4 artichokes, 8 baby artichokes (see Note, page 95), or two 9-ounce (270-g) packages
        frozen artichoke hearts, thawed

1. In a large, shallow salad bowl, whisk together the lemon juice and salt. Whisk in the oil and garlic. Taste for seasoning. Set aside.
2. Thoroughly drain the artichoke slices. Toss them with the lemon-oil-garlic mixture. (This can be done up to 2 hours in advance.) Set aside, uncovered, at room temperature.
3. Preheat the broiler. Transfer the artichokes in a single layer to a nonstick baking sheet. Place the baking sheet about 3 inches (12.5 cm) from the heat. Broil until the artichokes are golden and sizzling, 2 to 3 minutes. (Alternatively, grill over a gas, electric, or wood charcoal fire.) Transfer to a bowl and toss. Taste for seasoning. Serve.

FOUR SERVINGS

VARIATION: For a stovetop version, sauté the artichokes in a nonstick skillet with the dressing. Once cooked, toss with freshly grated Parmesan cheese and snippets of fresh flat-leaf parsley leaves.

FACING PHOTOGRAPH: *From top to bottom: Braised Whole Garlic (page 130); Barcelona Grilled Artichokes; and Braised Red Onions (page 130).*

MEATY GRILLED MUSHROOMS

Come October, our pine woods are filled with dozens of varieties of wild mushrooms. Everyone in the village seems to know "the" spot to find the freshest *girolles* (chanterelles), the reddest *lactaire delicieux* (lactarius), the plumpest *boletus* (bolete). Everyone except Walter and me. We can go out for hours at a time and spot not a single *champignon.* Finally, we got smart: We tired of everyone telling us how fertile

A "back from the market" still life: bright red currants or groseilles, *fresh radishes, and meaty* sanguines *mushrooms (*lactarius deliciousus*), named for the blood-red juice they give off when sliced.*

our woods were and began organizing group hunts, with a
fine meal to follow. One of our favorite methods for cooking mushrooms is a simple grill, with a difference: The
mushrooms are first grilled and then sautéed, making for
superbly moist, full-flavored mushrooms without a touch
of dryness. I learned the technique from Benoit Guichard,
chef Joël Robuchon's right-hand man in the kitchen. Any
good meaty variety of fresh mushroom can be used here,
including cultivated white mushrooms, cremini, or porto-
bello. These are also good at room temperature and as a
topping for pizzas or *fougasse.*

*At the Vaison market, a vegetable
merchant greets Patricia with a kiss.*

> 1 pound (500 g) meaty mushrooms, rinsed and
>   trimmed
> 2 tablespoons extra-virgin olive oil
> Sea salt and freshly ground black pepper to taste
> 1 teaspoon fresh thyme leaves
> 4 tablespoons (2 ounces; 60 g) unsalted butter

1. Cut each mushroom lengthwise into ⅛-inch (2.5-mm)
slices. Brush both sides of each mushroom slice with oil. Season with salt, pepper, and
thyme.

2. Preheat a gas, electric, or ridged cast-iron stovetop grill. Or prepare a wood or charcoal
fire. The fire is ready when the coals glow red and are covered with ash.

3. Place each mushroom on the grill at a 45-degree angle to the ridges of the grill. Grill
for 1 minute, pressing down firmly on the mushrooms with a baking sheet to accentuate
the impression of the grill marks. Still grilling the same side of the mushroom, reposition
each mushroom at the alternate 45-degree angle. Grill for 1 minute more, pressing down
firmly on the mushrooms with the baking sheet. (This will form a very even and attractive grill mark on the mushrooms.) Turn each mushroom over and grill on the other side,
positioning the mushrooms again at the two angles and pressing down firmly on the
mushrooms. Grill for a total of 2 minutes more.

4. In a large skillet, heat the butter over moderate heat until it sizzles. Add the grilled
mushrooms in several carefully arranged layers, sprinkle with thyme, and finish cooking,
covered, until soft and tender, about 5 minutes more. Do not turn the mushrooms but,
rather, baste regularly with the buttery cooking juices.

FOUR SERVINGS

 WINE SUGGESTION: From the Jura, a light and tasty white Arbois.

ARTICHOKE & BASIL RAGOUT

I make this dish often in the early fall, with end-of-season artichokes and the garden's final burst of basil. I've used wine in place of stock to connect the acidity of the lemon juice and the natural lemony tang of the artichoke, making for a very digestible dish. This is also delicious tossed with fresh pasta: You'll need about 8 ounces (250 g).

2 cups (50 cl) dry white wine, such as a white Rhône, Riesling, Aligoté, or Chenin Blanc

1 cup (25 cl) loosely packed fresh flat-leaf parsley leaves, carefully destemmed

8 plump, fresh garlic cloves, peeled and halved

Sea salt to taste

2 firm, ripe tomatoes, cored, peeled, and chopped

½ cup (12.5 cl) extra-virgin olive oil

4 artichokes, 8 baby artichokes (see Note, page 95), or two 9-ounce (270-g) packages frozen artichoke hearts, thawed

4 tablespoons fresh basil leaves, carefully destemmed and cut into julienne with a scissors or sharp knife

1. In a 3-quart (3-l) saucepan, bring the wine to a boil over high heat. Boil vigorously until all the alcohol has burned off and there is no alcohol aroma wafting from the saucepan, about 8 minutes.

2. With a large chef's knife, finely chop the parsley, garlic, and salt. Transfer to a heavy-duty saucepan. Add the tomatoes, oil, and wine. Thoroughly drain the artichoke slices and add to the saucepan. Cover and bring just to a simmer over moderate heat. Turn the heat to low, cover, and simmer very gently for 30 to 45 minutes for fresh artichokes, 10 to 15 minutes for thawed, frozen artichokes, until they are soft and offer no resistance when pierced with a knife. The ragout should not be dry but should be bathed in a fragrant, delicious sauce. Stir in the basil. Taste for seasoning.

3. To serve as a first course or vegetable side dish, transfer to warmed shallow soup bowls, spooning the sauce over the artichokes. Pass plenty of crusty bread for sopping up the soup. (To serve with pasta, toss the artichokes with 8 ounces [250 g] of cooked fresh linguine, using all the liquid as the sauce. The pasta does not require cheese.)

FOUR TO SIX SERVINGS

WINE SUGGESTION: Serve the same simple dry white wine as used in cooking the artichokes.

Zucchini, tomatoes, and peppers—a Provençal trinity.

⋋: WHAT'S A RAGOUT? :⋋   Sometimes I feel as though the French language was poetically designed around its cuisine. One of my favorite examples is the origins of the word *ragout.* Coming from the French verb *ragouter,* it denotes anything that stimulates or awakens the palate. This idea of reviving a tired palate leads to speculation that stews and ragouts were originally quite spicy, though they have since evolved into elegant dishes. Dating from the sixteenth century, a ragout is classically a stew made from any meat or fish cooked in a thickened sauce with aromatic flavorings. Essentially, there are two types of classical ragouts: the "brown" ragout, in which the meat or firm fish is seared in oil or butter and then cooked with flour and stock, and the "white" ragout, which is cooked without coloration and then treated in the same manner with flour and stock. Since all ragouts are formed with meats and flour, the final product is always thick and satisfying.

A *ragout* also means a basic garnish for filling tarts, *vol-au-vent,* and such. For vegetables, the same basic principle applies: A mix of vegetables is first seared and then cooked in their own juices. I like to think of a ragout as an ensemble of tightly bound flavors that emerge tasting greater than the sum of their parts. Here I've gathered my favorite flavors of early fall to enjoy as a hearty vegetable ragout.

PROVENÇAL ROAST TOMATOES

This variation of roast tomato recipes found in my previous books is included here because it is a classic Chanteduc dish, one that accompanies almost every roast leg of lamb and chicken that I cook in my wood-fired oven. Two important common cooking techniques are used to succeed here: First, the tomatoes are seared—meaning they are browned with intense heat to seal in the juices and impart color and more flavor. Next, they are deglazed with vinegar (sometimes a very hot, spicy one for extra punch)—a process of adding liquid to the pan in which the tomatoes have been seared. This is done to allow the deglazing liquid to absorb the glaze and the crusty browned bits formed on the bottom of the skillet. Deglazing should always be done off the heat to avoid burning those precious juices.

EQUIPMENT: One oval baking dish large enough to hold all the tomatoes in a single layer (about 10 x 16 inches; 25 x 41 cm)

¼ cup (6 cl) extra-virgin olive oil
12 firm tomatoes, cored and halved lengthwise
Sea salt to taste
¼ cup (6 cl) fresh mixed herbs, such as parsley leaves, tarragon, basil, and rosemary, snipped with a scissors
¼ cup (6 cl) best-quality red wine vinegar or *Pili Pili* Vinegar (page 313)

1. Preheat the oven to 400°F (200°C; gas mark 6/7).
2. In a very large skillet, heat the oil over moderately high heat. When hot, place as many tomatoes as will easily fit in the pan, cut side down. (If you crowd the pan, the tomatoes will steam, not sear). Sear without moving the tomatoes, until they are dark and almost caramelized, 3 to 4 minutes. Transfer the tomatoes, cooked side up, to the baking dish. Overlap them slightly since they will reduce as they bake. Continue until all the tomatoes are seared. Season the tomatoes lightly with salt. Remove the pan from the heat. Deglaze the remaining fat in the pan with the vinegar. Return the pan to high heat, scraping the bottom of the pan to loosen drippings into the liquid. Pour over the tomatoes. Sprinkle with fresh herbs.
3. Place the baking dish in the center of the oven and bake, uncovered, until the tomatoes are soft, shriveled, and even a bit black around the edges, about 30 minutes. Serve hot, warm, or at room temperature.

EIGHT SERVINGS

VARIATION: This recipe lends itself to endless variation. As a change of pace and an even more substantial dish, top the tomatoes with a dollop of Pistou (page 316) and a grating of Parmesan cheese before placing them in the oven.

JUNE VEGETABLE RAGOUT WITH HERB GARDEN PISTOU

One June morning the extraordinarily fresh array of vegetables on display at my vegetable merchant in Vaison-la-Romaine nearly knocked me out with its sheer beauty. I wanted to bring them all home, and so I did, combining the purple-tipped artichokes (known as *poivrades*), plump fava beans, last-of-season peas, and asparagus. I had made some pistou the day before and still had some in the refrigerator, so I added the lively sauce to this sunny ragout. The wine—both its fruit and its acid—links the varied flavors of the vegetables.

> 2 medium onions, peeled
>
> 6 tablespoons extra-virgin olive oil
>
> 1 head plump, fresh garlic, cloves peeled but left whole
>
> Sea salt to taste
>
> Bouquet garni: small bunch of summer savory or thyme and parsley, tied in a bundle with household twine
>
> 8 artichokes, 16 baby artichokes (see Note, page 95), or four 9-ounce (270-g) packages frozen artichoke hearts, thawed and quartered
>
> 2 pounds (1 kg) fava beans in their pods; 2 cups (50 cl) shelled beans, first skin removed
>
> 3 tomatoes, peeled, cored, seeded, and coarsely chopped
>
> 1½ cups (37.5 cl) white wine
>
> 2 pounds (1 kg) fresh peas in their pods; 2 cups (50 cl), shelled, blanched, and refreshed
>
> 20 fresh asparagus tips, blanched and refreshed
>
> 1 recipe Pistou (page 316)

1. Slice the onions in half lengthwise. Place each half, cut side down, on a cutting board and cut crosswise into very thin slices. Makes about 2 cups (50 cl).
2. In a large unheated skillet, combine the onions, oil, garlic, salt, and bouquet garni, and toss to coat the ingredients with the oil. Sweat over low heat, covered, until the onions are soft, about 10 minutes. Drain the artichokes, and add with the fava beans, tomatoes, and wine, and simmer, uncovered, for 10 minutes to burn off the alcohol. Add the blanched peas and asparagus, and cook for 1 minute more. Remove and discard the bouquet garni. Serve immediately, passing a bowl of Pistou and plenty of crusty homemade bread.

FOUR SERVINGS

 WINE SUGGESTION: Since this dish could be served as a main course, it deserves its own wine. Use the same wine as for cooking, such as a Sauvignon Blanc.

TIP: Blanch vegetables one to two minutes in boiling salted water, then refresh them for one minute in ice water so they will retain their lovely green color.

PATRICIA'S SPEEDY RATATOUILLE

I think of this dish as my speedy ratatouille since it's made in a flash and still possesses many of the great qualities of a painstakingly prepared ratatouille. No matter how big a batch I make, it disappears with great haste. It's equally good warm or cold, served as a vegetable dish or tossed with pasta. Just be certain that you use firm, young zucchini fresh from the garden. Old, worn, and wrinkled zucchini have no place here. Adding a drop of vinegar at the end lends a sharp touch, particularly refreshing when served slightly chilled on a very hot day.

¼ cup (6 cl) extra-virgin olive oil
10 small, very fresh zucchini (about 2 pounds; 1 kg), cut into thin rounds
2 teaspoons fresh thyme leaves, carefully stemmed
Sea salt to taste
3 plump, fresh garlic cloves, peeled and minced
2 pounds (1 kg) fresh plum tomatoes (Roma), cored, peeled, seeded, and chopped
2 tablespoons tomato paste
2 teaspoons best-quality red wine vinegar

1. In a very large skillet over moderately high heat, heat the oil until hot but not smoking. Add the zucchini and 1 teaspoon of thyme leaves and sauté, shaking the pan from time to time, until the zucchini is cooked through but still firm and just beginning to brown slightly, about 5 minutes. (The zucchini need not be in a single layer, but the rounds should not be piled high in the skillet.) The zucchini is done at the point it begins to taste like cooked zucchini and before it loses its brilliant green color.
2. Add the salt and garlic, and cook for 1 or 2 minutes more, just until the garlic begins to brown. (The salt will force the zucchini to give off liquid, which will prevent the garlic from burning.) Add the tomatoes, tomato paste, and vinegar, and, still over moderately high heat, continue cooking, uncovered, until ingredients are well blended and very little liquid remains in the skillet, about 10 minutes more. Add the remaining teaspoon of thyme and taste for seasoning. Serve warm or at room temperature.

SIX TO EIGHT SERVINGS

Cooking should be a carefully balanced reflection of all the good things of the earth.

JEAN AND PIERRE TROISGROS

TURNIP & CUMIN PUREE

It's time for turnips—with their subtle gingerlike flavor—to stand on their own. All too often this firm, dense root vegetable is relegated to the stockpot or acts as a minor character in boiled beef and vegetables, or pot-au-feu. Here—all on their own—turnips are paired with a gentle dose of cumin. Serve this with a simple roast duck.

> 2 tablespoons unsalted butter
> 12 ounces (750 g) turnips, peeled and cubed
> Sea salt to taste
> A pinch of sugar
> About 1 cup (25 cl) homemade Chicken Stock (page 322)
> ½ teaspoon cumin seeds

1. In a large skillet, heat the butter over moderate heat until it sizzles. Add the cubed turnips and salt lightly. Add the sugar and sauté, tossing until the turnips are lightly browned all over, about 7 minutes. Cover with chicken stock and cook over low heat until almost all the liquid has evaporated, about 30 minutes.

2. Transfer to a food mill or the bowl of a food processor and puree. Season to taste with cumin. Taste for seasoning. Serve warm, as a vegetable side dish. (The puree can be prepared several hours in advance. Keep warm in the top of a double boiler set over simmering water.)

FOUR SERVINGS

PURE TOMATO CONFIT: OVEN-ROASTED TOMATOES

Nothing can match the pure, wholesome flavor of tomatoes, and no method amplifies tomato essence like a reduction. These are the sun-dried tomatoes of the 1990s—fresh tomatoes that are baked for hours in a very slow oven until much of their moisture evaporates, creating tomatoes with a dense, haunting, rich, and pleasantly tangy flavor. Be sure to adjust the oven to the lowest possible heat so that the tomatoes actually melt more than bake. I use the tomatoes in soups, salads, on sandwiches, for pasta, or anywhere I want a rich, pure tomato flavor. Although fresh herbs have a tendency to burn when baked, both the liquid provided by the oil and the low oven temperature prevent this from happening.

> 2 pounds (1 kg) fresh plum tomatoes (Roma), peeled, cored, seeded, and quartered lengthwise
> Fine sea salt and freshly ground black pepper to taste
> A pinch of confectioners' sugar
> 2 sprigs of fresh thyme, stemmed
> 4 plump, fresh garlic cloves, peeled and slivered
> 2 tablespoons extra-virgin olive oil

1. Preheat the oven to the lowest possible setting, about 200°F (90°C; gas mark 1).
2. Arrange the tomato quarters side by side on a baking sheet. Sprinkle each side lightly with salt, pepper, and confectioners' sugar. Scatter the thyme leaves over the tomatoes and place a garlic sliver on top of each quarter. Drizzle with olive oil. Place in the oven and cook until the tomatoes are very soft, about 1 hour. Turn the tomatoes, baste with the juices, and cook until meltingly tender and reduced to about half their size, about 2 hours total. Check the tomatoes from time to time. They should remain moist and soft. Remove from the oven and allow to cool thoroughly.
3. Transfer the tomatoes to a jar along with the cooking juices and oil. Cover securely and refrigerate up to 1 week. Use in salads, on sandwiches, for pasta, or anywhere you want a rich, pure tomato flavor.

TWO CUPS (50 CL)

◡ **TWO WAYS TO PEEL A TOMATO** ∾ I have two schools of thought on peeling tomatoes: When serving tomatoes raw—as in a salad—I peel them with a vegetable peeler, using a back-and-forth sawing motion to remove the peel. This way the tomatoes are not subjected to heat and retain their delicious raw flavor.

When tomatoes will eventually be cooked, blanch them in boiling water for one minute, then refresh them in cold water, and the peel will slip off with ease.

It was in France that I first learned about food.
And that even the selection of a perfect pear, a ripe piece of Brie, the freshest butter,
the highest quality cream were as important as how the dish
you were going to be served was actually cooked.

ROBERT CARRIER

MONSIEUR HENNY'S EGGPLANT GRATIN

One spring weekday just before Easter, I was chatting with my butcher, Monsieur Henny. Along with my leg of lamb, he wrapped up a container of eggplant and tomato gratin from his *traiteur,* or delicatessen counter. The simple gratin was a revelation: He had taken baby eggplants, sliced them in half, and placed them, cut side up, in a gratin dish. A brush of olive oil, a sprinkling of fresh herbs, and fresh halved tomatoes, cut side down, nested on top of the eggplant. A long roasting in a hot oven and— *voilà!*—a marvelously dark, caramelized vegetable gratin full of the rich flavor of a fine ratatouille. When the dish comes bubbling and fragrant from the oven, even you are convinced the dish was laborious and complicated. I think of it as my "slice and forget it" gratin, for it takes no more than three of four minutes of preparation time. The possibilities with the dish are endless. I've added my own touch, a dusting of freshly grated Parmesan, to provide a bit of body and to bind the flavorful juices that flow from the tomatoes and the eggplant. If there is any left over, recycle by topping it with tomato sauce, fresh herbs, and another sprinkling of cheese. The dish is best made with tiny eggplants, weighing no more than 5 ounces (150 g). They generally have more flavor and are less likely to be bitter.

EQUIPMENT: One shallow 2-quart (2-l) gratin dish

   2 tablespoons extra-virgin olive oil
   3 small eggplants, each weighing about 5 ounces (150 g) or the equivalent weight in
      larger eggplants, trimmed at stem end
   Fine sea salt to taste
   3 tablespoons finely minced mixed fresh herb leaves, such as rosemary, sage, thyme,
      and basil
   A pinch of dried oregano
   ½ cup (2 ounces; 60 g) freshly grated Parmigiano-Reggiano cheese
   2 pounds (1 kg) fresh tomatoes, cored and halved crosswise

1. Preheat the oven to 450°F (230°C; gas mark 8).

2. Drizzle 1 tablespoon of oil over the bottom of the gratin dish. If the eggplants are small, slice them in half lengthwise. (If they are large, cut them into four lengthwise slices.) Place the eggplants, skin side down, in a single layer in the gratin dish. Lightly score them with a sharp knife. Sprinkle with the salt and minced fresh herbs and oregano. Sprinkle with about half the cheese. Place the tomato halves, cut side down, on top of the eggplants in a single layer. Brush the tomato skins with the rest of the oil and sprinkle with the remaining cheese.

3. Place the gratin dish in the center of the oven and bake until the vegetables are soft and almost falling apart, about 1 hour. The tops of the tomatoes should be almost black, and the juices from the eggplant and tomato should turn thick and almost caramelized. Serve warm or at room temperature, as a side dish or main vegetable dish. Use a spatula to cut and serve measured portions.

FOUR TO SIX SERVINGS

WINE SUGGESTION: A bright young red is ideal: Chianti, Côtes du Rhône, a California Zinfandel.

◦: **ON EGGPLANT** :◦ Eggplants are a tricky business because everything is hiding beneath the protective outer skin. In selecting the best eggplants, pick them up and test the weight: The best are firm, and heavy for their size. Select the smallest available since large eggplants not only are less tender but also contain larger seeds that contribute to a bitter aftertaste. (This is why I am opposed to salting eggplant to "rid them of bitterness." If the eggplant is fresh in the first place, it will never be bitter.) I am also of the "never peel an eggplant" school: Why discard something that's so beautiful and tastes so delicious? Note that the eggplant's porous, fat-free flesh is also capable of absorbing impressive quantities of oil, water, or any liquid, which is why I find broiling them in the oven the best way to enjoy them without drenching them in olive oil. The broiling helps eggplants to release their natural juices without drying them out. Baste the eggplants as they cook for added moisture and flavor.

Watch a French housewife as she makes her way slowly along the loaded stalls ...
searching for the peak of ripeness and flavor.... What you are seeing is a true artist at work,
patiently assembling all the materials of her craft, just as the painter squeezes
oil colors onto his palette ready to create a masterpiece.

KEITH FLOYD

BRAISED & GRATINÉED FENNEL

In Provence, fennel grows wild along the roadsides and is an easy garden vegetable. I often raid the garden of the delicate fronds for salad, being careful not to overdo it, for the fronds help provide the light and energy that keep this bulb vegetable growing. Since fennel is one of my favorite vegetables, no one need coax me to prepare this dish. Anything that comes bubbling from the oven with a nice coating of cheese wins my appetite! Much of the work can be done in advance: The fennel is lightly browned, then braised in a touch of broth. The drained fennel is then gratinéed at the last minute under the grill. The same dish can be prepared with many other vegetables, including celery, carrots, cauliflower, and cabbage, with approximately the same cooking times.

EQUIPMENT: One shallow 2-quart (2-l) gratin dish

> 6 tablespoons extra-virgin olive oil
> 2 pounds (1 kg) fennel bulbs, trimmed and quartered lengthwise
> Sea salt to taste
> 2 cups (75 cl) Potager Stock (page 321) or homemade Chicken Stock (page 322)
> ½ cup (2 ounces; 60 g) freshly grated Parmigiano-Reggiano cheese

1. In a large skillet, heat the oil over moderately high heat until hot but not smoking. Add the fennel and a touch of salt. Sweat, covered, over moderate heat until the fennel begins to brown lightly and becomes impregnated with the oil, about 5 minutes. Add the stock, cover, and simmer gently until the fennel is meltingly tender throughout, about 30 minutes. If any broth remains in the skillet, remove the fennel and reduce the liquid over high heat until just a few tablespoons of thick sauce remain. Reserve. Taste for seasoning. (The fennel can be prepared to this point up to 2 hours in advance.) Return the fennel to the skillet, cover, and set aside.
2. Preheat the broiler.
3. Transfer the fennel slices and any reserved sauce in a single layer to a large gratin dish. Sprinkle with cheese. Place the baking dish under the broiler about 3 inches

(8 cm) from the heat. Broil until the cheese is melted and fragrant, and the fennel sizzling, 1 to 2 minutes.

4. Serve immediately as a vegetable side dish. This is particularly delicious with a roast turkey or chicken, pork, or grilled fish, or all by itself as a vegetable main dish.

FOUR TO SIX SERVINGS

TIP: Never discard the delicate, feathery fronds that sprout from the top of a bulb of fennel. They can be minced and tossed into salads or scattered over this gratin when the fennel comes from the oven.

VARIATION: Top the fennel with a few quarters of Pure Tomato Confit (page 119) before sprinkling with cheese.

◡ **A WORD ON FENNEL** ⌁ "Florence" fennel is the term used to describe bulb fennel—*fenouil* in French and *finnochio* in Italian. It's a vegetable that responds brilliantly to braising, stewing, and even grilling. The compelling anise taste is tempered by the sweetness of the juices and the mellow, translucent texture. Etymologically, fennel comes from *feniculum* or *fenum,* meaning "little hay." This is perhaps an allusion to the wispy fronds at the top of the bulb. When storing fresh fennel, it is best to trim the larger stems and leave only a few small fronds intact. Otherwise, the stems continue to extract moisture from the bulbs, leaving the interiors spongy and stringy.

*The secret of good cooking is, first, having a love of it. . . . If you're convinced
that cooking is drudgery, you're never going to be good at it,
and you might as well warm up something frozen.*

JAMES BEARD

CELERY ROOT LASAGNE

Life works in strange ways. One day I was in New York cooking several recipes from my book *Bistro Cooking* for television. One show was on potato gratins, so I selected a potato and celery root gratin. I hadn't made the dish for years and had forgotten how much I loved the combination of tangy potato gratin and a touch of tomato, cream, and cheese. I couldn't wait to return home to Paris to create a new gratin using celery root. The very day of my return I dined at the wonderful Parisian restaurant L'Ambroisie where chef Bernard Pacaud prepared a "lasagne" of very thinly sliced celery root layered with white truffles, foie gras, and wild mushrooms. I went back to the tomato-cream mixture of my first gratin, but inspired to take the Italian accent of the dish even further, I replaced the traditional Gruyère cheese with freshly grated Parmesan. I always keep several batches of tomato sauce in my freezer, so dishes such as this are less of an ordeal. This lasagne can make a one-dish meal all on its own, or serve it as I have, with Sea Bass in Parchment with Warm Pistou (page 203).

EQUIPMENT: One shallow 2-quart (2-l) gratin dish

About 3 pounds (1.5 kg) celery root
2 tablespoons freshly squeezed lemon juice
Sea salt to taste
2 cups (50 cl) Tomato Sauce (page 325)
¾ cup (18.5 cl) heavy cream
Butter for preparing the gratin dish
1 cup (4 ounces; 120 g) freshly grated Parmigiano-Reggiano cheese

1. Preheat the oven to 400°F (200°C; gas mark 6/7).
2. Peel the celery root and cut it in half to make it more manageable. Using a mandoline, electric mandoline, or vegetable slicer, cut into paper-thin slices.
3. In a large pot, bring 6 quarts (6 l) of water to a rolling boil. Add the lemon juice, 3 table-spoons of salt, and the celery root, stirring to prevent it from sticking. Cook until tender but firm, about 7 minutes. Drain thoroughly, carefully pressing out any excess water.

4. Meanwhile, in a medium-size saucepan, combine the tomato sauce and cream, and warm over low heat. Taste for seasoning.

5. Butter the gratin dish. Layer ⅓ of the drained celery root on the bottom of the gratin dish. Top with ⅓ of the tomato sauce and ⅓ of the cheese. Repeat two more times until all the celery root, tomato sauce, and cheese have been used. (The dish can be prepared to this point several hours in advance. Bring to room temperature before baking.)

6. Place in the center of the oven and bake until golden brown, about 40 minutes. Serve immediately, cut into thick wedges.

SIX TO EIGHT SERVINGS

❧ **ON CELERY ROOT** ❧ Celery root is actually a vegetable of extremes: It's best either raw (as in a classic French *céleri remoulade,* a julienne of celery root tossed in a tangy mayonnaise) or in the form of a creamy puree or soup. The vegetable can be intimidating because, like turnips, it has several layers of skin that need to be thoroughly peeled before it can be used. The best way to begin is to cut off the top and bottom so it rests steadily on the cutting board. Then, with a sharp knife or vegetable peeler, cut around the edges from top to bottom, turning the celery as needed. Make sure to cut through and discard all the brown and light brown skin. Remove any large brown spots as well. The interior should be an off-white color. If peeled ahead of time, the celery will discolor and dry out. Store in water with a bit of lemon juice or vinegar until ready to use.

FRESH BEANS WITH GARLIC & HERBS

Fresh, white *cocos blancs* encased in pale celadon-green pods and the mottled red *cocos rouges* encased in brilliant red pods grow all over Provence in the summer. I love to serve the white beans as a simple salad, at room temperature, or as a warm dish to accompany roast lamb. I always mix both red and white beans for fresh summer pistou. For more complex flavors and varied colors, haunt your local farmer's market for fresh beans. They'll reward you with their creamy, nutty flavors, and you'll love the aromas that waft from the kitchen as fresh beans, garlic, and herbs fill the room with their mingled fragrances.

> 1 pound (500 g) fresh small white (navy) beans in the pod, shelled, or 8 ounces (250 g) dried small white beans, cooked
> 1 pound (500 g) fresh cranberry beans in the pod, shelled, or 8 ounces (250 g) dried cranberry beans, cooked
> 3 tablespoons extra-virgin olive oil
> 2 fresh bay leaves
> 3 plump, fresh garlic cloves, peeled and minced
> A large bunch of fresh thyme
> 2 quarts (2 l) cold water
> 1 teaspoon fine sea salt, or to taste

1. For dried beans: Rinse the dried beans, picking over them to remove any pebbles. Place the beans in a large bowl, add boiling water to cover, and set aside for 1 hour. Drain the beans, discarding the water.

2. For both fresh and dried beans: In a large, heavy-bottomed pan, combine the olive oil, bay leaves, garlic, and thyme and stir to coat with the oil. Cook over moderate heat until the garlic is fragrant and soft, about 2 minutes. Do not let it brown. Add the beans, stir to coat with the oil, and cook for 1 minute more. Add the water and stir. Cover, bring to a simmer over moderate heat, and simmer for 15 minutes for fresh beans or 30 minutes for dried beans. Season with salt. Continue cooking at a gentle simmer until the beans are tender, about 15 minutes more for fresh beans or 30 minutes more for dried beans. Stir from time to time to make sure they are not sticking to the bottom of the pan. Add water if necessary. (Cooking time will vary according to the freshness of the beans.) Taste for seasoning. Remove and discard the bay leaves and thyme. At serving time, pass a cruet of extra-virgin olive oil to drizzle over the beans.

SIX TO EIGHT SERVINGS

FACING PHOTOGRAPH: *A farmer with his homegrown produce.*

The onion is the truffle of the poor.
ROBERT J. COURTINE

ONION-PARMESAN GRATIN

I call this a dream recipe—it's low on labor and big on flavor. And it can be prepared quickly, with items a cook generally has on hand. This versatile vegetable dish, which tastes both light and rich at the same time, was inspired by chef Alain Passard, who serves it often in his elegant Parisian Left Bank restaurant Arpège. I find this onion gratin works miracles as a slightly sweet and mild accompaniment to strong-flavored dishes such as Beef Daube with Mustard, Herbs, & White Wine (page 258). The gratin is a good companion for both white and red wines, and can easily be prepared several hours in advance and then gratinéed just seconds before serving. The cloves, by the way, are a surprise ingredient and add a pleasantly unexpected flavor. For best results grind the whole cloves in a food mill or coffee grinder just before using.

EQUIPMENT: One shallow 1-quart (1-l) gratin dish

2 pounds (1 kg) onions, peeled
4 tablespoons (2 ounces; 60 g) unsalted butter
¾ teaspoon freshly ground whole cloves
½ teaspoon fresh thyme leaves
Fine sea salt to taste
2 large egg yolks
¼ cup (6 cl) heavy cream
½ cup (2 ounces; 60 g) freshly grated Parmigiano-Reggiano cheese

1. Slice the onions in half lengthwise. Place, cut side down, on a cutting board and slice crosswise into very thin slices. Set aside.
2. In a large nonstick skillet, combine the butter, cloves, onions, thyme, and salt. Cover and sweat over very low heat until the onions are very soft, about 10 minutes. Taste for seasoning.
3. Transfer the onion mixture to the gratin dish and smooth it with the back of a spoon. (The gratin can be prepared several hours in advance up to this point. Store, covered, at room temperature.)
4. Just before serving, preheat the oven broiler.
5. In a small bowl, combine the egg yolks and cream, and whisk with a fork to blend. Stir in the cheese. Pour the mixture over the onion mixture in the baking dish. Place the bak-

ing dish under the broiler, about 2 inches (5 cm) from the heat. Broil until the top is sizzling, fragrant, and golden, about 1 minute. Serve immediately as a vegetable course or as an accompaniment to such dishes as Beef Daube with Mustard, Herbs, & White Wine.

FOUR SERVINGS

WINE SUGGESTIONS: This gentle, harmonious dish reminds one of France's Loire Valley. The region's Savennières comes to mind, with its fruity, pleasantly acidic flavor. But any good red wine with a fine acid balance—a Beaujolais or Côtes du Rhône—would be fine.

⌁ THE MAGIC OF CLOVES ⌁   Cloves are actually the sun-dried, unopened, nail-like pink flower buds of a tropical evergreen tree native to Southeast Asia. The word "clove" comes from the Latin *clavus,* which literally means nail. In French, a clove is a *clou de girofle,* nail of the clove tree. (In fact, when someone is tiny and thin, they compare them to a *clou de girofle.*) Originally found in the Spice Islands, cloves were already in use in Asia long before they were discovered by the Dutch in the seventeenth century.

Long known for their medicinal value, cloves are still used to prevent nausea and to soothe aching eyes. Clove oil—distilled from the leaves and flower buds—is used as a flavoring, an insecticide, and to numb toothaches.

Though some compare the taste of clove to cinnamon or mace, its flavor is quite unique. The heat of cooking or a long marination helps to temper its intense spiciness. While in cooking the clove is primarily used for baking and for sweet wines, cloves are equally delicious when added to slow-cooked beef stews (where they bring out the flavor of beef nicely), meat sauces, even pickling vegetables. Traditionally, onions are studded with cloves when preparing soups or stocks. You will find cloves added to cold meats, such as sausages and hams, where they help aid digestion. Here I've experimented with mixing the clove's tangy bite with the warm comfort of milk. The pairing is dynamic.

Always purchase cloves whole and grind them yourself in a spice or coffee grinder. Never keep whole cloves for more than a year, for even the whole spice will lose its power and zest.

In cooking, as in the arts, simplicity is a sign of perfection.

CURNONSKY

BRAISED RED ONIONS

Vermilion red onions, roasted slowly in a warm oven, are a fine accompaniment to a simple roast pork, grilled sausages, or roast chicken. I like to make a large batch and use them on sandwiches and pizzas.

6 large red onions, in their skins
1 tablespoon extra-virgin olive oil
4 tablespoons water
Sea salt and freshly ground black pepper to taste

1. Preheat the oven to 275°F (135°C; gas mark 2).
2. Place the onions on a shallow baking sheet and drizzle with oil and water. Place in the center of the oven and bake, basting every 15 minutes, until soft, about 2 hours. To serve, remove the onion skins and either slice or leave the onions whole. Season with salt and pepper. For a spicy onion, drizzle with a few drops of hot oil or vinegar, or *Pili Pili* (page 313).

SIX SERVINGS

VARIATION: Substitute garlic for red onions. For delicious braised garlic, cut off and discard the top third from whole heads of garlic in their skins.

CELERY-PARMESAN GRATIN

O ften I feel like a one-woman band singing the praises of the world's most abused vegetable: celery. My garden in Provence harbors a special plot for growing the proud stalks, ready for transforming gratins, soups, and salads. Try letting celery star all on its own, as in this simple, refreshing gratin. You're not likely to regret it.

EQUIPMENT: One shallow 1-quart (1-l) gratin dish

Unsalted butter for preparing the gratin dish
5 cups (1.25 l) diced celery hearts, with leaves
Sea salt
½ cup (12.5 cl) heavy cream
Freshly ground black pepper to taste
¾ cup (3 ounces; 90 g) freshly grated Parmigiano-Reggiano cheese

1. Preheat the oven broiler.
2. Generously butter the gratin dish.
3. In a large pot, bring 6 quarts (6 l) of water to a rolling boil. Add 3 tablespoons of salt and the celery. Cook until tender but still firm, about 7 minutes. Drain thoroughly.
4. Toss the celery and cream in the gratin dish, and smooth the surface with the back of a spoon. Season generously with pepper. Sprinkle with the cheese.
5. Place the gratin dish about 5 inches (12.5 cm) from the heat. Cook until the cheese is melted and golden brown, 2 to 3 minutes. Serve immediately.

SIX TO EIGHT SERVINGS

*Our favorite street musician, Philippe, at the local market.
In honor of guest Julia Child's eightieth birthday,
he came up the hill with his barbary organ
for a special performance at Chanteduc.*

Large, naked raw carrots are acceptable as food only to those
who lie in hutches eagerly awaiting Easter.

FRAN LEIBOWITZ

CARROTS PROVENÇAL

Our friend Maggie Shapiro has been a frequent house guest over the years, and with each visit she seems to leave behind a recipe that becomes part of our repertoire. When she gave me this one, which she first ate years ago when her housekeeper Irma prepared it, she said, "Once you've tasted these, you'll never prepare carrots any other way." She's right. This beautiful dish—with a colorful contrast of black and orange—has become our traditional Thanksgiving vegetable. It's one with a personal Provençal touch: prepared with olives picked from our own trees. The carrots can be served warm or at room temperature, which means that you can make them in advance. Use baby carrots if available; cut them in half lengthwise.

> 2 tablespoons extra-virgin olive oil
> 2 pounds (1 kg) carrots, peeled and sliced diagonally
> 1 head plump, fresh garlic, cloves peeled and halved
> Sea salt to taste
> About 30 best-quality black olives (such as French Nyons), pitted and halved

1. In a large skillet, heat the oil over moderately high heat until hot but not smoking. Add the carrots, stir to coat with oil, and lower the heat to moderate. Cover and braise for 20 minutes, stirring regularly.
2. Add the garlic, season with salt, and stir. Reduce heat to low and continue cooking until the carrots are almost caramelized and the garlic is soft and tender, about 15 minutes more.
3. Sprinkle with the olives, stir, and taste for seasoning. Serve hot or at room temperature.

EIGHT TO TEN SERVINGS

VARIATION: Carrots and tarragon are natural partners. Try substituting about 4 tablespoons chopped fresh tarragon leaves for the black olives.

TENDER ROASTED SHALLOTS

Shallots grace the table with elegance and distinction. In this roasted version, the shallots are first simmered in milk, a procedure that serves to both soften and sweeten the root vegetable. This is a very tender vegetable accompaniment, one that is particularly delicious with Spit-Roasted Brine-Cured Pork (page 269).

> 18 shallots, in their skins
> 2 cups (50 cl) whole milk
> Sea salt to taste
> 1 tablespoon extra-virgin olive oil
> ½ teaspoon best-quality red wine vinegar

1. Preheat the oven to 400°F (200°C; gas mark 6/7).
2. In a shallow, heatproof, and ovenproof casserole, combine the shallots and milk. Bring to a simmer over moderate heat. Cover and simmer gently for 10 minutes. Drain the shallots, discarding the milk. Return them to the casserole and cover with aluminum foil.
3. Place in the center of the oven and roast until tender, about 35 minutes. Remove from the oven, season with oil and vinegar, and toss to blend. Serve whole, in their skins, as a vegetable accompaniment.

FOUR TO SIX SERVINGS

Corine and Josiane Meliani of Les Gourmandines, Vaison-la-Romaine's quality produce shop.

POTATOES ROASTED IN SEA SALT

In French, this potato preparation is known as *pommes de terre au diable* or *pommes de terre au sel,* a method of roasting tiny, whole potatoes in their skins with just a sprinkling of sea salt in an unglazed clay pot. The results of this ultra-simple preparation are astonishing: The potatoes emerge fragrant, with the skins just a bit crackly. The flesh of the potato is soft but not mushy, and is filled with the perfume of sea salt. As the potatoes cook, the clay absorbs some of their moisture, leaving behind a rich, almost primordial, earthy flavor. The dried clay pots, generally called devils or *diables,* come in several shapes. Sometimes they are twin round, flat-bottomed vessels with a pair of elongated clay handles. Other times they resemble a bean pot, with a flat bottom, a bulbous shape, a very tiny opening, and a very tiny lid. (The best substitute is Rompertof-brand unglazed clay pot.) I have an entire collection of these pots, some old, some new, because whenever I prepare this recipe, I never seem to manage to make enough potatoes for the crowd. I generally roast the potatoes in a clay pot in the oven, but traditionally the potatoes were cooked in the *diable* set in cinders in the fire. They can also be cooked on top of the stove over a very low flame set with a flame-tamer. This recipe allows for endless variations; I keep it very simple, with just a sprinkling of salt, tucking a few fresh bay leaves in for good measure. One might add whole garlic cloves in their skins, whole shallots in their skins, or a bunch of fresh thyme. Once the potatoes emerge from the clay cooker, they can be sampled with the sauce of whatever they are cooked with—a touch of olive oil, fresh butter, homemade mayonnaise, aïoli. The sky's the limit. The other beauty of this recipe is that the potatoes somehow know that they are not going to go into the oven alone. They sense that they will have to share the oven's heat, so they retain a very flexible attitude toward cooking time and temperature. This is a particularly "hostess friendly" dish, since the cook gets all the credit even though the honors really go to the potatoes and the clay cooker.

> About 4 teaspoons sea salt
> 2 pounds (1 kg) small, yellow-fleshed potatoes (such as Yukon Gold or Yellow Finn), scrubbed

1. Preheat the oven to 375°F (190°C; gas mark 5).
2. Sprinkle about 2 teaspoons of salt on the bottom of a dry clay cooker. Place the potatoes in the pot. Sprinkle with the remaining 2 teaspoons of salt. Cover. Place the clay cooker in the oven and roast. Once the potatoes present no resistance when pierced with a two-pronged fork, they are done, about 45 minutes. If the oven temperature is lowered, the potatoes will happily stay there until you are ready for them.
3. To serve, bring the clay pot to the table and uncover so that the guests can enjoy the pleasing, earthy aroma emerging from the pot.

SIX TO EIGHT SERVINGS

SMASHED POTATOES

After the fad of creamy mashed potatoes began to fade, Parisian palates moved on to what I call "smashed" potatoes and the French call *pommes écrasées*. Rather than reducing the potatoes to a puree, they are simply crushed with a fork and enriched with butter and oil. The dish shows up everywhere, from bistro tables to grand palaces, and plays a versatile role as a warming accompaniment to roast pork, chicken, lamb, or fish. It's a method that flatters the fragrance and flavor of very nutty, fruity, earthy yellow-fleshed potatoes. In France we use the fingerling *ratte* or yellow-fleshed Charlotte. Try this with fingerlings, such as banana or ruby crescents, or Yukon Golds. Be sure to have a large well-heated bowl on hand in which to crush the potatoes. The glory of this dish is the fragrance that wafts from the rising steam, so prepare and serve at the very last moment.

> 2 pounds (1 kg) firm, yellow-fleshed potatoes, scrubbed and peeled
> Coarse sea salt to taste
> 8 tablespoons (4 ounces; 120 g) unsalted butter
> 2 tablespoons extra-virgin olive oil
> Fine sea salt to taste
> 2 tablespoons fresh flat-leaf parsley, leaves only, snipped with a scissors

1. Place the potatoes in a large pot and fill with cold water to cover by at least 1 inch (3 cm). For each quart (l) of water, add 1 tablespoon (10 g) of coarse sea salt. Simmer, uncovered, over moderate heat until a knife inserted in a potato comes away easily, 20 to 30 minutes. Make sure the potatoes are fully cooked, or they will not mash properly. Drain the potatoes as soon as they are cooked. (If allowed to cool in the water, the potatoes will taste reheated.)

2. Transfer the potatoes to a warmed large serving bowl and dot with the butter and oil. With a large fork or a potato masher, coarsely crush the mixture to blend. Do not let it form a puree. Season with fine sea salt and parsley, and serve immediately.

FOUR TO SIX SERVINGS

VARIATION FOR GARLIC LOVERS: Simmer a head of peeled garlic cloves in cream until soft, then puree in the blender. When mashing the potatoes, add the garlic cream along with the butter and oil.

◌ **NEXT DAY TIP** ◌ Should you have any leftover potatoes, they are delicious cut into chunks and tossed in dressing—either fresh mayonnaise seasoned with herbs or an herb-flecked vinaigrette.

FAKE *FRITES*

Steamed and then roasted, these potatoes have the look and flavor of freshly cooked fries minus the excess fat. The potatoes can be steamed several hours in advance and roasted at the last minute. The steaming allows a fine, moist coating of starch to form on the surface of the potato, providing a very crisp texture when baked. Baking time will vary according to the variety of potato used as well as the cut. I like to cut my potatoes into fat, hefty fries. Serve with a simple roast, such as City Steak (page 255) or Spit-Roasted Brine-Cured Pork (page 269).

> 2 pounds (1 kg) baking potatoes, such as Idaho russets or Bintje, peeled and cut into thick fries, ¾ inch x 3 inches (1.75 cm x 7.5 cm)
>
> 2 to 3 tablespoons extra-virgin olive oil
>
> Fine sea salt to taste

1. Preheat the oven to 500°F (260°C; gas mark 9).
2. Bring 1 quart (1 l) of water to a simmer in the bottom of a steamer. Place the potatoes on the steaming rack, place the rack in the steamer, cover, and steam just until a knife inserted in a potato comes away easily, 10 to 12 minutes. (The potatoes should not be cooked through, or they will tend to fall apart.)
3. Transfer the steamed potatoes to a bowl and drizzle with oil. Carefully toss to coat evenly with oil. (The potatoes can be prepared to this point several hours in advance. Set aside at room temperature.)
4. With a large slotted spoon, transfer the potatoes in a single layer to a nonstick baking sheet. Discard any excess oil or liquid. Place the baking sheet in the oven and bake, turning so they brown evenly, until the potatoes are crisp and a deep golden brown, 15 to 20 minutes. Remove from the oven, season generously with salt, and serve immediately.

FOUR TO SIX SERVINGS

᷑ **THE POTATO OF CHOICE** ᷚ   Almost any potato can be roasted in this manner, but my choice is the Charlotte, a firm, yellow-fleshed potato the size of an egg. The variety has existed only since the early 1980s when farmers from Brittany made an immediate hit with this very tender, creamy, fine-fleshed potato. The most famous ones now come from the island of Noirmoutier, where their earthy flavor marries so well with the rare sea salt that is the gift of the island's shores. My second choice here is the tiny *ratte* variety, known in France since the ninth century but made newly famous in the 1980s. The *ratte* is a very tiny potato (some not much bigger than an almond) of uneven shape, with very fine golden skin and a very waxy, smooth flesh with a mild, buttery, earthy flavor.

GRATIN DAUPHINOIS

To wash or not to wash the potatoes, that is the question. There are two schools of thought on rules for a perfect gratin. Some cooks never wash the potatoes, preferring a starchier dish that creates a more unctuous liaison of starch, cream, and cheese to coat the potatoes. Others feel the clean potato flavor is enhanced by a careful rinse. I prefer the starchy version, but try it both ways and decide for yourself. This is a variation on my favorite and simplest of gratins, first published in my *Food Lover's Guide to Paris*. In France, I like to use the Charlotte potato. Just be sure they are nice firm-fleshed potatoes. And make sure the cheese is a good Swiss Gruyère.

EQUIPMENT: One shallow 2-quart (2-l) gratin dish

1 plump, fresh garlic clove, peeled and halved
2 pounds (1 kg) firm-fleshed potatoes, peeled and sliced very thin
4 ounces (125 g) Swiss Gruyère cheese, freshly grated
2 cups (50 cl) whole milk
½ cup (12.5 cl) heavy cream
Sea salt and freshly ground black pepper to taste

1. Preheat the oven to 375°F (190°C; gas mark 4/5).
2. Rub the inside of the baking dish with garlic.
3. In a large bowl, combine the potatoes, ¾ of the cheese, the milk, cream, salt, and pepper. Mix well. Spoon the mixture into the baking dish, pouring the liquid over the potatoes. Sprinkle with the remaining cheese.
4. Place in the center of the oven and bake until the potatoes are cooked through and the top is crisp and golden, about 1 hour and 15 minutes.

FOUR TO SIX SERVINGS

What I say is that, if a man really likes potatoes,
he must be a pretty decent sort of fellow.

A. A. MILNE

JR'S GRATIN DAUPHINOIS

Chef Joël Robuchon is one of the greatest cooks I know, and his version of any dish is sure to cause diners to exult. Not one to ever stint on butter or cream, he embellishes his potato gratin with plenty of both. Robuchon also cooks his potatoes in the creamy mixture first, making for a gratin that is ultimately rich and unctuous.

EQUIPMENT: One shallow 2-quart (2-l) gratin dish

2 cups (50 cl) whole milk
1 cup (25 cl) heavy cream
4 ounces (125 g) freshly grated Swiss Gruyère cheese
Sea salt and freshly ground black pepper to taste
Freshly grated nutmeg to taste
1 plump, fresh garlic clove, peeled and halved
2 pounds (1 kg) firm-fleshed potatoes, peeled and sliced very thin
3 tablespoons (1½ ounces; 45 g) unsalted butter

1. Preheat the oven to 375°F (190°C; gas mark 4/5).
2. In a large saucepan, bring the milk to a boil over moderate heat. Add the cream and ¾ of the cheese. Stir to blend. Season with salt, pepper, and a grating of nutmeg. Add the potatoes and mix well with a wooden spoon. Cook over low heat, stirring from time to time, until the potatoes are soft, about 20 minutes. Taste for seasoning.
3. Thoroughly rub the inside of the baking dish with garlic. Transfer the potatoes and their liquid to the baking dish. Sprinkle with the remaining cheese and the butter.
4. Place in the center of the oven and bake until the potatoes are cooked through and the top is crisp and golden, about 1 hour and 15 minutes. Serve immediately.

FOUR TO SIX SERVINGS

CREAMY OLIVE OIL & PARMESAN POTATO PUREE

Homey and elegant in the same breath, a perfect potato puree is pure, smooth, creamy gastronomic pleasure. This version is embellished with a touch of olive oil and enriched with a flavorful Parmesan cheese. Here I steam rather than boil the potatoes for a richer potato flavor. Serve this with a simple roast chicken and a nice bottle of red wine.

EQUIPMENT: A food mill

2 pounds (1 kg) baking potatoes, such as Idaho russets
1½ to 2 cups (37.5 to 50 cl) whole milk
Fine sea salt to taste
About 4 tablespoons extra-virgin olive oil
¼ cup (1 ounce; 30 g) freshly grated Parmigiano-Reggiano cheese

1. Scrub and peel the potatoes. Bring 1 quart (1 l) of water to a simmer in the bottom of a steamer. Place the potatoes on the steaming rack. Place the rack in the steamer, cover, and steam until a knife inserted in a potato comes away easily, 20 to 30 minutes. (Make certain the potatoes are cooked through, or they will be very difficult to put through the food mill.)
2. In a large saucepan, bring the milk just to a boil over high heat. Set aside.
3. Pass the potatoes through the medium grid of a food mill into a large, heavy-bottomed saucepan. Add a pinch of salt and the olive oil, little by little, stirring vigorously with a wooden spoon until the oil is thoroughly incorporated and the mixture becomes fluffy and light. Slowly add about ¾ of the hot milk in a thin stream, stirring vigorously, until the milk is thoroughly incorporated. Place the pan over low heat and continue to stir vigorously. If the puree seems a bit heavy or stiff, add additional oil and milk, stirring all the while. Stir in the cheese. Taste for seasoning. The puree may be made up to 1 hour in advance. Place in the top of a double boiler over simmering water. Stir occasionally to keep smooth.

SIX TO EIGHT SERVINGS

‿ **HEALTH TIP** ∾ Boiling potatoes robs them of over half their potassium content. To obtain maximum health benefits, steam them.

BRAISED ASPARAGUS

In the early spring, all of France waits for the first asparagus to appear from Provence. While the soil in Provence tends to be chalky and rocky, there are also vast patches of rich, sandy soil ideal for cultivating long, elegant rows of asparagus. Add to the equation the wealth of warm spring sun and you have an enviable asparagus culture. While fat, ivory-white asparagus are traditional, today many different varieties are found, including classic green asparagus and the delicate violet-tipped variety with white stems shading to a delicate spring green. The inspiration for this recipe comes from Paris chef Alain Passard: I spent a day in his kitchen early one spring, and noticed that rather than blanching asparagus, as is the French tradition, he braised them slowly in golden butter from Brittany, making for a vegetable that is particularly moist and rich with that grassy, pure asparagus flavor. During the slow braise the asparagus give up their mineral-like juices which concentrate and mingle with the butter, bathing the asparagus in a truly intense sauce. This method can be used with any variety of asparagus, just be certain they are all the same size, so they cook evenly.

> 3 tablespoons (1½ ounces; 45 g) unsalted butter
> 2 pounds (1 kg) medium-size green asparagus, tough ends trimmed
> Fine sea salt and freshly ground black pepper to taste
> Coarse sea salt to taste

1. In a large skillet, melt the butter over medium heat. Add the asparagus and shake the skillet until they fall into a single layer in the bottom of the pan. Raise the heat slightly and cook until the butter starts to sizzle, 1 to 2 minutes. Season with fine sea salt and pepper.
2. Reduce the heat to low. With a spatula, rotate the asparagus as they cook, turning them so they brown slightly on all sides. Cook for an additional 10 to 12 minutes, or until tender. Taste for seasoning. With a slotted spoon, gently transfer the asparagus to a platter. Sprinkle with a small amount of coarse sea salt. Serve immediately.

FOUR TO SIX SERVINGS

5

PASTA

WHERE WOULD THE MEDITERRANEAN PALATE be without pasta? The lineup of Provençal ingredients—ripe black olives, fresh Mediterranean clams, plump red tomatoes, rosemary, and thyme—all seem destined to share top billing with wheaty strands of pasta. During the winter months, I'll cook up a sauce of sausage, fennel, and red wine to toss with spirals of fusili, turn up the heat with a batch of Spicy Red Pepper Spaghetti, or warm our souls with rich helpings of Spaghetti alla Carbonara, inspired by a favorite trattoria in Rome. Should we unearth a fragrant black truffle in the vineyard, it will surely find its way into Hervé's Truffle Butter Pasta, a dish inspired by our local truffle maven, Hervé Poron. I rarely make fresh pasta at home anymore, since Giuseppina Giacomo, the village shopkeeper we've dubbed "Madame Pâtes Fraîches" provides us with golden sheets of fresh egg pasta for forming into rectangles of lasagne, or cutting into strands of fettucine for tossing with creamy Roquefort cheese, lemon zest, and a touch of fresh rosemary. Our local green olives go into a variation on the popular Puttanesca, while Monday evenings we'll be found near the fire, downing helpings of Monday Night Spaghetti, laced with an avalanche of fresh herbs—parsley, sage, rosemary, basil, and thyme.

FACING PHOTOGRAPH: *Old stone steps lead to the master bedroom, where a louvered shutter allows for a cool evening breeze. When the rosemary is freshly trimmed, the adjacent rooms are perfumed with the herb's heady, oil-rich scent.*

FETTUCINE WITH ROQUEFORT,
LEMON ZEST & ROSEMARY

It's really a shame that so much goes down the drain—pasta cooking water, that is. The starch and delicate flavor of the liquid, when used judiciously, can enhance the texture and flavor of many pasta dishes. I sampled a version of this dish one evening in Germany, at the then Michelin three-star restaurant of Heinz Winkler. The next day, chef Winkler kindly demonstrated his version, one that's surprisingly light despite the addition of rich Roquefort cheese. In fact, this is one of the lightest pastas I know, with just a gentle hint of Roquefort amplified by a generous dose of nutmeg, a ration of butter, and a soupçon of lemon zest. It's a "midnight" pasta if ever there was one!

> 3 tablespoons (1½ ounces; 45 g) unsalted butter, at room temperature
>
> 3 tablespoons (1½ ounces; 45 g) Roquefort cheese, at room temperature
>
> 3 tablespoons sea salt
>
> 1 pound (500 g) fresh or dried fettucine
>
> About 1 cup (25 cl) pasta cooking water
>
> Freshly grated nutmeg to taste
>
> Grated zest (yellow peel) of 1 lemon
>
> 1 tablespoon minced fresh rosemary
>
> Freshly ground black pepper to taste

1. Preheat the oven to the lowest possible setting, about 200°F (80°C; gas mark 1). Place a large heatproof bowl in the oven to warm.

2. In a small bowl, mash the butter and Roquefort with a fork until soft and well blended. Set aside.

3. In a large pot, bring 6 quarts (6 l) of water to a rolling boil. Add the salt and pasta, stirring to prevent the pasta from sticking. Cook until tender, 1 to 2 minutes for fresh; 3 to 5 minutes for dried. Carefully drain the pasta, leaving a few drops of water clinging to the pasta so that the sauce will adhere. Reserve 1 cup (25 cl) of cooking water.

4. Place the pasta in the warmed bowl and add the butter-Roquefort mixture. Toss the pasta slowly and gently until the pasta absorbs all of the mixture. Slowly add the cooking water, tablespoon by tablespoon, until the pasta is evenly coated with sauce. (Rather than thinning out the sauce, the starchy water will actually work to thicken it.) Season generously with nutmeg and toss with the lemon zest and rosemary. Taste, then season generously with pepper. Toss once more. Transfer to warmed shallow soup bowls and serve.

FOUR TO SIX SERVINGS

 WINE SUGGESTIONS: This is lovely with an Italian white wine: a golden, smooth Umbrian Orvieto, a Frascati from the Roman hills, or a nicely chilled Vernaccia di San Gimignano.

FUSILI WITH SAUSAGE, FENNEL & RED WINE

This hearty cold-weather pasta is a full-flavored blend of well-seasoned pork sausage and a hint of fennel, all held together with a silky red wine sauce. Just before serving, a few eggs are tossed with the pasta—carbonara style—as a gentle binder, producing a dense, clinging sauce. Search for the best sausage meat you can find, preferably a well-seasoned pork sausage sold either in bulk or in links (in which case you'll need to remove the meat from the casings). I make this dish with either fusili—the little corkscrew pasta—or the quill-like penne. They both have an ideal shape for trapping pieces of sausage and giving you equal amounts of sauce and pasta with each bite. It's a good idea to reserve a bit of pasta cooking water to even out the sauce at the end. Note that red wine replaces traditional water or stock in the sauce, adding additional balance, character, and flavor to the dish.

1 pound (500 g) bulk sausage meat, broken into small pieces

1 teaspoon fennel seeds

3 tablespoons tomato paste

2 cups (50 cl) dry red wine, such as Chianti

2 eggs, at room temperature

¼ cup (1 ounce; 30 g) freshly grated Parmigiano-Reggiano cheese

Freshly ground black pepper to taste

Sea salt

1 pound (500 g) dried Italian pasta, such as fusili or penne

About 1 cup (25 cl) pasta cooking water

1. In a skillet large enough to hold the pasta later on, brown the meat with no additional fat over low heat for 3 to 4 minutes. With the end of a spatula, continue to break up the sausage pieces into fine bits of meat. Add the fennel seeds and tomato paste, toss to blend, and cook over moderate heat for 2 minutes to allow the flavors to blend. Slowly add the wine, pouring it all over the surface of the pan. Adjust the heat to bring the liquid to a gentle simmer and cook, uncovered, until most of the wine—and alcohol—have cooked off, about 15 minutes from the time the liquid comes to a simmer. Taste for seasoning.

2. Place the eggs in a small bowl and whisk to blend. Whisk in the cheese and a generous grinding of pepper. Set aside.

3. In a large pot, bring 6 quarts (6 l) of water to a rolling boil. When the water boils, add 3 tablespoons of salt and the pasta, stirring to prevent the pasta from sticking. Cook until tender but firm to the bite, 9 to 11 minutes. Carefully drain the pasta, leaving a few drops of water clinging to the pasta so that the sauce will adhere. Reserve 1 cup (25 cl) of cooking water.

4. Add the pasta to the skillet with the sausage meat and use two forks to toss thoroughly, evenly coating the pasta with the sauce. Remove the pan from the heat and, working quickly with two forks, stir in the egg mixture. Continue to toss until each piece of pasta is evenly coated with sauce. (The pasta should not be dry; if it is, add the pasta water, tablespoon by tablespoon, tossing after each addition, to create a smooth, clinging sauce.) Serve immediately in warmed shallow soup bowls. Pass the pepper mill.

FOUR TO SIX SERVINGS

WINE SUGGESTION: This pasta can take a big wine. I love it with a fine Piedmont red, such as a Dolcetto d'Alba.

PENNE "RISOTTO"

This recipe was inspired by a visit to French chef Alain Ducasse's country hotel-restaurant, La Bastide de Moustiers, a lovely three-hour drive from our home across Provence's most stunning lavender fields. Before dinner I chatted with the resident chef, Sonja Lee, about the evening's menu. She began talking about penne cooked like risotto, and I conjured up an instant image of a bowl of dense, perfectly cooked pasta penetrated with the rich flavors of a tomato sauce. Rather than being boiled in water, the penne is actually cooked like risotto: It is browned lightly in oil, tossed with a thick coating of tomato paste, then cooked slowly by adding spoonfuls of stock, stirring and tossing until it is cooked through and only a veil of sauce remains. The end result is a pasta that is deeply flavored and very unusual. Ask your guests to guess how it was cooked. I'll bet few will get the right answer. The recipe is said to originate with the workers in the olive oil mills along the Mediterranean coast. Each time I prepare the dish, I vary it. For a vegetarian pasta, I substitute a rich herb broth for chicken stock. I once prepared this with a rich duck stock, and everyone kept looking for the bits of meat they were sure had been added to the sauce.

> About 2½ quarts (2.5 l) Potager Stock (page 321) or homemade
>   Chicken Stock (page 322)
> 1 pound (500 g) dried Italian tubular pasta, such as penne
> ½ cup (12.5 cl) extra-virgin olive oil
> ½ teaspoon fine sea salt
> 4 tablespoons tomato paste
> 2 tablespoons finely chopped fresh rosemary leaves
> ¼ teaspoon crushed red peppers (hot red pepper flakes), or to taste
> 2 teaspoons best-quality red wine vinegar
> ½ cup (2 ounces; 60 g) freshly grated Parmigiano-Reggiano cheese

1. In a large saucepan, heat the stock and keep it simmering, with barely an occasional bubble, while preparing the pasta.

2. In a heavy skillet large enough to hold all the pasta (it need not be in a single layer), heat the oil over moderately high heat. When it is hot but not smoking, add all the pasta, stirring continuously until the pasta begins to brown lightly around the edges, 3 to 4 minutes. Season with salt and add all the tomato paste and the rosemary, stirring constantly until the pasta is evenly coated with the sauce. Slowly add a ladleful of stock, stirring until most of the liquid is absorbed. Adjust the heat as necessary to maintain a gentle simmer. The pasta should cook slowly and should always be covered in at least a light film of stock. Continue adding ladlefuls of stock, stirring frequently and tasting regularly, until the pasta is tender and firm to the bite, about 17 minutes total. Add the red pepper

and vinegar and toss. Taste for seasoning. Add about half the cheese and toss to blend. Serve immediately in warmed shallow soup bowls. Pass a bowl with the remaining cheese to sprinkle over the pasta.

FOUR TO SIX SERVINGS

WINE SUGGESTIONS: I like a dense, meaty wine with this dish. Try a Gigondas from Provence, an Australian Shiraz, a spicy Rhône-style red from California, or a Montepulciano d'Abruzzo from Italy.

HOT WATER OR COLD? Following rules I somehow learned as a child, I always began with cold tap water—rather than hot—when filling a pan with water to bring to a boil. One day I decided to research the reason for this time-wasting habit. As it turns out, the concern stems from the existence of lead in pipes, which leaches out more readily in hot water than cold. Today, most lead pipes have been replaced with other harmless materials, so it's okay to fill your stockpots with steaming tap water. See how quickly even a "watched" pot will boil!

MONDAY NIGHT SPAGHETTI

Most stores are closed in Vaison-la-Romaine on Monday, and this is when I turn to the garden and pantry for sustenance. The bold, fresh flavors of just-picked herbs, a touch of spicy red pepper, and the soothing flavor of tomato sauce make this a favorite. Be sure the herbs are fresh, and use a good variety in the sauce and lots of rosemary, basil, and thyme as garnish.

¼ cup (6 cl) extra-virgin olive oil

6 plump, fresh garlic cloves, peeled and minced

½ teaspoon crushed red peppers (hot red pepper flakes), or to taste

Sea salt to taste

One 28-ounce (765-g) can peeled Italian plum tomatoes in juice, or one 28-ounce (765-g) can crushed tomatoes in puree

Bouquet garni: a generous bunch of fresh rosemary, parsley, bay leaf, thyme, and sage, tied with household twine

1 pound (500 g) Italian spaghetti

1 teaspoon best-quality red wine vinegar

A handful of minced fresh rosemary, parsley, thyme, sage, and basil, for garnish

Freshly grated Parmigiano-Reggiano cheese, for the table

1. In an unheated skillet large enough to hold the pasta later on, combine the oil, garlic, crushed red peppers, and salt, stirring to coat with the oil. Cook over moderate heat just until the garlic turns golden but does not brown, 2 to 3 minutes. Add the tomatoes: If using whole tomatoes, puree in a blender or food processor, or place a food mill over the skillet and puree the tomatoes directly into it. If using crushed tomatoes, add directly from the can. Add the bouquet garni, season with additional salt, and stir to blend. Simmer, partially covered (to capture the herbed infusion), until the sauce begins to thicken, about 15 minutes. Remove and discard the bouquet garni. Taste for seasoning.

2. Meanwhile, in a large pot, bring 6 quarts (6 l) of water to a rolling boil. Add 3 tablespoons of sea salt and the spaghetti, stirring to prevent the pasta from sticking. Cook until tender but firm to the bite, 11 to 14 minutes. Drain thoroughly.

3. Add the drained pasta to the skillet with the sauce. Toss, add the vinegar, cover, and let rest off the heat for 1 to 2 minutes to allow the pasta to absorb the sauce. Add about half of the minced fresh herbs and toss again. Transfer to warmed shallow soup bowls and sprinkle with the remaining herbs. Serve immediately, passing a bowl of cheese.

FOUR TO SIX SERVINGS

WINE SUGGESTION: Serve a sturdy red wine that will stand up to the spice of the sauce, such as a Dolcetto d'Alba or a spicy Côtes du Rhône.

SPAGHETTI WITH GREEN OLIVE PUTTANESCA

On one visit to our market in Vaison-la-Romaine, I counted no less than twenty different varieties of green olives, seasoned with herbs, spices, and vegetables and cured in many different ways. The fresh pungency of green olives is often ignored in cooking, where black olives often take a front seat. Here is a Provençal-inspired variation on the classic spaghetti alla puttanesca, substituting green olives for black, and fresh thyme for parsley, offering a new dimension to an old favorite.

3 tablespoons capers
¼ cup (6 cl) extra-virgin olive oil
3 plump, fresh garlic cloves, peeled and minced
½ teaspoon crushed red peppers (hot red pepper flakes), or to taste
One 28-ounce (765-g) can peeled Italian plum tomatoes in juice, or one 28-ounce
     (765-g) can crushed tomatoes in puree
20 best-quality green olives (such as French Picholine), drained, pitted, and chopped
Sea salt to taste
1 pound (500 g) Italian spaghetti
1 tablespoon fresh thyme leaves

1. Drain the capers, rinse well, and soak in cold water for 10 minutes to remove excess salt.
2. In an unheated skillet large enough to hold the pasta later on, combine the oil, garlic, and crushed red peppers. Cook over moderate heat just until the garlic turns golden but does not brown, 2 to 3 minutes. Add the tomatoes: If using whole canned tomatoes, place a food mill over the skillet and puree the tomatoes directly into it. Crushed tomatoes can be added directly from the can. Add the olives and capers. Season with salt, stir to blend, cover, and simmer until the sauce begins to thicken, about 15 minutes. Taste for seasoning.
3. Meanwhile, in a large pot, bring 6 quarts (6 l) of water to a rolling boil. Add 3 tablespoons of sea salt and the spaghetti, stirring to prevent the pasta from sticking. Cook until tender but firm to the bite, 11 to 14 minutes. Drain thoroughly.
4. Add the drained pasta to the skillet with the sauce. Toss, cover, and let rest off the heat for 1 to 2 minutes to allow the pasta to absorb the sauce. Add the thyme and toss again. Serve immediately in warmed shallow soup bowls. Traditionally, cheese is not served with this dish.

FOUR TO SIX SERVINGS

 WINE SUGGESTION: A dependable Chianti, such as those from the Antinori or Ricasoli estates.

INDIVIDUAL ZUCCHINI LASAGNE WITH SPICY PIZZA SAUCE

The inspiration for this dish comes from colleagues Johanne Killeen and George Germon of Al Forno restaurant in Providence, Rhode Island. This version is actually "constructed" in individual portions at serving time. Simply count on two strips of lasagne per serving.

4 tablespoons extra-virgin olive oil

3 tablespoons minced fresh rosemary leaves

½ teaspoon crushed red peppers (hot red pepper flakes), or to taste

10 plump, fresh garlic cloves, peeled and slivered

Sea salt to taste

One 28-ounce (765-g) can peeled Italian plum tomatoes in juice, or one 28-ounce (765-g) can crushed tomatoes in puree

1 medium zucchini, scrubbed, trimmed, and thinly sliced (do not peel)

½ teaspoon dried leaf oregano

2 tablespoons balsamic vinegar

8 sheets dried Italian lasagne (do not use the precooked variety)

1. In an unheated skillet, combine 3 tablespoons of the oil, the rosemary, red peppers, garlic, and salt. Cook over moderate heat just until the garlic turns golden but does not brown, 2 to 3 minutes. If using whole canned tomatoes, place a food mill over the skillet and puree the tomatoes directly into it. Crushed tomatoes can be added directly from the can. Stir to blend and simmer, uncovered, until it begins to thicken, about 15 minutes.

2. While the sauce is simmering, prepare the zucchini: In a large nonstick skillet, heat the remaining 1 tablespoon of oil over moderately high heat. When the oil is hot but not smoking, add the zucchini and sauté just until golden, about 5 minutes. Transfer to a colander to drain any excess oil, season with salt, and toss with oregano. Add the zucchini to the tomato sauce in the skillet and toss. Add the balsamic vinegar, toss, cover, and let rest over low heat to allow the zucchini to absorb the sauce, 1 to 2 minutes.

3. Meanwhile, in a large pot, bring 6 quarts (6 l) of water to a rolling boil. Add 3 table-spoons of salt and the lasagne, stirring to prevent the pasta from sticking. Cook until tender but firm to the bite, about 4 minutes. Drain thoroughly.

4. Place a spoonful of the sauced zucchini on a warmed dinner plate. Top with a layer of lasagne. Add a second layer of sauce, a second layer of lasagne, and a third layer of sauce. Repeat with additional servings until all the pasta and sauce have been used. Serve.

FOUR SERVINGS

 WINE SUGGESTION: A Barbera d'Alba young Italian red, or a white Pinot Grigio.

CATALAN FRIED NOODLES

Nearly each day in Provence I am reminded of the unity of Mediterranean cuisine and the realization that the related cuisines have virtually no borders. While garlic mayonnaise, or aïoli, is generally tied to Provence, I've had endlessly delicious versions in Spain, particularly in Barcelona, where it shows up as a tapas topping for potatoes and always with the ever-popular *fideos,* a pasta side dish that is prepared much like the Italian risotto. I serve it on days I'm looking for a quick and filling dish with a great hit of garlic. I first sampled this dish at Barcelona's El Dorado Petit, where they toss the pasta with cubes of monkfish and serve it with the garlic-rich sauce.

> 8 ounces *fideos* noodles (or dried angel's hair pasta, capellini, or vermicelli), broken
>   into 2-inch (5 cm) lengths
> 2 tablespoons extra-virgin olive oil
> 2 cups (25 cl) homemade Chicken Stock (page 322)
> 1 recipe Aïoli (page 314)

1. Preheat the oven to 350°F (175°C; gas mark 4/5).
2. In a large bowl, toss the pasta with the oil. Spread evenly on a rimmed nonstick baking sheet. Place in the center of the oven and bake, shaking from time to time, until golden brown, 5 to 7 minutes. Do not allow the pasta to burn. Remove from the oven and set aside.
3. In a large saucepan, bring the stock to a boil over high heat. Add the browned noodles, stir to blend, and cook, covered, until most of the liquid is absorbed, about 5 minutes.
4. Stir several tablespoons of the aïoli into the noodles. Transfer to warmed shallow soup bowls and serve immediately. Pass a bowl with additional garlic mayonnaise to add to the noodles.

FOUR SERVINGS

WINE SUGGESTIONS: To stand up to the intensity of the aïoli, you'll want a thirst-quenching wine: a young red from the Rhône, a rosé from Provence, or a pale white Italian Verdicchio.

No man is lonely while eating spaghetti: it requires so much attention.
CHRISTOPHER MORLEY

SPICY RED PEPPER SPAGHETTI

Brilliant red bell peppers remain gems of Provence's summer bounty. Here, red peppers are seared with onions, garlic, and a touch of pepper, enriched with chicken broth, and then turned into a slightly coarse puree. The method of tossing the pasta—first with the cheese, then with the sauce—results in a pasta with a greater depth of flavor, since the pasta first absorbs the cheese and then the rosy sauce. I often make a double batch for the freezer, for those days when I'm pressed for time in the kitchen.

4 red bell peppers
1 pound (500 g) onions
4 tablespoons extra-virgin olive oil
2 plump, fresh garlic cloves, peeled and finely chopped
½ teaspoon crushed red peppers (hot red pepper flakes), or to taste
2 cups (50 cl) homemade Chicken Stock (page 322) or Potager Stock (page 321)
Sea salt to taste
1 pound (500 g) Italian spaghetti
¾ cup (3 ounces; 90 g) freshly grated Parmigiano-Reggiano cheese

1. Halve the peppers, and trim and discard the core, veins, and seeds. Chop them coarsely and set aside.
2. Slice the onions in half lengthwise. Place, cut side down, on a cutting board and cut crosswise into very thin slices. Set aside.
3. In a large skillet, heat the oil over moderate heat until hot but not smoking. Add the peppers and a pinch of salt, and cook until softened, stirring regularly, about 5 minutes. Add the onions, garlic, red pepper flakes, and another pinch of salt, and cook over moderate heat until the onions begin to soften, about 5 minutes more. (Do not let the onions brown.) Add the stock and simmer over moderate heat, uncovered, until thickened, about 30 minutes.
4. Transfer the mixture in small batches to a food processor or blender, being careful to remove the plunger or lid so the liquid does not splatter. Process to a coarse puree. Return to the saucepan in batches and reheat gently over low heat.
5. Meanwhile, in a large pot, bring 6 quarts (6 l) of water to a rolling boil over high heat. Add 3 tablespoons of sea salt and the spaghetti, stirring to prevent the pasta from sticking. Cook until tender but firm to the bite, 11 to 14 minutes. Drain thoroughly.

6. Add the drained pasta to a large bowl and add about half the cheese. Toss gently and thoroughly until all the cheese has been absorbed. Add the pepper sauce and toss again, until all the sauce has been absorbed. Taste for seasoning. Serve immediately in warmed shallow bowls. Pass a bowl with the remaining cheese to sprinkle over the pasta.

FOUR TO SIX SERVINGS

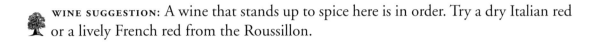 **WINE SUGGESTION:** A wine that stands up to spice here is in order. Try a dry Italian red or a lively French red from the Roussillon.

SOME LIKE IT HOT! Be careful when adding hot ingredients to the container of a food processor or blender. Always add in small batches and remove the lid or plunger so that the hot air and steam can escape. This way there are fewer splatters and easier clean-ups!

DON'T THROW AWAY THAT STARCH! Traditionally, the promise of a classical French sauce is to deliver strong flavor and smooth texture. Most sauces are thickened with a starch—in most cases flour—and then receive additional reducing to obtain a more concentrated flavor, or butter to give a glossy effect. Water drained from pasta provides a natural source of starch that acts as a thickening agent, so let the starch that is normally thrown away add body and life to the pasta sauce.

HERVÉ'S TRUFFLE BUTTER PASTA

Hervé Poron is our local truffle maven. He runs one of the world's largest truffle preserving operations. From November to March his little factory in Puymeras is in full operation, as he and his staff weigh, clean, trim, and calibrate the bountiful local truffle crop. On one visit he gave me a sample of the truffle butter he had

created. I tossed it on fresh pasta made by Giuseppina Giacomo, owner of the village pasta shop, and was instantly convinced that this is one of the finest ways to consume black truffles. Their fragrance and rich flavor are accentuated by the butter and fully absorbed into the pasta. I think of this as the classic black cocktail dress of food: simplicity as well as perfection. If you are truly smitten with the essence of truffles, prepare your own pasta, but first store the eggs enclosed in a jar with the truffles for a day or two. Pasta prepared with the eggs will take on a rich truffle flavor of its own. Since the dish is very rich, serve in small portions.

Fresh truffles infuse fresh eggs with their mysterious flavor and fragrance.

> 1 pound (500 g) fresh fettucine
> Sea salt to taste
> 8 tablespoons (4 ounces; 120 g) unsalted butter
> 1 ounce (30 g) fresh black truffles, finely minced

1. In a large pot, bring 6 quarts (6 l) of water to a rolling boil. Add 3 tablespoons of sea salt and the pasta, stirring to prevent the pasta from sticking. Cook until tender, about 1 minute. Drain thoroughly.
2. Meanwhile, in a skillet large enough to hold the pasta later on, melt the butter over the lowest possible heat. Add the truffles and toss to blend. Add the drained pasta to the skillet with the sauce. Toss, cover, and let rest off the heat to allow the pasta to absorb the sauce, 1 to 2 minutes. Transfer to warmed shallow soup bowls. Serve immediately.

SIX SERVINGS

WINE SUGGESTION: A rich white is ideal. Try one prepared with the Viognier grape, such as those from California or the Rhône Valley.

FACING PHOTOGRAPH: *Fresh truffle "sandwich": St. Marcellin cow's milk cheese is sliced in half, fresh sliced black truffles are slipped between the halves, then all is broiled just until the cheese melts. Miam!*

CHECCHINO DAL 1887'S SPAGHETTI ALLA CARBONARA

Spaghetti alla carbonara seems to have as many versions as there are cooks who prepare it. The best one I ever tasted was at Trattoria Checchino dal 1887 in Rome. They present it sauced with a blend of eggs, a good hit of freshly ground black pepper, crisp pancetta matchsticks, and a mixture of Pecorino and Parmigiano-Reggiano cheeses. Despite its popularity, spaghetti alla carbonara is often disappointing. Deceptively simply, it is an easily put together dish that demands great attention to detail. Think of it as a two-step process where you have to work quickly. First, thoroughly coat the pasta with the pancetta and oil, then turn off the heat and toss with the seasoned eggs. When I do it, I send everyone out of the kitchen so I can concentrate 100 percent.

> 4 large eggs, at room temperature
> Sea salt and freshly ground black pepper to taste
> 5 tablespoons extra-virgin olive oil
> 3½ ounces (100 g) pancetta, very thinly sliced and cut into matchsticks
> 1 pound (500 g) Italian spaghetti
> ¼ cup (1 ounce; 25 g) freshly grated Pecorino cheese
> ¼ cup (1 ounce; 25 g) freshly grated Parmigiano-Reggiano cheese

1. Place the eggs in a small bowl and whisk until smooth. Whisk in a pinch of salt and a generous grinding of pepper. Set aside.
2. In a skillet large enough to hold the pasta later on, combine the oil and pancetta, and sauté gently over moderate heat just until the pancetta begins to crisp and turn a very light brown, 4 to 5 minutes. Set aside.
3. In a large pot, bring 6 quarts (6 l) of water to a rolling boil over high heat. Add 3 tablespoons of sea salt and the pasta, stirring to prevent the pasta from sticking. Cook until tender but firm, or al dente, 11 to 14 minutes. With tongs or a slotted spoon, transfer the pasta to a colander to drain. Toss well to eliminate as much water as possible.
4. Add the spaghetti to the pancetta in the skillet and over low heat thoroughly toss to coat the pasta with the oil. Remove the pan from the heat and, working quickly, stir in the egg mixture and continue to toss until the mixture is thoroughly blended and each strand of pasta is coated with the thick, satiny, golden sauce. (If the pan is too hot, you will have scrambled eggs. To avoid this, be certain to add the eggs off the heat.) Serve immediately in warmed shallow soup bowls. Pass the cheeses and the pepper mill.

FOUR TO SIX SERVINGS

WINE SUGGESTION: A dry white from the Castelli Roman vineyards near Rome or a zesty white Pinot Grigio.

PROVENÇAL PENNE

In Provence, cooks often enliven their tomato sauce with a bit of orange zest, a practice I've followed for years. Going one step further, I enjoy bathing bulb fennel in a tomato and orange sauce, making for a dish that pleases the eye as well as the palate.

4 tablespoons extra-virgin olive oil

1 medium onion, minced

2 plump, fresh garlic cloves, peeled and minced

½ teaspoon crushed red peppers (hot red pepper flakes), or to taste

1 fresh bay leaf

Sea salt to taste

1 fennel bulb (about 8 ounces; 250 g), trimmed and cut into matchsticks

One 28-ounce (765-g) can peeled Italian plum tomatoes in juice, or one 28-ounce (765-g) can crushed tomatoes in puree

Grated zest (orange peel) of 1 orange, preferably organic, cut into matchsticks

1 pound (500 g) dried Italian tubular pasta, such as penne

¼ cup (6 cl) fresh flat-leaf parsley leaves, snipped with a scissors

1. In an unheated skillet large enough to hold the pasta later on, combine the oil, onion, garlic, red peppers, bay leaf, and a pinch of salt, and toss to coat with the oil. Place over moderate heat, cooking just until the garlic turns golden but does not brown, 2 to 3 minutes. Add the fennel, stirring so that the ingredients blend together and are evenly coated in the oil. Cover and sweat for 10 minutes over a moderate heat. Toss the fennel with a wooden spoon from time to time to assure that none of the pieces stick or burn.

2. Add the tomatoes: If using whole canned tomatoes, place a food mill over the skillet and puree the tomatoes directly into it. Crushed tomatoes can be added directly from the can. Add the orange zest. Stir to blend and simmer, uncovered, until the sauce begins to thicken, about 15 minutes. Taste for seasoning. Remove and discard the bay leaf.

3. Meanwhile, in a large pot, bring 6 quarts (6 l) of water to a rolling boil. Add 3 tablespoons of salt and the penne, stirring to prevent the pasta from sticking to the bottom. Cook until tender but still firm to the bite, about 12 minutes. Drain thoroughly.

4. Add the drained pasta to the skillet with the fennel sauce and toss. Cover, turn the heat to low, and let rest for 1 to 2 minutes, stirring to coat the pasta with the sauce. Taste for seasoning. Add the parsley and toss again. Transfer to warmed shallow soup bowls and serve immediately.

FOUR TO SIX SERVINGS

WINE SUGGESTION: A good-quality red that can stand up to the spice and the orange is ideal, such as a Chianti Classico from Tuscany or a California Zinfandel.

What you eat and drink is 50 percent of life.
GÉRARD DEPARDIEU

PATRICIA'S SPAGHETTI WITH CLAMS

Nearly two decades of living in France has helped give me a sense of building flavors in the kitchen. Often, a simple step—such as straining or reducing a liquid—can transform a dish from one that's ordinary to one that delivers big, substantial flavors. Here, the extra step of steaming the clams and then reducing the clam liquor results in a subtle, elegant fusion of flavors. The sweetness of the clam liquor balances nicely with the tomato's acidity, resulting in a wonderfully refined clam flavor.

2 pounds (1 kg) small fresh littleneck or Manila clams (about 40 clams)
Sea salt to taste
2 cups (50 cl) homemade Tomato Sauce (page 325)
1 pound (500 g) Italian spaghetti
2 tablespoons fresh thyme leaves

1. Scrub the clams thoroughly under cold running water with a stiff brush. Discard any with broken shells or shells that do not close when tapped. Since most clams come from sandy areas, they tend to be sandy themselves. Steam open a few and taste them. If they are gritty, purge them in a saltwater solution of 1 tablespoon per quart (l) of cold water. Allow them to soak for 3 hours at room temperature. Pick up the clams with your fingers, leaving behind the grit and sand. You will be amazed at the amount of sand they give up. Transfer them to a shallow dish and season generously with freshly ground pepper.

2. Prepare a large steamer: Fill the bottom portion with 1 cup (25 cl) water and bring to a boil. Transfer the clams to the steamer basket and steam, removing the clams one by one as they open. The entire process should take less than 10 minutes. Discard any shells that do not open. Reserve the liquid in the bottom of the steamer; this is your clam liquor. Remove the clams from their shells, discard the shells, and place the clam meat in a small bowl. Place a double thickness of moistened cheesecloth over a strainer and pour the clam liquor through the cheesecloth directly over the clams. Rinse the clams in the clam liquor to help remove any remaining sand and at the same time plump the clams in their own juices. With a slotted spoon, transfer the clams to another small bowl and cover so they do not dry out. Pour the clam liquor once more through the cheesecloth-lined strainer into a covered skillet large enough to hold the pasta later on.

3. Place the skillet over high heat and reduce the clam liquor to about 4 tablespoons, 6 to 7 minutes. Whisk in the tomato sauce and simmer to fuse the flavors, 2 to 3 minutes

(The recipe can be prepared up to this point several hours in advance. Reheat gently at serving time, tasting for seasoning.)

4. Cook the pasta: In a large pot, bring 6 quarts (6 l) of water to a boil. Add 3 table-spoons of salt. Add the pasta and cook just until tender but still firm to the bite, 11 to 14 minutes. With a slotted spoon, transfer the pasta to a colander to drain. Toss well to eliminate as much water as possible.

5. Add the drained pasta to the skillet with the clam-flavored tomato sauce and toss thoroughly. Add the reserved clams. Cover and warm gently over very low heat, allowing the pasta to absorb the sauce, 1 to 2 minutes. Taste for seasoning. Transfer to warmed individual shallow bowls, sprinkle with thyme, and serve immediately.

FOUR TO SIX SERVINGS

WINE SUGGESTIONS: The tomato sauce all but dictates a red wine here. Try an Italian Barbera, a California Zinfandel, or a light red Côtes du Rhône.

⌇ **HAPPY AS A CLAM!** ⌇ Actually the expression is "Happy as a clam at high tide." Since clams live in sand, they can't be gathered while the sand is under water.

6

BREAD

ON ANY GIVEN DAY IN PROVENCE I CAN BE found in the kitchen first thing each morning, mixing, kneading, concocting a bread, a biscuit, the makings of a bread tart or a pizzalike fougasse. I know of few acts that give a cook as much spiritual nourishment as making bread. With a batch of dough assembled in just minutes, I am rewarded with a feeling of true accomplishment before the sun is fully risen, before I've set down the road for a run or a trip to the market. Bread is patient, bread is flexible, bread is responsive. There's bread for breakfast (such as Baby Chocolate Brioche), bread for sandwiches we'll take on the train back to Paris (Golden Parmesan-Pepper Loaf) and those ideal for the cheese tray that accompanies each dinner (Fig, Apricot, Walnut, & Raisin Rye). In the winter months I crave the rich, warming density of a slice of Rita's Rye, while at Christmas time Provençal Olive Oil Brioche feeds the need for tradition. Pine Nut Rolls remind me of summer and the sun, while Oatmeal Biscuits appear on the menu when we're in the mood for a blue cheese feast, accompanied by a sip of sweet *vin doux naturel* from the nearby Domaine La Soumade.

FACING PHOTOGRAPH: *Walter unloads* ceps de vigne, *spent trunks of vines used as fuel for the outdoor bread oven that Patricia tends in the courtyard of their farmhouse.*

POMPE À L'HUILE: PROVENÇAL OLIVE OIL BRIOCHE

Years ago I made an olive oil brioche—known as *pompe à l'huile*—to celebrate our first Christmas in Provence. For some unknown reason I put the recipe on the back burner, so to speak, and forgot about it. I resurrected it recently, and in the period of a single week, made more than half a dozen versions. I paired the golden dough with quickly seared foie gras in a syrupy sherry, as I had savored it in Spain; I wrapped it around a truffled pork sausage and baked it, serving a traditional mustard sauce alongside; I served it with cheese and sweet-and-sour Mostarda: Fig & Prune Chutney (page 331) in place of dessert. Each morning, guests came down to breakfast and headed for the bread drawer, cutting off thick slices of brioche to toast and sample with homemade jam. Few recipes are as versatile as this one. I'm a brioche lover but pretty much stopped making it because of the high butter content. This recipe—using only extra-virgin olive oil as the fat— is ideal for today's world. It's light, only mildly sweet, and right at home on the breakfast, lunch, and dinner table—in short, a hit!

1 teaspoon active dry yeast
1 teaspoon sugar
1 cup (25 cl) lukewarm water (about 105°F; 40°C)
¼ cup (6 cl) extra-virgin olive oil
2 large eggs, at room temperature
2 teaspoons fine sea salt
Grated zest (orange peel) of 1 orange, preferably organic
Grated zest (yellow peel) of 1 lemon, preferably organic
1 tablespoon orange flower water or tap water (see Note)
About 5 cups (665 g) unbleached all-purpose flour
1 beaten egg yolk, for glazing

1. In the bowl of a heavy-duty electric mixer fitted with a paddle, combine the yeast, sugar, and water, and stir to blend. Let stand until foamy, about 5 minutes. Stir in the olive oil, eggs, salt, orange and lemon zests, and orange flower water, and stir to blend.
2. Add the flour, a little at a time, mixing at the lowest speed until most of the flour has been absorbed and the dough forms a ball. Continue to knead until soft and satiny but still firm, 4 to 5 minutes, adding additional flour to keep the dough from sticking.
3. Transfer the dough to a bowl, cover tightly with plastic wrap, and place in the refrigerator. Let the dough rise in the refrigerator until doubled or tripled in bulk, 8 to 12 hours. (The dough can be kept for 2 to 3 days in the refrigerator. Simply punch down the dough as it doubles or triples.)
4. About an hour before you plan to bake the brioche, remove the dough from the refrig-

(continued on next page)

erator. Punch down the dough, roll it into a circle, and shape in the form of a crown, forming a small hole in the center of the crown. Place on a nonstick baking sheet, with a small teacup in the hole to keep it from closing up as the dough rises. Cover with a clean towel and let rise until about double in bulk, about 1 hour.

5. Preheat the oven to 400°F (200°C; gas mark 6/7).

6. Remove the towel and the teacup, and brush the dough with the egg yolk glaze. Place the baking sheet in the center of the oven. Bake until the brioche is a deep golden brown, about 30 minutes, turning the baking sheet from time to time if the oven is heating unevenly.

7. Remove the brioche from the oven and transfer it to a rack to cool. If stored in a zipper-locked plastic bag the brioche will stay fresh for 2 to 3 days.

ONE LARGE BRIOCHE

VARIATIONS: In Provence the olive oil brioche may be seasoned with about 1 teaspoon of fennel grains or even rolled into two layers and flavored with several tablespoons of quince jam (*confiture de coings)* between the layers.

NOTE: Orange flower water can be ordered from King Arthur's Flour Baker's Catalog, P.O. Box 876, Norwich, VT 05055. Telephone (800) 827-6836.

༉ **A CHRISTMAS TRADITION** ༉ In the region of Aix-en-Provence it's known as the *gibassié;* in Manosque they call it fougasse; in the northern part of the Vaucluse it may be called *pogne;* but by any name *pompe à l'huile* is sacred in Provence, an essential element of Christmas Eve dinner. Prepared with the first-pressed olive oil of the season, the brioche was traditionally arranged in the bakery on straw baskets in threes, as a symbol of the trinity.

༉ **THE HONOR OF BREAD** ༉ For the French, bread is a staple of any good meal. Different types of bread are baked fresh daily all over France, and because of its common appeal, there are many expressions surrounding bread. My favorites include *Long comme un jour sans pain* ("As long as a day without bread") and *Il a mangé son pain blanc le premier* (Literally, "he ate the white bread first"—an expression that refers to someone who takes the best first and leaves the rest for last). More simply, *gagner son pain* ("earn his bread") is how someone makes a living, a saying that's comparable to our "bringing home the bacon."

Bread is the warmest, kindest of words. Write it always
with a capital letter, like your own name.
RUSSIAN CAFÉ SIGN

PINE NUT ROLLS

Early one July, friends invited us to dine at the Château Eza in Eza, an enchanting hill town near Monte Carlo. The evening had a special allure: We were beginning a two-week vacation, we were with friends we had not seen in a long time, and the meal offered many pleasant surprises—the best of which was the assortment of breads, including these tiny pine nut rolls. Pine nuts come from the parasol pines one sees looming all over the Mediterranean, so it seemed like a perfectly natural flavoring here. I love the creamy, almost haunting flavor of pine nuts. But beware: They become rancid if not properly stored. Be sure to buy from a reputable merchant and store them in the freezer until they are used. For best results, toast them for two to three minutes in a warm oven to bring out their mystical flavor.

> 1 recipe Bread Dough (page 185)
> 1 cup (4 ounces; 125 g) pine nuts, toasted and cooled

1. Prepare the bread dough according to the recipe directions through Step 3. About 1½ hours before you plan to bake the rolls, remove the dough from the refrigerator. Punch down the dough, place it in a bowl, cover with a clean towel, and let rise at room temperature for about 1 hour.
2. Preheat the oven to 450°F (230°C; gas mark 8).
3. Punch down the dough. Separate it into 15 equal portions, each weighing about 2 ounces (60 g). Press several teaspoons of pine nuts into each portion of dough and shape each into a neat round, pulling the dough around itself to form a tight ball. Place the balls of dough on a baking sheet. Cover with a clean towel and let rise for 30 minutes.
4. Remove the towel and place the baking sheet in the center of the oven. Using a large plant sprayer filled with water, spray the bottom and sides of the oven with water. Spray 3 more times in the next 6 minutes. (The spray will help give the rolls a good crust.) Bake until the dough turns a deep golden brown, 20 to 25 minutes, turning the baking sheet from time to time if the oven is heating unevenly.
5. Remove the baking sheet from the oven and transfer the rolls to a rack to cool. The rolls should be eaten the day they are prepared.

FIFTEEN ROLLS

*He lay back for a little in his bed thinking about the smells of food . . .
of the intoxicating breath of bakeries and dullness of buns. . . . He planned dinners,
of enchanting aromatic foods . . . endless dinners, in which one could alternate flavor
with flavor from sunset to dawn without satiety, while one breathed
great draughts of the bouquet of brandy.*

EVELYN WAUGH

BABY CHOCOLATE BRIOCHE

I can't think of a better way to begin a Sunday morning than with a few cups of thick espresso coffee and one of these delicate, fragrant, individual chocolate-filled brioches. This simple brioche recipe—a milk-based variation of *Pompe à l'Huile: Provençal Olive Oil Brioche* (page 167)—is best prepared a day in advance, allowing the dough to rise slowly in the refrigerator overnight. The long, leisurely rise makes for a more tender and flavorful brioche. Inevitably, some chocolate will seep out as the rolls bake, but don't worry—it builds character! I prefer to sweeten these with local lavender honey from my market in Vaison. The marriage of honey and chocolate was definitely made in heaven!

> 1 teaspoon active dry yeast
>
> 2 tablespoons lavender honey or other fragrant honey
>
> 1 cup (25 cl) lukewarm whole milk (about 105°F; 40°C)
>
> ¼ cup (6 cl) extra-virgin olive oil
>
> 2 large eggs, at room temperature
>
> 2 teaspoons fine sea salt
>
> About 5 cups (665 g) unbleached all-purpose flour
>
> 3 ounces (90 g) bittersweet chocolate, preferably Lindt Excellence, divided
> into 12 portions
>
> 1 egg yolk
>
> 1 tablespoon whole milk
>
> 1 tablespoon sugar

1. In the bowl of a heavy-duty electric mixer fitted with a paddle, combine the yeast, honey, and milk, and stir to blend. Let stand until foamy, about 5 minutes. Add the olive oil, eggs, and salt, and stir to blend.

2. Add the flour, a little at a time, mixing at the lowest speed until most of the flour has been absorbed and the dough forms a ball. Continue to mix until soft and satiny but still firm, 4 to 5 minutes, adding additional flour to keep the dough from sticking.

3. Cover the bowl tightly with plastic wrap and refrigerate. Let the dough rise until double or triple in bulk, 8 to 12 hours. (The dough can be kept for 2 to 3 days in the refrigerator. Simply punch down the dough as it doubles or triples.)

4. About an hour before you plan to bake the rolls, remove the dough from the refrigerator. Punch down the dough and divide into 12 equal portions, each weighing about 3 ounces (90 g). With the palm of your hand, flatten each portion into a disc. Press a piece of chocolate into each portion of dough and shape the dough around itself to form a tight ball so that the chocolate is completely covered with the dough. Place each ball of dough on a baking sheet. Cover with a clean towel and let rise for 30 to 45 minutes.

5. Preheat the oven to 400°F (200°C; gas mark 6/7).

6. Prepare the glaze: Place the egg yolk in a small bowl and beat lightly with a fork. Add the milk and sugar, and blend. Remove the towel from the dough and brush each piece with the glaze. Place the baking sheet in the center of the oven. Bake until the rolls are a deep golden brown, 15 to 20 minutes, turning the baking sheet from time to time if the oven is heating unevenly. Some chocolate may seep from the rolls, which is normal.

7. Remove the rolls from the oven and transfer to a rack to cool. Let rest for 10 to 15 minutes before serving. If stored in a zipper-locked plastic bag, the brioche will stay fresh for 2 to 3 days.

TWELVE INDIVIDUAL ROLLS

VARIATIONS: These little brioche can be made with a variety of flavorings. Additional sweet fillings might include almonds or hazelnuts rolled in honey or a combination of candied orange or lemon zest, or chopped prunes or dates. For a savory brioche, try filling them with olives, tapenade, or a mixture of fresh herbs, such as thyme, summer savory, and rosemary.

Bleu d'Auvergne (vache)

Roquefort (brebis)

Fourme d'Ambert (vache)

Bleu des Causses (vache)

OATMEAL BISCUITS

Whenever I travel to Britain, I forgo dessert in favor of biscuits, cheese, and a little glass of port. When the biscuits are crumbly and delicate, the cheese pungent and ripe, the port aged just right, the combination is ultimately memorable. These same biscuits—what Americans call crackers—are lovely with a sharp farm cheddar, an aged French Cantal, or any of the range of blue cheeses. To make the combination thoroughly European, serve a spoonful of Mostarda: Fig & Prune Chutney (page 331) alongside. The dough in this recipe is particularly easy and forgiving.

EQUIPMENT: One 2-inch (5-cm) scalloped cookie cutter

¾ cup (100 g) unbleached all-purpose flour
1 cup (100 g) old-fashioned oats
½ teaspoon fine sea salt
2 teaspoons brown sugar, firmly packed
½ teaspoon baking soda
5 tablespoons (2½ ounces; 75 g) unsalted butter, chilled and cubed
1 teaspoon freshly squeezed lemon juice
3 to 4 tablespoons whole milk

1. Preheat the oven to 400°F (200°C; gas mark 6/7).
2. In a food processor, combine the flour, oats, salt, brown sugar, and baking soda, and process just until blended. Add the butter and pulse just until the mixture resembles coarse crumbs, about 10 pulses. Through the feed tube, add the lemon juice and 3 tablespoons of milk and pulse just until the dough begins to hold together, about 10 times. Add additional milk if the mixture is too dry. Do not over-process. The dough should not form a ball.
3. With a pastry scraper, transfer the dough to a floured work surface. Roll about ⅛ inch (3 mm) thick. Cut out the dough with the cookie cutter. Transfer the rounds to nonstick baking pans. Pierce each round 4 or 5 times with the tines of a fork to create an attractive design.

Josiane Deal, owner of Lou Canestéou, our local cheese shop.

4. Place in the oven and bake until firm in texture, slightly puffed up, and lightly browned around the edges, 12 to 15 minutes. If your oven has a tendency to bake unevenly, rotate the baking sheets from top to bottom and front to back halfway through the baking period. The biscuits should rise slightly.

(continued on next page)

FACING PHOTOGRAPH: *An assortment of blue cheeses and a carafe of the local sweet fortified* vin doux naturel *to accompany Oatmeal Biscuits.*

5. Remove from the oven and let cool on the baking sheets for 1 minute, to firm up. Using a metal spatula, transfer the biscuits to wire racks to cool completely. The biscuits can be stored in an airtight container at room temperature for 1 week.

ABOUT TWENTY-FOUR BISCUITS

WINE SUGGESTIONS: Although port is a natural here (such as Churchill's Tawny Port, aged ten years, or any good vintage port), I also enjoy a rich Spanish sherry, such as Gonzalez Byass's Oloroso Dulce; a chilled, sweet fortified French wine, such as a *vin doux naturel* from Domaine La Soumade in Provence; or a sweet, sherrylike Marsala, such as a barrel-aged Soleras or Riserva from De Bartoli.

ON OATMEAL Oatmeal is a grain that instantly calls an image to mind: sitting at the breakfast table on a cold winter's day with a bowl of steaming hot porridge, topped with cinnamon and bits of brown sugar—one of the best comfort foods to exist. In fact, beyond that, oatmeal is more complex than it first appears. "Rolled oats" are, as the term implies, oats that have been flattened with a roller so they are easier to eat. An oat kernel, or groat—a term used to describe an oat kernel with only the hull removed—was originally rolled and blended as part of one big flake. The oats consumed at breakfast, most commonly "quick oats," are rolled and steel-cut to an even thinner consistency so that they can be cooked quickly and eaten immediately. Quick oats are not recommended for bread recipes; they are too thin and delicate to hold their own. Not only is oatmeal delicious, but it is an excellent source of soluble fiber, iron, and minerals.

ON BAKING SODA Baking soda, or sodium bicarbonate, has an almost indefinite shelf life as long as it is not exposed to humidity. It is used as a leavener in baking when joined with an acidic ingredient, such as sour milk, lemon juice, vinegar, sour cream, or molasses. The baking soda neutralizes some of the acidity and by that process causes the baked ingredients to rise.

GOLDEN PARMESAN-PEPPER LOAF

I first sampled a version of this zesty, aromatic bread at The Seafood Restaurant, Richard Stein's magnificent restaurant in the British village of Padstow, Cornwall, that looks onto the Atlantic Ocean. My variation is made along the lines of *pain de mie,* a fine-crumbed, refined bread with almost no crust, a rather grown-up version of what we consider "white bread." The addition of butter and milk makes for a softer, more delicate bread, a golden brown loaf that slices and toasts beautifully. I love to serve this bread toasted, with blue cheese and a glass of port.

EQUIPMENT: One bread pan or covered *pain-de-mie* mold, 9 x 5 inches (22.5 x 12.5 cm)

Butter for preparing the pan
1 teaspoon active dry yeast
1 teaspoon sugar
1½ cups (37.5 cl) lukewarm whole milk (about 105°F; 40°C)
1½ teaspoons salt
4 tablespoons (2 ounces; 60 g) unsalted butter, melted
4 to 5 cups (540 to 675 g) bread flour
½ cup (2 ounces; 60 g) freshly grated Parmigiano-Reggiano cheese
1 teaspoon freshly ground black pepper

1. Butter the loaf pan or the mold and cover of a *pain-de-mie* pan. If using a loaf pan, butter a piece of aluminum foil to use as a cover. Set aside.
2. In the bowl of a heavy-duty electric mixer fitted with a paddle, combine the yeast, sugar, and milk, and stir to blend. Let stand until foamy, about 5 minutes. Add the salt and butter, and stir to blend.
3. Add the flour, a little at a time, mixing at the lowest speed until most of the flour has been absorbed and the dough forms a ball. Add the cheese and pepper. Continue to mix at the lowest speed until soft and satiny but still firm, 4 to 5 minutes, adding additional flour to keep the dough from sticking. Scrape the paddle. Form the dough into a ball and return to the bowl. Cover and let rise until double in bulk, about 2 hours.
4. Punch down the dough and transfer to the baking pan. With your fingertips, press the dough down smoothly, being sure it fills the corners. Cover tightly. Let rise at room temperature until about double in bulk, about 2 hours.
5. About 30 minutes before the dough is ready to be baked, preheat the oven to 375°F (190°C; gas mark 5).
6. Cover the pan or mold and place in the center of the oven. Bake until the bread is golden brown, about 45 to 55 minutes. Remove from the oven, unmold, and place on a rack to cool.

ONE LOAF

*There is a communion of more than our bodies when bread is broken
and wine is drunk. And that is my answer when people ask me:
Why do you write about hunger, and not wars or love?*

M. F. K. FISHER

SESAME, FLAX & SUNFLOWER SEED BREAD

I bake bread every few days, usually a sourdough loaf filled with various seeds or grains, which provide an extra bit of wholesomeness, flavor, and crunch. Since I know that not everyone has the time or desire to keep a sourdough starter active, I have developed a yeast version of my daily loaf. It uses only a small amount of leavening (so there's more wheat and less yeast flavor) and takes on its substantial character from long rising in the refrigerator. This loaf is kneaded by mixer rather than by hand, creating a glutinous, high-rising, more polished loaf with even air holes.

> 1 teaspoon active dry yeast
> 1 teaspoon sugar
> 4 cups (1 l) lukewarm water (about 105°F; 40°C)
> About 9 cups (1 kg 215 g) bread flour
> 1 tablespoon fine sea salt
> ½ cup (75 g) hulled sesame seeds
> ½ cup (75 g) flax seeds
> ½ cup (75 g) sunflower seeds

1. In the bowl of a heavy-duty electric mixer fitted with a paddle, combine the yeast, sugar, and 1 cup (12.5 cl) of water, and stir to blend. Let stand until foamy, about 5 minutes.

2. Stir in the salt and 1 cup (12.5 cl) of the water, and mix at low speed for 1 minute. Mix in the remaining 2 cups (25 cl) of water. Slowly add 4 cups (540 g) of the flour and mix until incorporated, about 3 minutes. Slowly add the remaining 5 cups (675 g) of flour and mix for about 3 minutes. A slow, steady addition of flour will make for a dense, well-constructed loaf. Add the sesame, flax, and sunflower seeds, and mix for 1 minute more, until the dough pulls away from the sides of the bowl and begins to form a loose but cohesive ball. Scrape the paddle.

3. Cover the bowl with plastic wrap and refrigerate until double in bulk, about 8 hours.

4. Transfer the dough to a lightly floured work surface and knead by hand for 2 minutes. Return the dough to the bowl, cover, and refrigerate until doubled again, about 8 hours or overnight.

5. Punch the dough down. Place in a clean bowl, cover, and set aside at room temperature in a draft-free spot until double, 3 to 4 hours.

6. Shape the dough into a large round loaf. Place a large floured cloth in a large loaf pan or rectangular basket and place the dough, smooth side down, in the pan or basket. Loosely fold the cloth over the dough. Let rise at room temperature until doubled, about 1 hour and 15 minutes.

7. At least 40 minutes before placing the dough in the oven, preheat the oven to 500°F (260°C; gas mark 9). If using a baking stone, place it in the oven to preheat.

8. Lightly flour a baking paddle or rimless baking sheet and turn the dough over onto the paddle or sheet. Slash the top of the dough several times with a razor blade, so it can expand regularly during baking. With a quick jerk of the wrists, slide the bread onto the baking stone or onto a baking sheet. Using a garden mister, generously spray the bottom and sides of the oven with water, then spray 3 more times during the next 6 minutes. The steam created will help give the loaf a good crust and will give the dough a boost during rising. Once the bread is lightly browned—about 10 minutes—lower the heat to 400°F (210°C; gas mark 7) and rotate the loaf so that it browns evenly. Bake until the crust is a dark golden brown and the loaf sounds hollow when tapped on the bottom, about 45 minutes more, for a total baking time of about 55 minutes. Transfer to a rack to cool. Do not slice the bread for at least 1 hour, for it will continue to bake as it cools.

ONE LARGE LOAF

❧ A WORD ON FLAX ☙ Flax seed has taken on new importance in recent years because it has been found to be excellent in combating high cholesterol levels. Obviously, it is also quite rich in fiber. The stalk of the flax plant is still used in the fabrication of cloth, and when treated and prepared for weaving, it is a rich golden yellow—thus, the term "flaxen-haired maiden" from fairy tales. Flax seed is commonly found at health-food stores.

Talk of joy: There may be things better than beef stew and
baked potatoes and homemade bread—there may be.
DAVID GRAYSON

CRUSTY WHEAT & POLENTA BREAD

I am always searching for new, natural flavors for my repertoire of breads. One day I had polenta on my mind and created this version, which is rich in corn flavor but not heavy, as many corn breads can be. Serve this golden, crusty bread with Shelia & Julian's Quick Foie Gras (page 32), in toasted cheese sandwiches, or as a special bread for the cheese course.

> 1 teaspoon active dry yeast
> 1 teaspoon sugar
> ¾ cup (17.5 cl) lukewarm milk (about 105°F; 40°C)
> 1 tablespoon fine sea salt
> 1 tablespoon extra-virgin olive oil
> 2¼ cups (30 cl) lukewarm water (about 105°F; 40°C)
> About 6 cups (810 g) bread flour
> 2 cups (300 g) polenta

1. In the bowl of a heavy-duty electric mixer fitted with a paddle, combine the yeast, sugar, and milk, and stir to blend. Let stand until foamy, about 5 minutes. Add the salt, oil, and water, and stir to blend.
2. Very slowly add about 2 cups of the flour to the mixing bowl, a little at a time, mixing well after each addition at the lowest speed. Add the polenta a little at a time, still at the lowest speed, mixing well after each addition. Add as much of the remaining bread flour as necessary, mixing at the lowest speed, until most of the flour has been absorbed and the dough begins to form a ball. Continue to mix for a full 5 minutes at the lowest speed.
3. Cover the bowl with plastic wrap and refrigerate. Let the bread rise in the refrigerator until doubled in size, about 8 hours, or overnight.
4. Remove the dough from the refrigerator, punch it down, and cover again with plastic wrap. Let rise at room temperature until about doubled in size, 2 to 3 hours.
5. Punch down the dough and knead it for about 30 seconds. Shape the dough into a tight rectangle by rolling the ball of dough and folding it over itself. Place a large floured cloth in a large loaf pan or rectangular basket, sprinkle generously with cornmeal, and place the dough, smooth side down, in the pan or basket. Loosely fold the cloth over the dough. Let

rise at room temperature until doubled in size, about 1 hour and 15 minutes. (Alternatively, form into 2 round loaves and let rise on a baking sheet, covered with a clean towel.)

6. At least 40 minutes before placing the dough in the oven, preheat the oven to 475°F (245°C; gas mark 8/9). If using a baking stone, place it in the oven to preheat.

7. Lightly flour a baking paddle or rimless baking sheet and turn the dough over onto the paddle or sheet. Slash the top of the dough several times with a razor blade, so it can expand evenly during baking. With a quick jerk of the wrists, slide the dough onto the baking stone or onto a baking sheet. Using a garden mister, generously spray the center of the oven with water (don't worry about the bread turning soggy). Then spray 3 more times during the first 6 minutes of baking. The steam created will help give the loaf a good crust and will give the dough a boost during rising. Once the bread is lightly browned—about 10 minutes—lower the heat to 400°F (200°C; gas mark 6/7) and rotate the loaf so it browns evenly. Bake until the crust is a dark golden brown and the loaf sounds hollow when tapped on the bottom, about 20 to 25 minutes more, for a total baking time of about 30 to 35 minutes.

8. Remove the bread from the oven and transfer to a cooling rack. Do not slice the bread for at least 1 hour, for it will continue to bake as it rests. The bread can be stored in a zipper-locked plastic bag for 3 to 4 days.

ONE LARGE LOAF OR TWO MEDIUM LOAVES

↶ **WHAT'S IN A WORD?** ↷ A lot of words are thrown around loosely without any investigation of their real meaning. Semolina? Polenta? Cornmeal? Semolina is the general term used to describe any cereal that is coarsely ground into granules. Though most semolina are made from a durum wheat base, others, such as white semolina, are ground from rice. In this case, yellow semolina is ground from cornmeal to make both polenta and cornmeal. Polenta is coarsely ground cornmeal and yields a grainy texture when cooked. Cornmeal is almost powdery in comparison and is consequently used for different kinds of cooking—in breads and cakes, for example.

WALNUT, RYE & CURRANT LOAF

Bread, cheese, and wine. I could live on them! And nothing brings out the flavor of a rich, golden cheese like a perfectly dense, firm, and crusty toasted slice of bread studded with walnuts and currants. Here's my favorite version. (If dried currants cannot be found, substitute raisins.) Note that as in all my bread recipes, a minimum of yeast is used here, so the bread tastes of wheat and rye, walnuts and currants, not yeast. One teaspoon is equal to about half a package of yeast.

> 1 teaspoon active dry yeast
> 1 teaspoon sugar
> 2½ cups (62.5 cl) lukewarm water (about 105°F; 40°C)
> 2 teaspoons fine sea salt
> 1 cup (125 g) rye flour
> About 5 cups (675 g) unbleached bread flour
> 1 tablespoon honey
> 1 cup (125 g) walnut pieces
> 1 cup (125 g) dried currants or raisins

1. In the bowl of a heavy-duty electric mixer fitted with a flat paddle, combine the yeast, sugar, and water, and stir to blend. Let stand until foamy, about 5 minutes.

2. Add the salt, rye flour, and wheat flour, a little at a time, mixing at the lowest speed until most of the flour has been absorbed and the dough forms a ball. Add the honey and continue to mix until soft and satiny but still firm, 4 to 5 minutes, adding additional flour to keep the dough from sticking. Add the walnuts and black currants, and mix until evenly blended into the dough. Scrape the paddle. (If the walnuts and currants are not evenly mixed into the dough by machine, knead them in by hand.)

3. Cover the bowl with plastic wrap and refrigerate until double in bulk, about 8 hours, or overnight.

4. Transfer the dough to a lightly floured work surface and knead by hand for 2 minutes. Return the dough to the bowl, cover, and let rise at room temperature until double in bulk, 2 to 3 hours.

5. Shape the dough into a large round loaf. Place a large floured cloth in a large loaf pan or rectangular basket and place the dough, smooth side down, in the pan or basket. Loosely fold the cloth over the dough. Let rise at room temperature until double in bulk, 2 to 3 hours.

6. At least 40 minutes before placing the dough in the oven, preheat the oven to 500°F (260°C; gas mark 9). If using a baking stone, place it in the oven to preheat.

7. Lightly flour a baking paddle or rimless baking sheet, and turn the dough over onto the paddle or sheet. Slash the top of the dough several times with a razor blade so it can

expand regularly during baking. With a quick jerk of the wrists, slide the bread onto the baking stone or baking sheet. Using a garden mister, generously spray the bottom and sides of the oven with water. Then spray 3 more times during the next 6 minutes. The steam created will help give the loaf a good crust and will give the dough a boost during rising. Once the bread is lightly browned—after about 10 minutes—lower the heat to 400°F (210°C; gas mark 7) and rotate the loaf so that it browns evenly. Bake until the crust is a dark golden brown and the loaf sounds hollow when tapped on the bottom, about 30 minutes more, for a total baking time of about 40 minutes. Transfer to a rack to cool. Do not slice the bread for at least 1 hour, for it will continue to bake as it cools.

ONE LOAF

A loaf of Sesame, Flax & Sunflower Seed Bread (page 176), with three local cheeses. Left to right: cow, sheep and goat.

If God had not made brown honey,
men would think figs much sweeter than they do.
XENOPHANES

FIG, APRICOT, WALNUT & RAISIN RYE

I love the way recipes develop. One afternoon in April, I was reorganizing my pantry and came across several small bags of dried fruit. There wasn't enough in any of the bags to amount to much, so I gathered them all up to create a dense loaf that goes well with fresh cheese, especially our fresh local goat's cheese. But the guests who were at our house that weekend couldn't wait for the cheese course: They wanted this bread for breakfast, lunch, and dinner. What better compliment can you pay a cook? Of course I complied! You don't need to follow the amounts and varieties of dried fruits and nuts to the letter. Use what you have on hand, mixing and matching dried fruits and nuts to your taste. Just be sure they are of top quality.

 1 teaspoon active dry yeast

 1 teaspoon sugar

 2½ cups (62.5 cl) lukewarm water (about 105°F; 40°C)

 10 dried apricots (about 50 g), quartered

 ½ cup (75 g) golden raisins

 4 dried figs (75 g), quartered

 ¼ cup (25 g) quartered walnuts

 About 5 cups (670 g) unbleached bread flour

 1 cup (135 g) rye flour

 2 teaspoons fine sea salt

 1 tablespoon raw honey

1. In the bowl of a heavy-duty electric mixer fitted with a flat paddle, combine the yeast, sugar, and water, and stir to blend. Let stand until foamy, about 5 minutes.

2. Meanwhile, in a small bowl, combine the apricots, raisins, figs, nuts, and toss with 1 tablespoon of flour. This will prevent them from sticking together and allow them to be more evenly distributed throughout the dough. Set aside.

3. Add the bread flour, rye flour, and salt to the yeast mixture, a little at a time, mixing at the lowest speed until most of the flour has been absorbed and the dough forms a ball. Add the honey and continue to mix until soft and satiny but still firm, 4 to 5 minutes, adding additional flour to keep the dough from sticking. Add the dried fruit and nuts,

(continued on next page)

and mix just until incorporated into the dough. Scrape the paddle. (If the fruit and nuts are not evenly mixed into the dough by machine, knead them in by hand.)

4. Cover the bowl with plastic wrap and refrigerate until double in bulk, about 8 hours.

5. Transfer the dough to a lightly floured work surface and knead by hand for 2 minutes. Return the dough to the bowl, cover, and let rise at room temperature until double in bulk, 2 to 3 hours.

6. Shape the dough into a large round loaf. Place a large floured cloth in a large loaf pan or rectangular basket and place the dough, smooth side down, in the pan or basket. Loosely fold the cloth over the dough. Let rise at room temperature until double in bulk, 2 to 3 hours.

7. At least 40 minutes before placing the dough in the oven, preheat the oven to 500°F (260°C; gas mark 9). If using a baking stone, place it in the oven to preheat.

8. Lightly flour a baking paddle or rimless baking sheet, and turn the dough over onto the paddle or sheet. Slash the top of the dough several times with a razor blade so it can expand regularly during baking. With a quick jerk of the wrists, slide the bread onto the baking stone or baking sheet. Using a garden mister, generously spray the bottom and sides of the oven with water. Then spray 3 more times during the next 6 minutes. The steam created will help give the loaf a good crust and will give the dough a boost during rising. Once the bread is lightly browned—after about 10 minutes—lower the heat to 400°F (210°C; gas mark 7) and rotate the loaf so that it browns evenly. Bake until the crust is a dark golden brown and the loaf sounds hollow when tapped on the bottom, about 30 minutes more, for a total baking time of about 40 minutes. Transfer to a rack to cool. Do not slice the bread for at least 1 hour, for it will continue to bake as it cools.

ONE LOAF

BREAD DOUGH

This is the simple, basic dough that I use in preparing pizzas, the base of rolls (Pine Nut Rolls, page 169), and bread tarts (Onion Caraway Bread Tart, page 191).

1 teaspoon active dry yeast
1 teaspoon sugar
1⅓ cups (33 cl) lukewarm water (about 105°F; 40°C)
2 tablespoons extra-virgin olive oil
1 teaspoon fine sea salt
About 4 cups (540 g) bread flour

1. In the bowl of a heavy-duty electric mixer fitted with a paddle, combine the yeast, sugar, and water, and stir to blend. Let stand until foamy, about 5 minutes. Stir in the oil and salt.

2. Add the flour, a little at a time, mixing at the lowest speed until most of the flour has been absorbed and the dough forms a ball. Continue to mix at the lowest speed until soft and satiny but still firm, 4 to 5 minutes. Add additional flour, if necessary, to keep the dough from sticking. The dough will be quite soft.

3. Transfer the dough to a bowl, cover tightly with plastic wrap, and place in the refrigerator. Let the dough rise in the refrigerator until doubled or tripled in bulk, 8 to 12 hours. The dough can be kept for 2 to 3 days in the refrigerator. Simply punch down the dough as it doubles or triples. Proceed with the individual recipes for pizzas, bread tarts, and rolls.

ENOUGH DOUGH FOR FOUR SMALL PIZZAS, ONE BREAD TART, OR FIFTEEN ROLLS

I was taught from childhood the sanctity of food.
Not a piece of bread could be thrown away without kissing it
and raising it to one's eyes as with all things holy.

ATTIA HOSAIN

RITA'S RYE

Years ago my friend Yale Kramer sent me this recipe, one he dedicated to his wife, Rita. He baked it late one night, then presented it to her as a gift in the morning. "I think it is delicious as a breakfast bread to go with Gruyère or Gouda, and it is, in my opinion, the perfect bread for *croque monsieur,*" he wrote. Later, when I prepared it for all of us at Chanteduc, he added to his commentary: "This is definitely a specialty bread, not a dinner bread, but one for toasting with butter or as part of a cheese course." Yes!

    1 teaspoon active dry yeast
    1 teaspoon sugar
    3 cups (75 cl) lukewarm water (about 105°F; 40°C)
    1 tablespoon fine sea salt
    About 4 cups (540 g) rye flour
    4 to 5 cups (540 to 675 g) unbleached bread flour
    4 tablespoons caraway seeds
    1 tablespoon fennel seeds
    2 tablespoons raw honey

1. In the bowl of a heavy-duty electric mixer fitted with a flat paddle, combine the yeast, sugar, and 1 cup (25 cl) of water, and stir to blend. Let stand until foamy, about 5 minutes. Add the salt and remaining 2 cups (50 cl) of water, and mix to blend. Slowly add the rye flour and mix at the lowest possible speed until the flour is thoroughly incorporated. Add the bread flour slowly. Add the caraway seeds, fennel seeds, and honey, continuing to mix at the lowest speed until the dough begins to form a ball. Continue to mix until soft and satiny but still firm, 4 to 5 minutes, adding additional flour to keep the dough from sticking. The dough should barely clean the sides of the bowl. Scrape the paddle.

2. Cover and set aside at room temperature to rise until about double in bulk, 2 to 3 hours. Punch down and let rise one more time, until double in bulk, 2 to 3 hours.

3. Shape the dough into a large round loaf. The dough will be quite sticky. To make it easier to handle the dough, dust your hands with flour before working with it. Place a large floured cloth in a large loaf pan or rectangular basket and place the dough, smooth

Assorted breads for sale at the Vaison market.

side down, in the pan or basket. Loosely fold the cloth over the dough. Let rise at room temperature until double in bulk, 2 to 3 hours.

4. At least 40 minutes before placing the dough in the oven, preheat the oven to 500°F (260°C; gas mark 9). If using a baking stone, place it in the oven to preheat.

5. Lightly flour a baking paddle or rimless baking sheet, and turn the dough over onto the paddle or sheet. Slash the top of the dough several times with a razor blade so it can expand regularly during baking. With a quick jerk of the wrists, slide the bread onto the baking stone or baking sheet. Using a garden mister, generously spray the bottom and sides of the oven with water. Then spray 3 more times during the next 6 minutes. The steam created will help give the loaf a good crust and will give the dough a boost during rising. Once the bread is lightly browned—after about 10 minutes—lower the heat to 400°F (210°C; gas mark 7) and rotate the loaf so that it browns evenly. Bake until the crust is a dark golden brown and the loaf sounds hollow when tapped on the bottom, about 30 minutes more, for a total baking time of about 40 minutes. Transfer to a rack to cool. Do not slice the bread for at least 1 hour, for it will continue to bake as it cools.

ONE LOAF

CARAWAY CORN-RYE BREAD

This is a "memory lane" recipe. One of my favorite tastes from childhood is caraway and rye, often in the form of firm, round rolls topped with coarse salt. Here is my grown-up interpretation. Rye flour has very little gluten and is often difficult to work with, for it tends to become quite sticky. By beginning with a rye "sponge," the bread is easier to work.

SPONGE

    1 teaspoon active dry yeast

    1 teaspoon sugar

    1 cup lukewarm water (about 105°F; 40°C)

    1½ cups (about 200 g) rye flour

THE BREAD

    2 cups (50 cl) water

    1 tablespoon fine sea salt

    ½ cup (75 g) polenta or cornmeal

    1 cup (135 g) rye flour

    About 4 cups (540 g) unbleached bread flour

    6 tablespoons caraway seeds

    1 egg plus 1 tablespoon water

    1 teaspoon coarse sea salt

1. Prepare the sponge: In the bowl of a heavy-duty electric mixer fitted with a flat paddle, combine the yeast, sugar, and water, and stir to blend. Let stand until foamy, about 5 minutes. Add the rye flour and mix at the lowest possible speed until the flour is thoroughly incorporated. Scrape the paddle. Leave the sponge in the bowl. Cover securely and refrigerate 8 hours or overnight.

2. Make the bread: Remove the sponge from the refrigerator. Return the bowl to the mixer and add the 2 cups (50 cl) of water, fine sea salt, polenta, and 1 cup (135 g) of rye flour, a little at a time, mixing at the lowest speed until all the flour has been absorbed. Add the bread flour slowly and 5 tablespoons of caraway seeds, continuing to mix at the lowest speed until the dough begins to form a ball. Continue to mix until soft and satiny but still firm, 4 to 5 minutes, adding additional flour to keep the dough from sticking. Scrape the paddle.

3. Shape the dough into a large round loaf. Place a large floured cloth in a large loaf pan or rectangular basket and place the dough, smooth side down, in the pan or basket. Loosely fold the cloth over the dough. Let rise at room temperature until double in bulk, 3 to 4 hours.

4. At least 40 minutes before placing the dough in the oven, preheat the oven to 500°F (260°C; gas mark 9). If using a baking stone, place it in the oven to preheat.

5. Bake the loaf: Lightly flour a baking paddle or rimless baking sheet, and turn the dough over onto the paddle or sheet. Slash the top of the dough several times with a razor blade so it can expand regularly during baking. Glaze with the egg and water mixture. Sprinkle with the remaining 1 tablespoon of caraway seeds and the coarse sea salt. With a quick jerk of the wrists, slide the bread onto the baking stone or baking sheet. Using a garden mister, generously spray the bottom and sides of the oven with water. Then spray 3 more times during the next 6 minutes. The steam created will help give the loaf a good crust and will give the dough a boost during rising. Once the bread is lightly browned—after about 10 minutes—lower the heat to 400°F (210°C; gas mark 7) and rotate the loaf so that it browns evenly. Bake until the crust is a dark golden brown and the loaf sounds hollow when tapped on the bottom, about 30 minutes more, for a total baking time of about 40 minutes. Transfer to a rack to cool. Do not slice the bread for at least 1 hour, for it will continue to bake as it cools.

ONE LOAF

◡: **AN ANISE-RICH SPICE** :◠ Caraway seeds are a spice most notably appreciated by the Germans. The Germans use them to perfume breads, sauerkraut, and their famous liqueur *kummel,* where caraway plays the lead role. However, this liking for the rich, anise-flavored spice makes its way into a wide span of world cuisines, including the Dutch, who add the fragrant seeds to certain cheeses such as Gouda, and the Alsatians, who add it to Munster. Although caraway responds well to cooking and baking, it should not be heated for an extended period of time because it can turn bitter and upset the balance of a dish. In slow-cooking recipes such as borscht, it is added only during the last few minutes of cooking.

In Hungary and England, caraway is added to such menu staples as cooked potatoes and "seed cakes," small sugar-coated pound cakes that attained the height of popularity in Victorian times. These cakes are even referred to in great literary works of the time, including Charles Dickens's *David Copperfield*: "I cut and handed the seed-cake."

Caraway, spelled "carvey" in Scotland, coming from the French *carvi,* was also used as both a digestive aid and an after-meal breath sweetener. The French have numerous nicknames for the spice, including "mountain cumin," "fool's aniseed," and "meadow cumin."

ONION CARAWAY BREAD TART

I've always had a love affair with homemade bread, but ever since I moved to France, that romance has been fed to an even greater extent by the bread-loving world that surrounds me. Bread tarts are such a simple solution to both appetizers and desserts that I make them frequently. This onion and caraway variation—makes for a lovely first course or even a main luncheon dish, accompanied by a tossed green salad. The tart is enhanced with a generous hit of freshly ground black pepper, preferably the top-grade Tellicherry pepper with its complex, balanced, elegant flavors. The peppercorn has hints of ginger and pine, and although it's a rich and bold seasoning, it is far from aggressive.

1 recipe Bread Dough (page 185), prepared with 1 teaspoon caraway seeds

4 medium onions (about 1½ pounds; 750 g), peeled

6 tablespoons extra-virgin olive oil

1 teaspoon sea salt

2 teaspoons sugar

Bouquet garni: several sprigs of fresh rosemary and 1 fresh bay leaf, tied to a bundle with household twine

1 large egg

1 teaspoon caraway seeds

Freshly ground black pepper to taste, preferably Tellicherry

1. Prepare the Bread Dough, adding the caraway seeds.

2. Slice the onions in half lengthwise. Place each half, cut side down, on a cutting board and cut crosswise into very thin slices for about 4 cups (100 cl).

3. At least 40 minutes before baking the tart, preheat the oven to 450°F (230°C; gas mark 8).

4. In a large, shallow skillet, combine the onions, oil, salt, sugar, and bouquet garni, and toss to coat the onions with oil. Cover and sweat over the lowest possible heat until the onions are very soft and slightly golden, about 30 minutes. Remove the bouquet garni. Taste for seasoning. Crack the egg into a small bowl, whisk to blend, then stir the egg into the onion mixture. Add the caraway seeds and toss to blend.

5. Punch down the prepared dough and shape into a rectangle. On a lightly floured surface, roll the dough into an 11½ x 15½-inch (30 x 40-cm) rectangle, or large enough to fit a standard nonstick baking sheet. Place the dough on the baking sheet and press it flat to fit the pan.

6. Spread the onion mixture evenly on the bread dough, going right to the edge. Place in the center of the oven and bake until the bread is firm and the onion mixture golden, about 25 minutes. Remove from the oven and sprinkle generously with pepper. Transfer to a cutting board and cut into squares or rectangles. Serve immediately.

TEN TO TWELVE SERVINGS

FOUGASSE

The lyrical, ladderlike bread known as fougasse is my Provençal pizza. I take my favorite bread dough, shape it into individual breads, then flavor them with whatever delicious toppings I might have on hand—black or green olives, home-cured anchovies, marinated baby artichokes, capers, bits of fresh goat cheese, a touch of hot *pili pili* oil, or simply a brush of olive oil and a scattering of fresh thyme and coarse sea salt. The most traditional fougasse is flavored with bits of browned pork fat (what we call cracklings), but one also finds sweet versions prepared with a butter-rich dough or briochelike butter and egg dough flavored with orange flower water. The origin of the word is a mystery, though in the rest of France a *fouace* can refer to any sort of flat, baked galette, either sweet or savory.

1 recipe Bread Dough (page 185)

Fougasse from the Vaison market.

1. At least 40 minutes before placing the assembled fougasse in the oven, preheat the oven to 500°F (260°C; gas mark 9).

2. Punch down the prepared dough and divide it evenly into 5 pieces. Shape each piece into a ball. On a lightly floured surface, roll each ball of dough into an 8-by-5 inch (20-by-12.5 cm) rectangle. Using a pastry scraper, cut lengthwise slashed into the bread, with 3 slashes at the bottom half of the dough and a single slash at the top, so that the slashes resemble the veins of a leaf.

3. Sprinkle a baking sheet with coarse cornmeal and carefully transfer the rectangles of dough to the baking sheet. Gently pull apart at the slashes. Cover with a clean towel and let rest for 10 minutes.

4. Assemble the fougasse: Brush lightly with olive oil or honey, then sprinkle with preferred toppings.

VARIOUS SAVORY TOPPING SUGGESTIONS: Brush the dough with olive oil, then—either alone or in combination—sprinkle dough with the following: pitted and halved black or green olives; drained capers; drained anchovy fillets; soft goat's cheese, crumbled; a thin layer of tomato sauce; drained marinated artichokes.

VARIOUS SWEET TOPPING SUGGESTIONS: Brush the bread with melted honey, then add—either alone or in combination—chopped walnuts; whole almonds; strips of chopped dried figs, apricots, kumquats, candied orange or lemon peel; sprinkle with whole fennel seeds, if desired.

Patricia prepares fougasse in her farm kitchen.

Patricia purchases fish at the Vaison market.

7

FISH & SHELLFISH

OUR LANDLOCKED VILLAGE MAY BE HOURS from the Mediterranean, yet the profusion of miniature whitebait, anchovies, sea bass, monkfish, dorade, and tuna in the Vaison market attests to the Provençal appetite for the fruits of the sea. And thanks to the wonders of modern transportation, lobster, crab, scallops, and oysters from Brittany waters are mine for the asking. Local fishmonger Eliane Berenger is a constant wealth of recipes and tips, while the glistening array of ultra-fresh fish at the stalls at the Tuesday market entice one to feast on Monkfish "Carpaccio," to take roast fish whole (such as silvery Bonito in Parchment with Warm Pistou), to bake it buried in salt (as in Whole Fish Roasted in a Crust of Sea Salt), or to sear Pancetta-Wrapped Cod. Mint from the garden is tossed into Minted Crabmeat Salad, while first-of-season Picholine green olives serve to flavor Steamed Salmon with Warm Lemon Vinaigrette.

MARIA'S GINGER SHRIMP

This dish is an homage to my editor, Maria Guarnaschelli. It's a zesty combination of ginger, garlic, and white wine, and is full of character and depth, just like dear Maria. I created it one spring Sunday on the way to my Paris market on rue Poncelet. I had seen giant fresh shrimp (gambas) there the day before and thought of all the flavors I wanted to enjoy for lunch that day. So I combined many of my cherished aromas, ingredients, and tastes in a single dish. At the same time it seemed that a dish as fragrant as this demanded a perfumed accompaniment, and then I remembered the package of basmati rice that Maria had given me on a recent trip to New York. Quite coincidentally, the contract for this book had just been signed and returned to New York the day before. Well, my husband, Walter, and I savored this dish and toasted Maria, saddened only because she wasn't with us to celebrate! In this recipe, the wine—either a Sauvignon blanc or a young white Rhône—is slightly reduced, adding depth of flavor as well as character to the sauce.

1 pound (500 g) large shrimp, shelled and deveined (about 16 to 20)
2 tablespoons extra-virgin olive oil
4 tablespoons grated fresh ginger
7 plump, fresh garlic cloves, peeled, halved, and slivered
Fine sea salt to taste
2 cups (50 cl) dry white wine
Basmati Rice (page 273)
4 tablespoons fresh basil leaves, cut into a chiffonnade

1. Rinse the shrimp and pat them dry. In a skillet large enough to hold all the shrimp in a single layer, heat the oil until hot but not smoking. Add 3 tablespoons of ginger, the garlic, and a pinch of salt. Cook over moderately high heat just until the garlic turns golden but does not brown, 2 to 3 minutes. Pour the wine all over the surface of the pan, bring to a simmer, and cook until reduced to 1 cup (25 cl), about 8 minutes.

2. Add the shrimp in a single layer and cook, stirring occasionally, just until the shrimp turn pink, about 4 minutes.

3. Prepare the Basmati Rice. Serve the shrimp with its juices spooned over the rice in shallow bowls. Sprinkle with the remaining ginger and basil.

FOUR SERVINGS

 WINE SUGGESTIONS: A nicely chilled floral wine is a great match here. A French or California Viognier or a white Châteauneuf du Pape are my choices.

SHERRY & GINGER LOBSTER

Inspired by Parisian chef Alain Passard, this recipe suggests a new, modern approach to lobster: Rather than presenting the entire tail in a single piece, the meat is quartered into long strips—still attached to the shell—making for an unusual and elegant presentation. There are also gustative and practical advantages to cutting the tail meat in this manner: The moist strips of meat better absorb the zesty sherry-ginger sauce (so delicious you could drink it alone!), and are less cumbersome to eat. To keep the tail straight as it cooks, a classic French technique is used: A stainless steel spoon is tied to the tail. The lobster is boiled briefly, then the meat is cooked in the oven and warmed in a fragrant, sherry and ginger sauce sweetened with honey. While Passard prepares his sauce with the sherry-like *vin jaune* of the Jura region, as well as hazelnut oil, my version combines a reduction of sherry wine blended with honey, olive oil, and a hint of ginger. For special occasions in Provence, I order live fresh "blue" lobsters from the Brittany shores and serve this dish as a romantic main dish for two.

Sherry & Ginger Lobster.

(continued on next page)

EQUIPMENT: An immersion mixer

2 live lobsters (1 pound; 500 g each)
2 cups (50 cl) best-quality dry Spanish fine dry sherry, such as Gonzalez Byass's
    Tío Pepe or Pedro Domecq's La Ina *fino*
2 tablespoons raw honey, or to taste
6 tablespoons extra-virgin olive oil
Fine sea salt
½ teaspoon best-quality ground ginger, or to taste

1. Prepare the lobsters: Thoroughly rinse the lobsters under cold running water. Bring a large pot of water to a rolling boil over high heat. Hold a lobster by the neck between your thumb and index finger. Place a metal spoon down the length of the interior of the tail. Wrap string around each articulation of the tail, pulling so the string winds around tightly. Tie the string in a secure knot. With scissors, remove the rubber bands restraining the claws. Repeat for the remaining lobster.

2. Cook the lobsters: Plunge the lobsters, head first, into the boiling water. Counting from the time the lobster hits the water, cook for 4 minutes. (The lobsters may be cooked one at a time.) Carefully remove the lobsters from the water, drain and set aside to cool for 10 minutes, to allow the lobster meat to firm up.

3. Preheat the oven to 425°F (220°C; gas mark 7/8).

4. Place the lobsters in a large, shallow pan with a fitted cover. Place in the center of the oven and cook for 10 minutes. Remove the pan from the oven and transfer the lobsters to a clean, flat work surface. Strain the juice in the pan through a fine-mesh sieve into a small bowl. Set aside.

5. Prepare the sauce: In a large, nonreactive saucepan, bring the sherry to a boil over high heat. Reduce the heat and simmer until the wine is reduced to about ½ cup (25 cl) and all the alcohol has burned off, about 5 minutes. Add the reserved lobster-cooking juices and cook for 2 minutes more. Add the honey and stir to dissolve. Remove from the heat and add 1 tablespoon of olive oil at a time, blending to a thick emulsion with an immersion mixer. (Alternatively, blend in a blender. Return to the saucepan.) Add the ginger, and taste for seasoning. Set aside.

6. Remove the meat from the claws: Twist each large claw off the body of the lobster. Gently crack the shells with a nutcracker or hammer, trying not to damage the meat. Extract the meat with a seafood fork, toothpick or lobster pick: It should come out in a single piece. Set aside. Gently detach the tail from the rest of the body. Remove and reserve the pale green tomalley (liver) from the upper portion of the body cavity. Remove and carefully reserve the deep red coral, if present. (The tomalley and coral will not be used in this recipe. They can be reserved—and frozen—to add to a lobster sauce for another preparation.) Discard the heat. Repeat for the remaining lobster.

7. Prepare the tail meat: Remove the spoon and string wrapped around each lobster tail. Place a lobster tail with the interior facing upward on a flat work surface. With a large, sharp chef's knife, make a cut through the middle down the length of the tail. By applying additional pressure on the knife, you should be able to cut through the outer shell, cutting the lobster tail in half lengthwise. Cut each half in half again so that each tail yields four long strips. (The meat should remain connected to the shell.) Set aside carefully. Repeat for the remaining lobster.

8. To finish: Transfer the sauce to a large, shallow skillet and warm over moderate heat. Carefully add the strips of lobster and shell in a single layer, along with the claw meat. Roll the pieces around in the sauce to warm them up and finish cooking, 3 to 4 minutes.

9. To serve: Arrange four pieces of tail meat lengthwise in the center of each warmed dinner plate. Place a claw on both sides of the tail meat. Repeat for the remaining plate. Spoon the sauce between, over and around the pieces of lobster. Serve immediately.

TWO SERVINGS

WINE SUGGESTION: This dish deserves a regal white Burgundy. My preference is for a Chassagne-Montrachet from the house of Olivier Leflaive, a wine that seems to flatter everything with which it comes in contact.

MONKFISH "CARPACCIO"

I first tasted a version of this dish at Paul Minchelli's extraordinary fish restaurant on Paris's Left Bank. The monkfish, cut into thin, horizontal slices, is arranged like petals on a large platter atop a drizzle of oil and a sprinkling of fine sea salt, and then anointed with another trace of oil. The fish is passed under the grill rapidly and, before bringing it to the table, sprinkled with a touch of fresh lemon juice and chives. Slip a piece of crusty home-made bread into the toaster as the fish goes in the oven, and you'll have an instant feast.

Because the tastiness of the dish depends on the pure flavor of utterly fresh fish, there is a caveat: Do not make this dish with anything but the very best ingredients. If you are in doubt, simply ask your fishmonger which is the freshest fish available that day.

> 2 tablespoons extra-virgin olive oil
> Fine sea salt to taste
> 8 ounces (250 g) fresh monkfish in one piece, membranes removed, or substitute red
>   snapper, sea bass, sea scallops, or cod
> 2 teaspoons freshly squeezed lemon juice
> 2 tablespoons chives, snipped extra-fine with a scissors

1. Preheat the broiler.
2. Drizzle a large ovenproof platter with about 1 tablespoon of oil, shifting the plate back and forth so it is evenly coated. Sprinkle very lightly with fine sea salt.
3. Using a very sharp knife (a flexible fish boning knife is ideal), cut the monkfish horizontally into slices ⅛ inch (2 mm) thick. (The length and width of the pieces is not important, but the thinness is.) Place the slices of fish side by side on the oiled platter, very slightly overlapping. Drizzle with the remaining 1 tablespoon of oil.
4. Place the baking dish under the broiler, about 2 inches (5 cm) from the heat. Broil until the fish turns pearly, opaque, and tender, 30 seconds to 1 minute. (The sweet, deliciously milky juice the monkfish exudes will merge into a golden, creamy mass as it cooks and combines with the oil.) Remove the platter from the oven. With a slotted spatula or spoon, transfer the pieces of fish in a single layer to warmed individual dinner plates. Drizzle with lemon juice and sprinkle with chives. Transfer the juices from the platter to a small pitcher or gravy boat with a pouring spout. Serve immediately, passing the pitcher of juices and additional oil, salt, and lemon juice, if desired. Serve with crusty grilled bread alongside.

FOUR SERVINGS AS A FIRST COURSE; TWO SERVINGS AS A MAIN COURSE

WINE SUGGESTIONS: The quick grill calls for a lovely white or even an exceptional rosé, a young and perfumed wine that will pay homage to the fresh fish. My choices include a rosé from Provence, a Sauvignon Blanc from California or Washington, a Pinot Grigio from Italy, or a Muscadet-sur-Lie from France.

Local farm-raised trout for sale at the Vaison market.

◌ **LIKE A CARPACCIO PAINTING** ◌ The legend behind the word *carpaccio* tells the story of an Italian chef with a small dilemma. Apparently, a certain contessa, Nagi Mocenigo, a regular customer, was ordered by her doctor to avoid cooked meats. The chef, Giuseppe Cipriani, the original owner of Harry's Bar in Venice, rose to the challenge and crafted the simplest and most delicious of tastes. Supposedly inspired by the painter Carpaccio, famous for his brilliant combination of reds and whites, Cipriani combined thin slices of fresh raw beef drizzled with a translucent white variation of mayonnaise.

The modern interpretation of carpaccio allows it to be applied not only to raw meats but also to raw and cooked fish, even vegetables. Here, thin slices of fish are layered Carpaccio-style on a plate and cooked in just seconds.

SEA BASS IN PARCHMENT WITH WARM PISTOU

One sunny Provençal Friday just before Christmas, I attended a luncheon sponsored by olive growers from the region of Les Baux. Each course included the newly pressed oil from one of the mills. My favorite dish of the day was a whole *loup de mer,* or sea bass, steam-roasted in parchment, accompanied by a basil puree and tomatoes. It may have been winter, but the dish made me feel as though it were a summer day by the sea, bright with the flavors of ripe tomatoes, fresh basil, and fragrant rich olive oil. Luckily, on returning home I was able to harvest some pistou from my freezer, the fishmonger turned up a tiny whole bonito, and there were willing guests on hand to share the feast. Other whole fish to use here include mackerel and bluefish. If whole fish are hard to find, this dish can be prepared with a variety of fish and a variety of cuts. Try cooking individual parchment packages of tuna, mahimahi, or swordfish steaks, placing the pistou and herbs on top of the fish and baking for just 10 minutes each.

1 whole sea bass (about 1½ pounds; 750 g), cleaned but with head and tail on, rinsed, and patted dry; or substitute whole bonito, red snapper, bluefish, or tuna, mahimahi, or swordfish steaks
Sea salt and freshly ground black pepper to taste
5 tablespoons Pistou (page 316), plus additional for garnish
Large sprig of fresh thyme
4 whole fresh bay leaves
2 medium tomatoes, peeled, cored, seeded, and chopped
3 tablespoons extra-virgin olive oil
Freshly squeezed lemon juice to taste

1. Preheat the oven to 450°F (230°C; gas mark 8).
2. Cut a sheet of baking parchment large enough to comfortably wrap the fish. Center it on a baking sheet. Place the fish to one side of the parchment. Season the fish inside and out with salt and pepper. Fill the cavity of the fish with 3 tablespoons of the pistou. Tuck the thyme and bay leaves inside. Carefully fold the other half of the paper over the fish, closing it like a book. To seal the package, plait or crimp-fold the parchment to form a neat package. Alternatively, double-fold the edges and secure each side with several staples.
3. Place in the center of the oven and bake for 20 minutes.
4. Meanwhile, just lightly warm the chopped tomatoes with the olive oil and remaining 2 tablespoons of pistou. Taste for seasoning, adding a touch of lemon juice.
5. Remove the package from the oven and with a scissors carefully cut it open. Watch out—there will be plenty of steam. Let it sit for about 3 minutes so the fish firms up and becomes easier to fillet. Carefully fillet the fish (see The Art of Filleting a Whole Baked

(continued on next page)

Fish, below) and place a portion on each of 4 warmed dinner plates. Arrange a spoonful of pistou on top of the fish. Spoon the warmed tomato sauce around the fish. Pass with a cruet of olive oil. I first served this with a Celery Root Lasagne (page 124), a vegetable dish that perfectly matches the character of the fish and pistou.

FOUR SERVINGS

WINE SUGGESTIONS: The first time I prepared this, we enjoyed it with an aged red Bandol from Domaine Tempier, a wine whose exuberance and sophistication paired beautifully with the sturdy bonito. The dish is also lovely with the lemony flavor of a select white Viognier. My favorite comes from the Domaine les Gouberts in Gigondas.

ᴥ **THE ART OF FILLETING A WHOLE BAKED FISH** ᴥ Not long ago I made my first real attempt to fillet a cooked fish, a small task that I always left for my husband, Walter, who is generally more adept than I am. He coached me along as I made the first cuts and gave me a few words of invaluable advice. "Remember," he began matter-of-factly, "a fish is two-dimensional and the same on both sides." Basic but invaluable. The best way to attack a small- to medium-size fish is with an ordinary fork and knife. The "two spoon" method is also a possibility, as they do in the fancy fish restaurants in Paris. Lay the fish on its side on a flat surface and press the back of the fork gently against the top fillet to hold the fish steady. Begin at the head end of the fillet and cut ½ inch (1 cm) deep down the length of the back to the tail end. Place the knife around the belly area of the fillet and delicately push the knife further into the fish until the flesh is completely dislodged from the bone. Use the fork to hold up the ventral part that is now separated and run the knife down to the tail so that the bottom half of the fillet is now off the bone. Gently work the knife upward, lifting the upper half of the fillet off as well. Transfer immediately to a serving platter. For the second fillet, use the tines of the fork to gradually lift the backbone off. Begin at the tail end and work upward. The fork does the lifting as the knife gradually elevates and dislodges the bones. The head is removed forcibly when the backbone has been removed. Lay the second fillet next to or on top of the other on the serving dish and enjoy!

NOTE: The removal of skin is important for many varieties of fish, though some can be eaten with the skin intact. As a general rule, remove the skin before removing the fillet from the bone. That way, the fillet will not have to be touched or fiddled with once it is intact off the bone. Some varieties of fish can be eaten with the skin. For example, red snapper, sea bass, and salmon all have skin that is delicious as a flavor contrast to the flesh. Some flatfish, such as sole and turbot, are eaten with the black skin removed from one side but the white skin on the underside intact. Other fish, such as bluefish, tuna, and skate, have edible skin, but it can be overpowering and bitter in flavor.

Local fish merchants Aymar and Eliane Berenger at work outside their village shop.

⌇ **ON COOKING WITH PARCHMENT** ⋋ The virtues of cooking in parchment paper are many. The first and foremost is that it provides moist, perfectly cooked fish. Encasing the fish in a protective layer steams it as it cooks and prevents it from drying out or losing flavor. Cooking *en papillote,* or with parchment, is also an impressive way to present fish to guests. Imagine a simple country restaurant on a cold autumn day. The waiter emerges with the puffed-up paper gift and cuts it open, letting the steaming aroma waft out to tempt the nostrils. It is this steam which accumulates in the paper case as the fish, sauce, and vegetables cook that creates the dramatic result. The steam has no way to escape, so the ingredients have no choice but to mingle and cook together. Cooking in parchment also allows for low-fat cooking that is high in flavor. Whole small fish are very receptive to this method.

STEAMED SALMON WITH WARM LEMON VINAIGRETTE

For all those cooks out there who have a fear of cooking fish—and even those who don't—I advise steaming. It's easier and more precise than poaching, and the steam's gentle, moist heat is ideal for the delicate flesh of fish. This recipe was devised one winter day soon after the local Picholine olives had been harvested and cured. I love their bright green color, assertive fennel flavor, and almost slippery feel on the palate. The meaty olives are paired here with the tang of capers, bathed in olive oil, a touch of lemon juice, and a shower of dill, making for a quick, easy, delicious dish we savor time and again.

> 1 cup (125 g) best-quality green olives (such as French Picholine), or substitute best-quality Spanish or Greek olives
> 4 tablespoons capers
> 4 salmon fillets, about ¾ inch thick and weighing about 7 ounces (200 g) each
> Fine sea salt and freshly ground black pepper to taste
> 4 tablespoons extra-virgin olive oil
> 4 tablespoons freshly squeezed lemon juice
> Fresh fennel fronds or fresh dill, snipped with a scissors, for garnish

1. Bring a large pan of water to a boil. Add the olives and blanch in the boiling water for 2 minutes to rid them of excess salt. Drain well and set aside.
2. Drain the capers, rinse well, and soak in cold water for 10 minutes to rid them of excess salt. Set aside.
3. Bring 1 quart (1 l) of water to a simmer in the bottom of a steamer. Place the salmon fillets, skin side down, on the steaming rack. Season very lightly with salt and generously with pepper. Place the rack over simmering water, cover, and steam until the salmon is opaque, 5 to 6 minutes for medium-rare, 6 to 8 minutes for medium. To test the salmon, insert the tip of a sharp knife into the thickest part of the fish. The salmon will flake easily once cooked.
4. Meanwhile, drain the capers. In a small saucepan, combine the oil, lemon juice, capers, and blanched olives, stir to blend, and warm gently over low heat.
5. To serve, transfer the salmon to 4 warmed individual plates and spoon the sauce on top and around the fish. Sprinkle with the fennel fronds or dill. Serve immediately, with steamed potatoes in their jackets.

FOUR SERVINGS

WINE SUGGESTIONS: The first time I prepared this we sampled the salmon with a chilled Sablet Blanc from the nearby village of Sablet, but any white wine of character will do fine. If the budget permits, a good white Burgundy (Meursault or a Chablis Grand Cru) would be a delight, as would an Australian or California Chardonnay.

*A friend…showed me into the kitchen of her new home with the words,
"This is my office." I knew what she meant. This is where I do
the work I want to, the work I like and enjoy.*

SHASHI DESHPANDE

MINTED CRABMEAT SALAD

Crab and mint are lively companions, reminding me of complicity of the garden and the sea. Each ingredient has a sort of proud elegance, a fresh, clean taste. This dish, quickly prepared, makes for a lovely main-course lunch or supper dish. Be certain to allow the mint leaves to infuse for a full thirty minutes in the warmed vinaigrette, allowing for a mellow, subtle mingling of fresh mint and mellow crab. Slices of freshly toasted *Pompe à l'Huile:* Provençal Olive Oil Brioche (page 167) are a perfect accompaniment.

4 tablespoons best-quality cider vinegar
6 tablespoons extra-virgin olive oil
2 ounces (30 g) fresh mint leaves, snipped with a scissors
1 pound (500 g) fresh lump crab meat, drained, picked over, and flaked into generous
    bite-size pieces
Fine sea salt and freshly ground black pepper to taste

In a small saucepan, combine the cider vinegar and oil, and bring just to a boil over moderate heat. Add half of the mint, remove from the heat, cover, and set aside to infuse for 30 minutes. This will allow the mint to gently flavor the vinaigrette. Strain the vinaigrette into a bowl, discarding the mint. Place the crab meat in a bowl, pour the liquid over the crab, add the remaining mint leaves, and toss to blend. Season with salt and pepper. (The mint must be added at the very last minute, or it may turn brown and, potentially, bitter.) Transfer to 4 small, chilled salad plates and serve immediately.

FOUR SERVINGS

WINE SUGGESTIONS: If you're in a festive and frivolous mood, serve the salad with flutes of bubbly champagne. Otherwise, a chilled white, such as a Sauvignon Blanc or a dry California or Australian Riesling, a Riesling or Semillon from the Pacific Northwest, a California or French Viognier, or a flinty French Pouilly-Fumé from the Loire Valley.

Food can look beautiful, taste exquisite, smell wonderful, make people
feel good, bring them together, inspire romantic feelings....
At its most basic, it is fuel for a hungry machine.

ROSAMOND RICHARDSON

PETITE FRITURE: FRIED BABY FISH

Each Tuesday in the Vaison-la-Romaine market, there are more than half a dozen exquisite fish stalls, not to mention the stand outside my local fishmonger, La Poissonnerie des Voconces. Miniature silvery fish, sold simply as *petite friture,* can be had fresh for a song. The tiny fish, dusted with seasoned flour and fried ever so quickly, have become the center of our standard after-market lunch, served simply with lemon wedges and plenty of baby-fine sea salt. After much experimentation, I find that the fish taste more of the sea if they are not rinsed first, though I leave that choice up to the individual cook. I love to prepare these as guests gather around, devouring the fish as soon as they are sprinkled with salt.

EQUIPMENT: A deep-fry thermometer

1 cup (135 g) superfine flour (such as Wondra)
Fine sea salt to taste
¼ teaspoon cayenne pepper
1 to 1½ quarts (1 to 1.5 l) vegetable oil (sunflower, soybean, grapeseed, peanut, or a
    blend of oils), for deep-frying
1 pound (500 g) mixed small fish, such as sardines, smelt or whitebait (rinsed and
    drained, if desired)

1. In a plastic bag, combine the flour, ½ teaspoon of salt, and the cayenne pepper. Shake to blend.
2. Preheat the oven to 200°F. (100°C; gas mark 1).
3. Pour the oil into a wide 6-quart (6-l) saucepan, or use a deep-fat fryer. (The oil should be at least 2 inches [5 cm] deep.) Place a wire skimmer into the oil, so that when you lift the fish from the oil, they will not stick to the skimmer. Place a deep-fry thermometer in the oil. Heat the oil to 375°F (190°C).
4. Dip a handful of fish into the bag of flour and shake to coat with the flour mixture. Transfer the coated fish to a fine-mesh sieve and shake off excess flour. Carefully drop the

(continued on next page)

FACING PHOTOGRAPH: *Fresh baby fish, ready for frying.*

Petite Friture: *Fresh baby fish are dusted with seasoned flour, then quickly deep fried.*

fish by handfuls into the hot oil. Cook until lightly browned, 1 to 2 minutes. With a wire skimmer, lift from the oil, drain and transfer to paper towels. Immediately season with fine sea salt. Place them in the oven—the door slightly ajar—to keep warm. Continue frying until all of the fish are cooked, allowing the oil to return to 375°F (190°C) each time before adding another batch. Serve immediately, with lemon wedges.

SIX TO TWELVE SERVINGS AS AN APPETIZER

WINE SUGGESTION: We enjoy serving this with our local white, a Sablet blanc from the Domaine Les Gouberts in Gigondas. Other light whites that go well with light fried foods include a Sauvignon Blanc, a white Bordeaux, or an Alsatian Riesling.

SEARED PANCETTA-WRAPPED COD

Inspired by London chef Alastair Little—who served me a version of this one winter evening in his London SoHo restaurant—this simple, flavorful dish can be prepared in a matter of minutes. Fish fillets are given a protective wrapping—either pancetta, ham, or bacon—that adds a touch of needed fat and also helps create a brilliant contrast of color and texture. The wrapping acts as a second skin, protecting and imparting flavor and texture to the final dish. I always keep a piece of Provençal "pancetta" (peppered rolled pork sold as *poitrine roulé*) on hand and wrap my fish with paper-thin slices—sliced as thin as humanly possible without creating pieces of lace! The end result is a lovely blending of the land and the sea, the crunchy and the soft, a splash of red, white, and green.

4 codfish fillets, each about 6 ounces (180 g) or substitute monkfish, tilefish, grouper, or striped bass
4 very thin slices of pancetta, unsmoked ham, or unsmoked bacon
3 tablespoons capers
6 tablespoons extra-virgin olive oil
2 tablespoons freshly squeezed lemon juice
Freshly ground black pepper to taste
Fresh parsley leaves, snipped with a scissors, for garnish

1. Wrap the pieces of fish in ham, bacon, or pancetta. Secure with toothpicks at each end.
2. Drain the capers, rinse well, and soak in cold water for 10 minutes to remove excess salt.
3. In a large nonstick skillet, heat 2 tablespoons of oil over moderately high heat until hot but not smoking. Sear the wrapped pieces of fish for about 3 minutes on each side, or until the fish are firm to the touch and offer little resistance when pressed with the fingertip.
4. While the fish is cooking, in a small saucepan combine the drained capers, the remaining 4 tablespoons of oil, and the lemon juice. Stir to blend and warm gently over low heat.
5. Transfer the fish to 4 warmed plates, season very generously with pepper, and spoon the sauce on top and around the fish. Sprinkle with parsley.

FOUR SERVINGS

WINE SUGGESTION: This dish calls for a rich, dry white wine: a Rhône Valley white, such as a Châteauneuf du Pape, or a California or Australian Chardonnay.

WHOLE FISH ROASTED IN A CRUST OF SEA SALT

One New Year's Eve I told my husband, Walter, that I would prepare anything in the world for him for our traditional dinner for two. I anticipated his wish list would include caviar, maybe a lobster or foie gras. But no, his sole request was for my *Bar en croute de sel*. I could not have been a happier cook that evening, enveloping a glistening sea bass, in handfuls of fragrant sea salt from Brittany.

This is, in fact, my preferred method of preparing any fish: roasted whole, encased in fragrant sea salt. Easy, uncomplicated, unfussy, it is a method that allows the fish—cooked whole and on the bone—to preserve its integrity, retaining maximum moistness, flavor, and texture.

The salt, with its high water content, firms up as it bakes, encasing the fish in a clay-like, hermetic package. (Any coarse salt can be used here, with equally good results.) Many varieties of fish can be roasted in this manner, including red snapper, dorade or porgy, or even salmon. Do not scale the fish, for the scales will not only add flavor to the fish and protect it as it cooks, but adhere to the salt, making it easier to fillet after cooking. In Provence, where bay leaves grow in profusion, I usually stick several fresh bay leaves in the cavity of the fish, as well as layer them within the mound of salt to perfume the dish even more. Leftover fish is delicious the next day, served with Pistou (page 316).

EQUIPMENT: One ovenproof baking dish large enough to hold the fish

> One 2-pound (1-kg) whole sea bass, gutted, but not scaled, head left on, tail and fins trimmed
> Several fresh bay leaves (optional)
> 7 to 8 cups (about 4 pounds; 2 kg) coarse sea salt or kosher salt
> Extra-virgin olive oil and fresh lemon sections, for garnish

1. Preheat the oven to 450°F (230°F; gas mark 8).
2. Rinse the fish thoroughly inside and out until there is no trace of blood. If the gills have not been removed, do so to avoid bitterness. Pat dry. Season the cavity of the fish with salt and, if desired, tuck in a few bay leaves as well.
3. Evenly spread 1 cup (250 g) of the salt in the bottom of the baking dish. Place the fish on top of the salt, and pour the remaining salt over the fish to completely cover it from head to tail. It should look as though you have a baking dish mounded with nothing but salt. (If the fish is large, there's a chance the tail fin will extend outside the baking dish. That won't alter the baking of the fish.)
4. Place the dish in the center of the oven, and bake for 10 minutes per pound (500 g), or 20 minutes for a 2-pound (1-kg) fish. Adjust baking times by 5 minutes either way for each ½ pound (250 g) of fish.

(continued on next page)

5. Remove the dish from the oven. Allow it to sit for 3 minutes to firm up the flesh and make it easier to fillet. Brush away as much salt as possible from the fish, so it will not fall into the flesh when you remove the skin. Using the blade of a sharp knife, gently scrape away and discard the skin from the top fillet of the fish. Remove and discard the bay leaves from the cavity of the fish.

Using the knife, gently trace along the backbone of the fish to divide the top fillet in half. Begin at the head end of the top fillet and cut ½ inch (1 cm) inch deep down the center, the full length of the fish. Trim off and discard any fat, extraneous flesh and skin from the sides of the fillet. This will make for neater filets and easier removal. Using two large spoons, gently remove one half of the top fillet in neat pieces and transfer to two warmed dinner plates. Repeat for the other half of the top fillet. With the spoons, carefully remove and discard the center bone. Repeat for the bottom fillet, dividing it into two and removing the halves of the fillet in pieces. Transfer to two additional warmed dinner plates.

6. Serve immediately, passing a cruet of olive oil and a bowl of lemon wedges for seasoning.

FOUR SERVINGS

WINE SUGGESTION: This regal dish demands a regal white, such as a rich, dry Chassagne-Montrachet from Burgundy.

Any variety of fish can be roasted in salt: Here, a single daurade *or porgy and a pair of small* bar *or sea bass are prepared for roasting.*

GINGER & LIME SCALLOP SEVICHE

Seviche has always seemed to me a miracle. How easy, to toss fresh fish or shellfish with citrus juice and have the acid actually cook it. In traditional seviche recipes, lime is preferred to lemon juice since it is usually more flavorful, slightly more fragrant, and pairs naturally with any fresh, firm white fish or shellfish. I have prepared this recipe with sea scallops, monkfish, as well as a Northern Atlantic fish found in my Paris markets called *beryx,* or *bérix,* a fish similar to a dorade or porgy. Be certain to tell your fishmonger you are making a seviche so he understands you need extremely fresh fish.

    8 ounces (250 g) fresh white fish, such as red snapper, sea bass, or scallops
        (avoid cod and other relatives, which have a higher parasite level in relation
        to other types of fish)
    Fine sea salt to taste
    4 tablespoons freshly squeezed lime juice
    1 tablespoon grated fresh ginger

Using a very sharp knife (a flexible fish boning knife is ideal), cut the fish horizontally into slices ⅛ inch (2 mm) thick. (The length and width of the pieces is not important, but the thinness is.) Sprinkle a large platter lightly with salt. Place the slices of fish side by side, very slightly overlapping, on the platter or on individual dinner plates. Spoon the lime juice over the fish and shower with ginger. Cover and refrigerate for 20 minutes. With a slotted spatula or spoon, transfer the fish to chilled individual dinner plates. Serve with a green salad and plenty of freshly grilled country bread.

FOUR SERVINGS AS A FIRST COURSE; TWO SERVINGS AS A MAIN COURSE

BEVERAGE SUGGESTION: My choice here is a nice chilled beer. The acid of the lime is a bit much to compete with a fine wine, but beer can certainly do the trick in quenching one's thirst.

SEVICHE What is it? A dish that has its origins in Chilean or South American cooking, seviche is more a technique for treating raw fish than a recipe. Essentially, a seviche is a piece of raw fish that is marinated in some form of acid—lemon or lime juice, or vinegar—and then served raw. The fish is cooked by the acid, though no heat is involved in the process, much in the way the Japanese dip their raw fish in soy sauce, a seasoning that adds flavor and slightly cooks the fish as well.

If man be sensible and one fine morning, while he is lying in bed,
counts at the tips of his fingers how many things in this life truly will give him enjoyment,
invariably he will find food is the first one.

LIN YUTANG

CATALAN TUNA DAUBE

Tuna is often called the pot roast of the sea since it takes so well to long, slow cooking, a method that beautifully tenderizes its meaty fish. This version—a daube that simmers slowly in the oven—takes advantage of many ingredients that combine to make a dish of very intense, complex flavors. In this dish which I first sampled in Spain, black peppercorns are crushed with garlic, then accented by hints of lemon, anchovy, garlic, and caper. I also enjoy the grassy flavors that green bell peppers impart. Due to the popularity of red bell peppers, green peppers have been mistakenly eclipsed in the modern kitchen. Lemon, tomatoes, and wine all work their magic in tenderizing this meaty, flavorful fish. The tuna is equally delicious the next day, served cold.

EQUIPMENT: A mortar and pestle

4 flat anchovy fillets in olive oil
4 tablespoons whole milk
1 tablespoon capers
1 medium onion, peeled
4 plump, fresh garlic cloves, peeled and halved
20 whole black peppercorns
Fine sea salt to taste
3 green bell peppers
6 tablespoons extra-virgin olive oil
2 pounds (1 kg) tuna steaks, cut about 2 inches (5 cm) thick
Freshly ground black pepper to taste
Grated zest (yellow peel) of 1 lemon, cut in wide strips
Bouquet garni: several parsley stems, celery leaves, and sprigs of thyme, wrapped in
    the green part of a leek and securely fastened
1½ cups (37.5 cl) dry white wine, such as a white Rhône, Riesling, Aligoté, or
    Chenin Blanc
1 small can (14½ ounces; 400 g) imported whole plum tomatoes in juice
½ teaspoon ground cayenne pepper, or to taste

1. Rinse the anchovies, discarding any visible bones. Pat them dry and chop finely. Place in a small bowl with the milk and set aside for 15 minutes. Drain, discarding the milk, and set aside.

2. Drain the capers, rinse well, and soak in cold water for 10 minutes. Drain and set aside.

3. Slice the onion in half lengthwise. Place each half, cut side down, on a cutting board and cut crosswise into very thin slices.

4. In a mortar, crush the garlic, peppercorns, and ½ teaspoon of salt with a pestle to form a paste. Set aside.

5. Char the skin of the peppers over a gas flame or under the grill. Peel, seed, and cut into strips, reserving as much juice as possible. Set aside.

6. Preheat the oven to 350°F (175°C; gas mark 4/5).

7. In a large skillet, heat 2 tablespoons of oil over high heat. When the oil is hot but not smoking, add the tuna, searing over high heat for 2 minutes. Turn the tuna to sear the other side. Season this side generously with salt and pepper. Transfer the tuna to a platter and season the second side generously with salt and pepper.

8. In a large, unheated ovenproof casserole, combine the remaining 4 tablespoons of oil, the onion, crushed garlic and peppercorns, lemon zest, and bouquet garni. Toss to coat evenly with oil. Cook over moderate heat until the onions are soft and the mixture is well blended, about 10 minutes. Add the wine, pouring it all over the surface of the pan. Adjust the heat to bring the liquid to a gentle simmer and cook, uncovered, until the alcohol has cooked off, about 7 minutes from the time the liquid comes to a simmer. Add the seared tuna slices. Add the tomatoes and their juice, cayenne pepper, green peppers and their juice, anchovies, and capers.

9. Cover the casserole and place in the center of the oven. Cook until the tuna is very tender, about 1 hour. Remove from the oven. Remove and discard the bouquet garni. Remove the pieces of tuna from the casserole and discard the skin of the tuna. Place a portion of tuna on a warmed dinner plate and, with a slotted spoon, spoon the solid ingredients over the tuna. Spoon a bit of the sauce over and around the fish. Serve with steamed rice or baked potatoes.

SIX TO EIGHT SERVINGS

 WINE SUGGESTION: Serve with a hearty red Rhône wine, such as Vacqueyras.

THE VAISON FISHMONGER'S FRESH TUNA CASSEROLE

One Tuesday in March, one of the fishmongers at the local Vaison-la-Romaine market was ecstatic over the arrival of the season's first red tuna from the seaside village of Sete. The fish was gorgeous—rosy and sweet-smelling, and you could see the "marbling" of fat. I asked for a thick steak, and he said, "Of course you'll do it *à la cocotte*." Then without missing a beat, he quickly reeled off this recipe. The fishmonger advised me *not* to sear the tuna—as is usual practice—for it can easily dry out. In this dish the tuna cooks quickly in the tomato sauce, just enough to soften the onions and make for a richly flavored sauce. Later, I thought about how *cocotte* is the word for casserole, but this is a far cry from the canned tuna casserole of my youth, garnished with canned fried onion rings!

1 small tuna steak, cut about 1½ inches (4 cm) thick (about 2 pounds; 1 kg)

Sea salt and freshly ground pepper to taste

4 small onions, peeled and quartered

1 small can (14.5 oz; 400 g) imported whole tomatoes in juice

2 teaspoons capers, rinsed

2 tablespoons extra-virgin olive oil

Bouquet garni: several parsley stems, celery leaves, and sprigs of thyme, wrapped in the green part of a leek and securely fastened

2 teaspoons best-quality red wine vinegar or sherry vinegar

Select a skillet just slightly larger than the tuna. Generously season both sides of the tuna with salt and pepper. Place the tuna in the pan, tuck the onion quarters around the tuna, and cover with the tomatoes and their juice, capers, oil, and bouquet garni. Cover, simmer over low heat just until the tuna is cooked through and flakes with a fork, about 25 minutes. Drizzle the vinegar over the tuna, cover, and let rest off the heat for 1 to 2 minutes to allow the fish to absorb the vinegar. To serve, remove and discard the skin of the tuna and the bouquet garni, quarter the tuna, and serve on warmed dinner plates surrounded by the vegetables.

FOUR SERVINGS

 WINE SUGGESTIONS: Try this with a medium-bodied red wine, such as a Chinon from the Loire Valley, a Merlot from Bordeaux, or a Santenay from Burgundy.

WALTER'S THANKSGIVING OYSTER CASSEROLE

In the 1970s when I met my husband, Walter, he was a much better cook that I was—at least he had a lot of impressive "gourmet" gadgetry I hadn't yet collected, such as fish poachers, stockpots, sharp knives, and an impressive collection of regional cookbooks, especially those from the South. With our move to Paris in 1980, Walter's cooking career was abruptly halted by the demanding schedule at the *International Herald Tribune.*

Yet each Thanksgiving by popular demand he prepares his now-famous oyster casserole. The recipe was adapted from *Charleston Receipts,* the cookbook published in 1950 by the Charleston Junior League and credited to Jane Christie Hammond. But when Walter decided to put the casserole back on the menu after we moved to France, we found a decided absence of one of the casserole's main ingredients, saltine crackers. We quickly found that the easy-to-find matzos gave the dish even more texture and flavor—hardly kosher but, as the French would say, *pas catholique non plus!*

EQUIPMENT: One square baking dish, 12 inches (30 cm) by 2 inches (5 cm)

1 quart (1 l) oysters, freshly opened and in their own liquor (3 to 4 dozen)
1 cup (25 cl) heavy cream
½ teaspoon freshly ground nutmeg
8 tablespoons (4 ounces; 120 g) unsalted butter
2 cups medium-coarse cracker crumbs (saltines or matzos) (about 4 ounces; 125 grams—one sleeve of saltines)
Sea salt and freshly ground black pepper to taste

1. Preheat the oven to 350°F (175°C; gas mark 4/5).
2. Drain the oysters. Strain the oyster liquor through dampened cheesecloth and reserve.
3. In a small bowl, combine the cream and nutmeg. Set aside.
4. In a small saucepan over low heat, melt the butter. Add the cracker crumbs and mix thoroughly. Season to taste with salt and pepper.
5. Spread half of the crumbs in the bottom of the baking dish. Arrange all the oysters on top of the cracker mixture. Add the remaining cracker crumbs. Pour the cream mixture over all. Drizzle lightly with about 2 tablespoons of the reserved oyster liquor. Place in the center of the oven and bake until most of the liquid has evaporated and the top is crisp and golden, 20 to 25 minutes. (Take care not to overcook; the oysters should poach until tender and not become rubbery.) Serve immediately as a side dish to roast poultry or, as we do, with the Thanksgiving turkey.

SIX TO EIGHT SERVINGS

8

POULTRY & GAME

Plump chickens and turkeys from the Bresse region, local pigeon and quail, fresh and wild rabbit, and moist mallard duck raised by our very own winemaker make up the family poultry larder from season to season. Give me a whole chicken and I'll turn it into a feast, gently coaxing handfuls of herbs beneath the skin, tucking it into the bread oven to roast to a crispy, golden tenderness. Rabbits have long been part of the history and lore of our farmhouse, so naturally they find their way to the table, with a Provençal version (Chanteduc Rabbit with Garlic & Preserved Lemons) as well as one from Italy's Piedmont (Pina's Braised Rabbit.) My butcher, Roland Henny, adds his expertise, supplying us with his version of Rabbit Bouillabaisse, while a trip to Switzerland and lunch at grand chef Fredy Girardet's inspired me to create a new family favorite, Duck with Lime & Honey.

FACING PHOTOGRAPH: *A corner of the Chanteduc kitchen, with an assortment of wooden kegs for homemade vinegars.*

POULET AUX FINES HERBES: BUTTER-ROASTED HERBED CHICKEN

Every time I roast a chicken, I learn something new. Perhaps my greatest "training" came when I was taught the following "rotation" method by chef Joël Robuchon. Roasting the bird on both sides, then breast side up, then finally breast side down, results in a bird that is evenly, uniformly browned and roasted. I've also added a final step: roasting it breast side down at the end, tail in the air, so the juices begin to run to the breast even as it is still roasting. I also find that the bird roasts more evenly if it is set on a rack in the roasting pan, allowing the heat to circulate around the chicken.

In this recipe I've given the breast—which tends to dry out in roasting—a protective coating of butter, which is slipped beneath the skin with the fingers, creating a stunning presentation and a very moist chicken. Basting is not necessary here; in fact, the chicken skin will be crisper if you do not baste at all. This is a good picnic bird, for the dish is truly wonderful served the next day at room temperature.

EQUIPMENT: One oval baking dish, just slightly larger than the chicken (about 9 x 13 inches; 23 x 33 cm), fitted with a roasting rack

1 lemon, preferably organic
1 free-range roasting chicken (about 5 pounds; 2.5 kg), with giblets
Sea salt and freshly ground black pepper to taste
1 bunch of fresh thyme
5 tablespoons very finely minced fresh herbs, carefully stemmed, preferably a mix of chervil, tarragon, chives, and parsley
5 tablespoons (2½ ounces; 75 g) unsalted butter, softened

1. Preheat the oven to 425°F (220°C; gas mark 7/8). (See Note below.)
2. Rinse the lemon in cold water and dry. Soften the lemon by rolling it back and forth along a flat surface. Using a two-pronged fork, a trussing needle, or a toothpick, pierce the skin of the lemon at least 20 times, to help the lemon release its juices during roasting. Generously season the cavity of the chicken with salt and pepper. Place the giblets, lemon, and thyme in the cavity and truss.
3. In a small bowl, combine the herbs, ½ teaspoon each of salt and pepper, and 4 tablespoons (2 ounces; 60 g) butter. Mash with fork and blend evenly.
4. Before putting the butter beneath the skin of the chicken be sure to remove any rings from your fingers, for they might pierce the skin. Entering from the neck end of the chicken, push your fingers through the skin over one side of the breast to separate the skin from the flesh. Be gentle so as not to tear the skin. Working with the tips of your fingers, spread half of the butter and herb mixture over one side of the breast meat. Repeat

the same process on the other breast side. Pressing down on the exterior of the skin, even out the butter mixture and pat the skin back into place. Rub the skin of the chicken with the remaining 1 tablespoon of butter. Season all over with salt and pepper.

5. Place the chicken on its side on the roasting rack in the baking dish. Place in the center of the oven and roast, uncovered, for 20 minutes. Turn the chicken to the other side and roast for 20 minutes more. Turn the chicken breast side up, and roast for 20 minutes more, for a total of 1 hour roasting time. By this time the skin should be a deep golden color. Lower the heat to 375°F (190°C; gas mark 5). Turn the chicken breast side down, at an angle if at all possible, with the neck down and the tail in the air. (This heightens the flavor by allowing the juices to flow down through the breast meat.) Roast until the juices run clear when you pierce a thigh with a skewer, about 15 minutes more.

6. Remove from the oven and season generously with salt and pepper. Transfer the chicken to a platter and place on an angle against the edge of an overturned plate, with the neck down and the tail in the air. Cover loosely with foil. Turn off the oven and place the platter in the oven, with the door open. Let rest a minimum of 10 minutes and up to 30 minutes. The chicken will continue to cook during this resting time.

7. Meanwhile, prepare the sauce: Place the baking dish over moderate heat, scraping up

(continued on next page)

any bits that cling to the bottom. Cook for 2 to 3 minutes, scraping and stirring until the liquid is almost caramelized. Do not let it burn. Spoon off and discard any excess fat. Add several tablespoons of cold water to deglaze (hot water will cloud the sauce). Bring to a boil. Turn the heat to low and simmer until thickened, about 5 minutes.

8. While the sauce is cooking, carve the chicken and place on a warmed platter.

9. Strain the sauce through a fine-mesh sieve and pour into a sauce boat. Serve immediately with the chicken. (If serving the chicken at room temperature, use the sauce to prepare a vinaigrette for an accompanying salad.)

FOUR TO SIX SERVINGS

 WINE SUGGESTION: A dry white or a fine old red are perfectly at home here. My choice is a good Burgundy, such as a silky Volnay.

NOTE: When you don't have time to wait for your oven to warm up, try the cold oven method. Turn the oven to 425°F (220°C; gas mark 7/8) and follow the recipe, allowing about 15 additional minutes of roasting time. Since some ovens heat up more quickly than others, roasting time may vary.

✌ **HOW'S YOUR HERB AWARENESS?** ∿ A little quiz to test your herb awareness: Do you know the difference between *herbes de Provence* and *fines herbes? Herbes de Provence* is usually a mixture of dried fennel, rosemary, sage, savory, and wild or domestic thyme. *Fines herbes* are composed of fresh chervil, tarragon, chives, and parsley.

FRENCH COUNTRY GUINEA HEN & CABBAGE

Few dishes embody classic country French as this warming specialty. It can be prepared with a whole chicken, but a plump and meaty guinea hen—the domesticated poultry that is closest to wild game—is one of the world's great culinary treats.

Sea salt and freshly ground black pepper to taste
1 guinea hen (about 2 pounds; 1 kg), or substitute chicken
2 shallots, peeled and halved
1 thin slice of smoked ham, minced
Bouquet garni: a bunch of flat-leaf parsley, celery leaves, bay leaves, and thyme
6 tablespoons (3 ounces; 90 g) unsalted butter
2 tablespoons olive oil
1 onion, minced
1 carrot, minced
2 cups homemade Chicken Stock (page 322)
1 large cabbage, quartered lengthwise
1 tablespoon sherry wine vinegar

1. Season the exterior and cavity of the hen with salt and pepper. Place the shallots, ham, and bouquet garni in the cavity and sew up the opening. Set aside.

2. In a large covered casserole, melt 1 tablespoon of the butter and the oil over moderate heat until hot but not smoking. Add the hen and brown on all sides, about 10 minutes. Transfer the bird to a platter and discard the fat in the pan. Season the exterior generously with salt and pepper. Stirring over moderate heat, add 1 tablespoon of butter to the casserole and scrape up the bottom of the pan. Add the onion and carrot, and cook until soft, about 5 minutes. Return the hen to the pan, add the chicken stock, cover, and braise at a gentle simmer over low heat until the hen is cooked through, about 50 minutes.

3. Meanwhile, in a large pot, bring 6 quarts of water to a rolling boil. Add 3 tablespoons of salt and the cabbage, and blanch, uncovered, for 5 minutes. Drain and set aside.

4. In a large skillet, melt the remaining butter over moderate heat. Add the vinegar and cabbage; add salt and pepper. Turn, trying to keep the pieces of cabbage intact and well coated with sauce. Cover and cook over low heat until soft, about 20 minutes. Taste for seasoning.

5. Carve the hen and arrange on a warmed platter. Discard the bouquet garni. Spoon the stuffing and sauce over the sliced poultry. Place the cabbage over the hen and serve.

FOUR TO SIX SERVINGS

WINE SUGGESTION: With this dish, which makes me think of the Alsatian region, I love a nicely chilled Riesling.

CHICKEN WITH TARRAGON & SHERRY VINEGAR

Chicken with vinegar is a classic specialty of France's Bresse region, which is famous for its pampered poultry, a special breed of bird that sports pure white plumes and amazing blue feet. Chicken with tarragon is another classic Bresse preparation, and in this dish I've combined these national treasures, adding a rich flavor base of onions, shallots, and garlic. The sauce is also enriched with reduced stock and a touch of mustard and cream, creating a thick, sensuous sauce that matches the simple elegance of this homey chicken dish. Serve with plenty of fresh pasta or rice to absorb the fragrant sauce.

2 medium onions, peeled
1 chicken (3 to 4 pounds; 1.5 to 2 kg), at room temperature, cut into 8 serving pieces
Sea salt and freshly ground black pepper to taste
3 tablespoons extra-virgin olive oil
1 tablespoon unsalted butter
4 shallots, peeled and cut into thin rounds
1 head plump, fresh garlic, cloves peeled but left whole
Bouquet garni: several generous sprigs of fresh tarragon, parsley, and rosemary, and several bay leaves and celery leaves, tied in a bundle with household twine
6 tablespoons best-quality sherry wine vinegar
2 cups (50 cl) homemade Chicken Stock (page 322)
1 tablespoon tomato paste
1 tablespoon imported Dijon mustard
4 tablespoons fresh tarragon leaves, snipped with a scissors
½ cup (12.5 cl) heavy cream

1. Slice the onions in half lengthwise. Place each half, cut side down, on a cutting board and cut crosswise into very thin slices. Set aside.
2. Liberally season the chicken on all sides with salt and pepper. In a large skillet, combine the oil and butter over high heat. When hot, add several pieces of chicken, skin side down (do not crowd the pan but instead brown the chicken in several batches), and cook until they turn an even golden color, about 5 minutes. Turn the pieces and brown them on the other side, 5 minutes more. Carefully regulate the heat to avoid scorching the skin. When all the pieces are browned, use tongs—to avoid piercing the meat—to transfer them to a platter.
3. Pour off and discard all but about 2 tablespoons of fat from the skillet. Add the onions, shallots, garlic, and bouquet garni, and season lightly with salt. Sweat by cooking over low heat without coloring, for about 5 minutes. Add the chicken pieces. Pour about 3 tablespoons of vinegar over the chicken pieces and cover. Cook very gently over low

heat, stirring to make sure the vegetables do not burn, until the chicken is cooked through, about 25 minutes. Remove and discard the bouquet garni.

4. Transfer the chicken pieces to a warmed platter. Cover with foil and keep warm in a low oven.

5. There should be a thin film of sauce remaining in the skillet. Leave the vegetables in the pan. Over moderate heat, slowly add the remaining 3 tablespoons of vinegar, scraping up any bits that stick to the bottom of the skillet. Add the chicken stock, tomato paste, mustard, and half of the tarragon. Stir to blend. Increase the heat to high and bring to a boil. Cook vigorously until the sauce is thick and glossy, about 7 minutes. Off the heat, stir in the cream and stir to blend. Return to low heat just to warm through. The resulting sauce should be thick, creamy, and fragrant. Taste for seasoning.

6. To serve, transfer the chicken pieces to warmed dinner plates. Spoon the sauce and vegetables over and alongside the chicken. Sprinkle with the remaining tarragon. Serve immediately, accompanied by rice or fresh fettucine.

FOUR TO SIX SERVINGS

WINE SUGGESTION: A light but elegant Bordeaux. I've loved this with a well-aged Pommard.

Happy and successful cooking doesn't rely only on know-how; it comes
from the heart, makes great demands on the palate, and needs
enthusiasm and a great love of food to bring it to life.
GEORGES BLANC

CHICKEN WITH SHALLOTS, LEMON & THYME

Few dishes are as welcoming as a moist whole chicken, browned and then braised in wine in an covered casserole with mountains of herbs and an avalanche of perfectly shaped, whole shallots. Here, white wine creates the base of the sauce, adding good balance to the dish. Choose an assertive wine—such as a French or California Riesling or a white Burgundy—that will cut through the rich flavors of the cream and eggs.

> 1 free-range roasting chicken (about 3 pounds; 1.5 kg), at room temperature
> Sea salt and freshly ground black pepper to taste
> 1 lemon, preferably organic
> 2 large bunches of fresh thyme
> 3 tablespoons (1½ ounces; 45 g) unsalted butter
> 2 tablespoons extra-virgin olive oil
> 3 cups (75 cl) white wine (see Wine Suggestions)
> Bouquet garni: a generous bunch of fresh tarragon, flat-leaf parsley, celery leaves, bay leaves, and sprigs of thyme, tied in a bundle with household twine
> 20 best-quality shallots, peeled but left whole
> 2 tablespoons heavy cream
> 3 large egg yolks
> 2 to 3 tablespoons freshly squeezed lemon juice
> About ¼ teaspoon freshly grated nutmeg
> 1 tablespoon fresh thyme leaves, carefully stemmed

1. Generously season the cavity of the chicken with salt and pepper. Rinse the lemon in cold water and dry. Pierce it with a two-pronged fork about a dozen times. Place the lemon and 1 bunch of thyme inside the cavity of the chicken and sew up the opening using household twine. Truss and set aside.

2. In a large, covered casserole, melt the butter and oil over moderate heat until hot but not smoking. Add the chicken and brown carefully on all sides, about 10 minutes. Adjust the heat to avoid scorching the skin. Use tongs to turn the chicken to avoid piercing the skin. Transfer the chicken to a platter and season generously with salt and pepper. Dis-

card the fat in the pan. Still over moderate heat, deglaze the pan with the wine. Bring the wine to a boil and boil vigorously until the alcohol has burned off and no alcohol aroma is wafting from the casserole (give it a good sniff from time to time!), about 5 minutes. Return the chicken to the pan, breast side up. Surround the chicken with the bouquet garni, the remaining bunch of thyme, and the shallots. Cover and simmer very gently over very low heat until the chicken is cooked through, 40 to 50 minutes.

3. Meanwhile, in a large bowl, combine the cream, egg yolks, 2 tablespoons of lemon juice, and nutmeg. Stir to blend. Set aside.

4. Transfer the chicken and shallots to a warm serving platter, cover with foil, and set in a warm oven to keep warm. Discard the bouquet garni and thyme. Pass the remaining cooking liquid through a fine-mesh sieve and return to the pan. It should measure about 1½ cups (37.5 cl). Return the pan to the heat and whisk in the crème fraîche and egg yolk mixture. Simmer gently—do not let the sauce boil—whisking regularly for about 5 minutes, until the sauce begins to thicken slightly. Taste for seasoning, adding additional lemon juice if desired. Strain the sauce through a fine-mesh sieve into a bowl.

5. Carve the chicken and transfer the pieces to a large warmed serving platter. Arrange the shallots alongside. Drizzle about half of the sauce over the chicken and shallots. Sprinkle with fresh thyme leaves. Serve warm, with Basmati Rice (page 273), passing the remaining sauce.

FOUR TO SIX SERVINGS

WINE SUGGESTIONS: The choice of cooking and drinking wines here is endless. I am partial to the fragrant whites of the Rhône, where the vines share the soil with such wild natural herbs as rosemary and thyme and pair so well with their pungent flavors and aromas. Any wine with a nice balanced acidity is good: a French Riesling, a white Burgundy, a not-too-oaky California Chardonnay, a Rhône Valley Viognier or simple Côtes du Rhône blanc de blanc.

THE LOVE OF THYME   If I had to grow only one herb in the garden, thyme would be it. In Provence, where the herb grows wild at will, it is called *farigoule*. Sometimes when I run in the warm summer mornings, the surrounding woods around Chanteduc smell like grilled thyme. The herb will grow in almost no soil at all, and the leaves fall from the stems as soon as they are picked. In the intense summer heat of Provence, fresh thyme becomes almost dried.

*In light of what Proust wrote with so mild a stimulus, it is the world's loss
that he did not have a heartier appetite. On a dozen Gardiner's Island oysters, a bowl of
clam chowder, a peck of steamers, some bay scallops, three sautéed soft-shell crabs, a few ears
of fresh-picked corn, a thin swordfish steak of generous area, a pair of lobsters,
and a Long Island duck, he might have written a masterpiece.*

A. J. LEIBLING

THE WINEMAKER'S DUCK WITH OLIVES & ARTICHOKES

A few days before Christmas, our winemaker, Daniel Combe, telephoned to say that some of his barnyard poultry were ready for the table and suggested a duck, a goose, or a chicken. What an embarrassment of riches! I hadn't cooked a duck in a long time, so that was my choice. I quickly scanned a stack of old Provençal cookbooks and adapted a recipe for duck with olives and artichokes, two of my favorite ingredients. That duck was the best I'd ever tasted. We cooked it in the bread oven in our courtyard, and you could hear the sizzling of the fat against the brick oven walls all the way to the kitchen. For months to come, the fat I collected from the duck that day was used to prepare the most delicious, golden sautéed potatoes.

4 large artichokes, 8 baby artichokes (see Note, page 95), or two 9-ounce (270-g)
    packages frozen artichoke hearts, thawed
4 tablespoons freshly squeezed lemon juice
4 tablespoons extra-virgin olive oil
1 cup (about 4 ounces; 125 g) best-quality black olives (such as French Nyons),
    drained and pitted
1 cup (about 4 ounces; 125 g) best-quality green olives (such as French Picholine),
    drained and pitted
Sea salt and freshly ground black pepper to taste
1 duck (about 5 pounds; 2.25 kg), liver reserved, trimmings (neck, heart, wing tips),
    chopped (see Note, page 235)
Bouquet garni: Generous branch of fresh tarragon, thyme, rosemary and parsley,
    secured with cotton twine
3 plump fresh garlic cloves, peeled and halved
1 small carrot, cut into thick diagonal slices
1 small onion, cut into thick slices

(continued on next page)

1. Preheat the oven to 425°F (220°C; gas mark 7/8).

2. Thoroughly drain the artichoke slices. In a small bowl, combine the artichokes, lemon juice, olive oil, and olives and stir to blend. Set aside.

3. Liberally season the exterior of the duck on all sides, as well as the cavity, with salt and pepper. Place the duck liver, the chopped trimmings, bouquet garni and garlic, carrot and onion in the cavity. Truss.

4. Place the duck on its side on a roasting rack in the roasting pan. Place in the oven with the fullest part of the duck, the breast portion, toward the back of the oven. Roast, uncovered, for 10 minutes. Turn the duck on the other side and roast for 10 minutes more. (If the duck releases great quantities of fat, pour off and discard about ⅔ of it.) Turn the duck on its back, breast side up, and roast for 10 minutes more. Remove from the oven and surround the duck with the olives and artichokes. Baste with the cooking juices 3 or 4 times so that the duck remains moist as it continues to roast. Remove the trussing string from the bird and season the legs with salt. (At this point the bird will hold its shape on its own. By removing the string, the legs will cook more evenly.) Return to the oven to roast for a total of 13 to 15 minutes per pound (500 g). If there is not enough fat to keep the trimmings from browning too much, add a few tablespoons of cold water. Roasting time will vary according to the size of the duck and your flavor preference. Select the shorter roasting time per pound for a large duck, the longer time for a smaller duck. Thus, total roasting time for a 2½-pound (1.25-kg) duck will be about 38 minutes; for a 5-pound (2.5-kg) duck it will be 1 hour and 5 minutes.

5. Remove the duck from the oven and *once again season generously.* Transfer to a platter and place at an angle against the edge of a baking dish, with its neck down and tail in the air. This heightens the flavor by allowing the juices to flow down to the breast meat. Cover with aluminum foil. Turn off the oven and place the duck in the oven, with the door slightly ajar. At the same time, transfer the olive and artichoke mixture to a pan. Cover and place in the oven with the duck. Let the duck rest a minimum of 20 minutes and up to 1 hour. The duck will continue to cook during the resting time.

6. To serve: Carve the duck and arrange in the center of the platter. Arrange the olives and artichokes around the duck. Serve immediately.

FOUR TO SIX SERVINGS

WINE SUGGESTION: This festive dish makes me want to take out a festive local wine, such as a heady Gigondas, one that sings of the thyme-flecked hills of Provence.

DUCK WITH LIME & HONEY

On assignment in Switzerland, I found myself without a dining partner for a few days and admit I didn't look forward to sitting alone at one of the world's greatest restaurants, Fredy Girardet's in Crissier. But one sip of his house champagne, and my mood changed. Suddenly I felt like a queen with a bevy of footmen. I chatted with the waiters and sommeliers and relished the regal feast. When a whole duck arrived, I almost gasped, realizing this extraordinary chef had cooked a whole duck just for me. I thought about that duck for weeks. Girardet has a great affection for lime and uses it liberally throughout his repertoire. I let the dish dance around in my head for a while, then I came up with a combination of whole lime, lime zest, a touch of honey and vinegar, and a whisper of tarragon. Since poultry meat readily absorbs the flavors placed in the cavity of the bird, the whole pierced limes exude their juices as the duck roasts. When the lime juice, tarragon, and moist duck meat converge, the flavors taste faintly Asian yet distinctly French. Whenever I prepare this dish, people walk into the kitchen and exclaim, "It smells like a Chinese restaurant in here." Serve this with a simple green salad.

> 4 whole limes, preferably organic
> 1 duck (2½ to 4 pounds; 1.25 to 2 kg), liver reserved and trimmings
>   (neck, heart, wing tips) chopped (see Note)
> Sea salt and freshly ground white pepper to taste
> Generous branch of fresh tarragon
> 3 plump, fresh garlic cloves, peeled and halved
> 1 small carrot, cut into thick diagonal slices
> 1 small onion, cut into thick slices
> 1 generous sprig of fresh thyme
> 1 tablespoon creamy honey, or to taste
> 4 to 5 tablespoons best-quality sherry or red wine vinegar
> 3 tablespoons (1½ ounces; 45 g) unsalted butter

1. Preheat the oven to 425°F (220°C; gas mark 7/8).
2. Rinse the limes in cold water and dry. Soften 2 of the limes by rolling them back and forth along a flat surface. Using a two-pronged fork, a trussing needle, or a toothpick, pierce the skin of the 2 limes at least 20 times, to help release the juice. Season the duck inside and out with salt and pepper. Place the duck liver, the 2 whole limes, and tarragon, in the cavity. They will serve to enrich the final flavor of the meat. Truss.
3. Zest the remaining 2 limes. In a separate bowl, juice the limes and set aside.
4. Place the duck on its side on a roasting rack in the roasting pan. Place in the oven with the fullest part of the duck—the breast portion—toward the back of the oven. Roast, uncovered, for 10 minutes. Turn the duck on the other side and roast for 10 minutes more.

(continued on next page)

(If the duck releases quantities of fat, pour off and discard about ⅔ of it.) Turn the duck on its back—breast side up—and roast for 10 minutes more. Remove from the oven and surround the duck with chopped trimmings: garlic, carrot, onion, and thyme. Baste with the lime juice and spoon the cooking juices over the duck 3 or 4 times so that it will remain moist as it continues to roast. Remove the trussing string from the bird and season the legs with salt. (At this point, the bird will hold its shape on its own. By removing the string, the legs will cook more evenly.) Return to the oven to roast for a total of 13 to 15 minutes per pound (500 g). (If there is not enough fat to keep the trimmings from browning too much, add a few tablespoons of cold water.) Roasting time will vary according to the size of the duck and your flavor preference. Select the shorter roasting time per pound for a large duck, the longer time for a small duck. Thus, total roasting time for a 2½-pound (1.25-kg) duck would be about 38 minutes; a 5-pound (2.5-kg) duck would be 1 hour and 5 minutes.

5. Meanwhile, prepare the zest: Bring a medium-size saucepan of water to a boil. Place the zest in a fine-mesh sieve and submerge in the boiling water for 2 minutes to blanch. Rinse under cold running water. Drain. Set aside.

6. Remove the duck from the oven and, once again, season generously. Transfer to a platter and place at an angle against the edge of a baking dish, with the neck down and tail in the air. This heightens the flavor by allowing the juices to flow down through to the breast meat. Cover loosely with aluminum foil. Turn off the oven and place the duck in the oven, with the door slightly ajar. Let rest a minimum of 20 minutes and up to 1 hour. The duck will continue to cook during the resting time.

7. To prepare the sauce: Place the roasting pan with the trimmings over high heat. Cook until the trimmings are nicely browned, 1 to 2 minutes. Drain and discard all the liquid in the pan, for it will be mostly fat. (Do not omit this step, or you will have a fat, greasy, inedible sauce.) Add the honey, stir, and cook for 1 to 2 minutes more. Deglaze with several tablespoons of vinegar and cook for 1 minute. Add about ½ cup (12.5 cl) of water (or enough to make a rich sauce) and simmer for 5 minutes more.

8. Strain the sauce through a fine-mesh sieve placed over a clean skillet, pressing down on the trimmings to extract as much juice and flavor as possible. Add any cooking juices that have drained from the duck as it rests. Bring the sauce to a boil over high heat. Taste and, if necessary, add 1 to 2 teaspoons of vinegar. Remove the pan from the heat and add the butter, a few pieces at a time, whisking constantly after each addition until thoroughly incorporated. Stir in the reserved zest.

9. To serve: Carve the duck, discarding the whole limes, and arrange in the center of the platter. Spoon about half of the sauce over the duck. Pour the reserved sauce into a warmed sauce boat. Serve immediately.

FOUR SERVINGS

WINE SUGGESTIONS: This duck is ideal with a robust wine of France's southwest. Try to lay your hands on a top-grade Madiran, such as Château Montus, from the duck-raising department of the Gers. It will echo the density and richness of the duck, a wine and food marriage made in heaven. I have also loved this with a lemon-zesty Viognier, a grape that's newly fashionable in Provence and California.

✌ TECHNIQUE FOR CARVING A DUCK ∿

When the duck has had ample time "to rest" after cooking and all of the juices have settled into place, it is ready to be carved for the table. Begin with the wing bone: Locate the shoulder joint that holds the wing in place and pierce the skin with a sharp knife at this point. Press heavily on the knife; the pressure will be needed to cut through the joint and free the wing. This will make it easier to carve the leg since there will be more free space for removal. Cut through the skin around the joint between the leg and the thigh in a semicircular shape, beginning the semicircle on the underside of the duck and finishing at the top outside. With a little pressure on the bone and a cut into the joint, the thigh is easily detached. Now the breast is all that remains to be removed: Cut down the middle of the bird, being sure to keep each breast piece intact. Once this initial cut has been made, slice deeply along the breast bone in order to free each side of the breast meat. When both sides of the breast have been removed, place them on the cutting board and cut them at an angle into lengthwise slices.

✌ A TRUSSING TIP ∿

A handy tip when trussing a duck or any other bird for roasting: When tying the knots to secure the different parts of the duck, tie a regular knot but loop the string an extra time through the knot before pulling it taut. This extra step will keep the knot tighter and the bird in better shape for even roasting.

NOTE: To extract the maximum flavor from all poultry trimmings—such as the neck, heart, and wing tips—chop them with a cleaver as finely as possible. For a quick and delicious sauce, sauté them quickly in fat, add aromatics such as carrots, onions, garlic, and thyme, and then deglaze with a bit of water or wine. Reduce over low heat for 4 to 5 minutes, then strain.

Even were a cook to cook a fly, he would keep the breast for himself.
POLISH PROVERB

CUMIN-RUBBED GRILLED QUAIL

I love the fragrant, slightly exotic essence of freshly toasted cumin. Here, I use it to infuse quail meat, then enhance it with even more flavor, with a "dipping" mix of coarse salt, lemon zest, fresh leaf coriander, and more ground cumin. I serve both grilled quail and pigeon often since they cook up quickly and make for elegant, individual portions. This dish is equally good hot or at room temperature. I often prepare a huge batch of grilled quail as part of a large buffet. Note that although the bird is split down the back to flatten it for grilling, it remains whole, in a single piece.

4 large fresh quail (each about 6 ounces; 180 g); if fresh quail cannot be found,
   substitute fresh squab (pigeon) or cornish game hens and increase grilling time
   to about 20 minutes
2 tablespoons roasted and freshly ground cumin seeds (see Note)
3 tablespoons extra-virgin olive oil
Sea salt to taste

GARNISH
Coarse sea salt
Grated zest (yellow peel) of 1 lemon, preferably organic
About 4 tablespoons fresh leaf coriander leaves (cilantro), snipped with a scissors

1. Place the quail, breast side down, on a flat surface. With a pair of poultry shears, split the bird lengthwise along the backbone. Open it flat and press down with the heel of your hand to flatten it completely. Turn the quail skin side up and press down once more to flatten. With a sharp knife, make tiny slits in the skin near the tip of each drumstick. Tuck the opposite drumstick through the slit, to cross the bird's legs. The bird should be as flat as possible to ensure even cooking. Set aside.

2. In a small bowl, combine 1 tablespoon of the cumin seeds with the oil and stir to form a wet paste. With a pastry brush, apply the paste evenly over all sides of the quail. Cover loosely with plastic wrap and set aside to marinate for about 30 minutes.

3. Preheat the oven broiler or prepare a wood or charcoal fire. The fire is ready when the coals glow red and are covered with ash.

4. Season the quail generously with salt. With the skin side toward the heat, place the

quail beneath the broiler or on the grill about 5 inches from the heat so that it cooks evenly without burning. Cook until the skin is evenly browned, about 5 minutes. Using tongs so you do not pierce the meat, turn and cook the other side, about 5 minutes more. Continue cooking and turning until the juices run clear when the thigh is pierced with a skewer, about 15 minutes total cooking time.

5. Remove the quail from the heat and season once more with salt. Cover loosely with foil and let rest, breast down and tail in the air, for at least 5 minutes.

6. To serve, arrange a whole quail on each of 4 warmed dinner plates. Arrange tiny mounds of coarse salt, ground cumin, grated lemon zest, and fresh coriander alongside. Invite guests to dip small pieces of the quail in one or more of the garnishes with each bite. Be sure to provide good steak knives. Offer finger bowls and a fresh extra napkin for each guest.

NOTE: To roast cumin seeds, heat a small, heavy-duty frying pan over medium heat for 2 minutes. Add the cumin and roast over medium heat, stirring and shaking the pan constantly in order to prevent burning. For the first minute or two the cumin will give up its liquid, and it will appear that nothing is happening. Watch carefully, for the cumin will brown quickly. (Lower the heat if the cumin appears to be browning too quickly.) Roast just until the cumin fills the kitchen with its fragrance and turns dark brown, about 4 minutes total roasting time. Immediately transfer the cumin to a plate to cool. Place the cooled spice in a clean coffee grinder, spice mill, or electric blender and grind to a fine powder.

FOUR SERVINGS

WINE SUGGESTION: I enjoy this with an Alsatian Riesling, which stands up nicely to the cumin-enhanced quail.

⌣ DON'T FORGET THE FINGER BOWLS! ⌣ I think we all love permission to eat with our fingers, especially to savor every nugget of flavor of poultry and meats cooked on the bone. When serving foods that will be picked up and eaten with one's fingers, be sure to provide finger bowls, small vessels of tepid water to which you've added a slice of fresh lemon. Out of consideration, also provide a second fresh napkin for each diner.

When I asked the charismatic chef Gigi what exactly it consisted of,
he replied, "Don't worry, you going to "'ave eet.'" And "'ave eet," indeed I did.

GILLIAN BEAL

MONSIEUR HENNY'S RABBIT BOUILLABAISSE

One spring morning I was standing in line at my village butcher shop, and as soon as the owner, Roland Henny, spied me, he ushered me upstairs to his kitchen. M. Henny was so proud of his latest creation, he not only had me taste the rabbit bouillabaisse but he insisted I "write it down." He knew this was a dish after my own heart. Who could resist a combination of tender rabbit, colorful saffron, and fragrant fennel, laced with rouille, or spicy aïoli? "Print it!" my editor husband said as he tasted the dish, and so we did. The dish could also be prepared just as successfully with chicken.

I whole fresh rabbit (about 3 pounds; 1.5 kg), cut into serving pieces
Sea salt and freshly ground black pepper
3 tablespoons extra-virgin olive oil
I head plump, fresh garlic, cloves separated and peeled
A pinch of saffron threads
I teaspoon fennel seeds
Several sprigs of fresh thyme
4 fresh bay leaves
2 tablespoons tomato paste
2 tablespoons anise liqueur, or pastis
I pound (500 g) small yellow-fleshed potatoes, peeled and thinly sliced
3 cups (75 cl) water
I cup (25 cl) dry white wine, such as a Riesling, a white Burgundy, a not-too-oaky
    California Chardonnay, or a white Côtes du Rhône
I recipe Rouille (page 315)

1. Generously season the rabbit pieces with salt and pepper. In a large, deep-sided skillet, heat the oil over moderately high heat. When hot but not smoking, add the rabbit pieces. Turn the heat immediately to low (to keep the rabbit meat from drying out), cover, and cook gently but shake the pan from time to time until the rabbit is tender but still moist, about 5 minutes per side. (Cooking time will vary according to

(continued on next page)

FACING PHOTOGRAPH: *Roland Henny, the model village butcher.*

the size of the pieces.) With tongs, transfer the rabbit to a platter, cover with foil, and set aside.

2. Add to the skillet the garlic, saffron, fennel, thyme, bay leaves, tomato paste, anise liqueur, water, and wine, scraping up any browned bits that cling to the bottom of the pan. Cover and simmer for 30 minutes. Remove and discard the bay leaves and thyme. Puree in batches in a blender or food processor.

3. Return the rabbit to the skillet. Add the potatoes, cover, and simmer very gently for 25 minutes. Taste for seasoning. The liquid should be souplike and tinged with colors or saffron-orange.

4. Prepare the rouille according to the recipe directions and set aside, covered.

5. To serve, transfer portions of the rabbit and potatoes into warmed shallow soup bowls. Spoon the sauce over the rabbit. Pass the rouille, allowing the guests to swirl in a few spoonfuls to thicken and season their soup. Serve with plenty of toasted homemade bread.

FOUR SERVINGS

 WINE SUGGESTION: Serve with a chilled Bandol rosé from Domaine Tempier.

✧ **TIP ON COOKING RABBIT** ✧ Although rabbit can successfully be replaced by chicken in most recipes, it should not be cooked in exactly the same manner. While chicken benefits from a good browning or searing before cooking, rabbit has no skin or covering of fat to protect its tender meat. Rather, begin cooking the rabbit over low heat, then cover it to assure moist, evenly cooked meat.

I hate people who are not serious about their meals.

OSCAR WILDE

PINA'S BRAISED RABBIT

Close your eyes and imagine yourself in a trattoria in the Piedmont. There's no sign, just a double wooden door covered with immaculate white curtains. There's no menu, just a series of staunchly traditional Piedmontese specialties, prepared with love. A single room and a menu that changes little from day to day, season to season. The food? All subtle, simple dishes—with flavors at once rich and intense—that come from the kitchen of a remarkable cook, Pina Bongiovanni, at the Osteria dell'Unione in Tresio, near Alba. Pina's favorite dish is also her best, an exquisite platter of rabbit braised in Barolo with sweet red peppers spiked with cloves and cinnamon—a dish for cooks short on money, rich on time. The rabbit meat all but falls off the bone; the sauce nearly reduces to a thick syrup, the spice reminiscent of deep, dark game dishes of days long past. For best results, be certain to use a rather high alcohol wine, 13 or 14 percent. What's amazing here is the depth of flavor Pina achieves with so few ingredients. The brief marinade tenderizes the meat without robbing it of its delicate flavors. The red wine also gives what no other liquid in the world can: flavor, acidity, color, and richness.

> 1 whole fresh rabbit (about 3 pounds; 1.5 kg), cut into serving pieces
> 2 cups (50 cl) tannic red wine, such as Barolo, Barbera, or Côtes du Rhône
> 3 tablespoons extra-virgin olive oil
> Bouquet garni: 2 fresh bay leaves and a large bunch of thyme, fastened with household twine
> 1 cinnamon stick, halved
> 2 whole cloves
> 1 onion, peeled and halved
> 2 large red bell peppers
> Sea salt and freshly ground black pepper to taste

1. In a large, shallow bowl, combine the rabbit, wine, 2 tablespoons of oil, bouquet garni, and cinnamon stick. Press a clove into each of the onion halves and add to the bowl. Cover and marinate at room temperature for 1 to 2 hours. Turn the rabbit from time to time, making sure the pieces evenly absorb the marinade.

2. Meanwhile, roast the bell peppers directly over a gas flame or under a broiler, as close to the heat as possible, turning often, until charred all over. Transfer to a paper bag and let

(continued on next page)

steam for 10 minutes. Scrape off and discard the blackened skins, and remove and discard the stems, seeds, and ribs. Cut the peppers into thin strips. Set aside.

3. In a large, covered casserole, heat the remaining tablespoon of oil over moderately high heat. Remove the individual rabbit pieces from the marinade and pat them dry. When the oil is hot but not smoking, add the rabbit. Turn the heat immediately to low (to keep the rabbit meat from drying out), cover, and cook gently but shake the casserole from time to time until the rabbit is tender but still moist, about 5 minutes per side. Do not crowd the casserole; this may have to be done in batches. (Cooking time will vary according to the size of the pieces.) As each piece of rabbit is cooked, transfer it to a platter and season lightly with salt and pepper.

4. Return all the cooked rabbit pieces to the casserole. Add the marinade ingredients and red pepper strips. Bring just to a simmer, then turn the heat to very low. Simmer gently, covered, turning the meat from time to time and cooking until the rabbit is fork-tender, about 1 hour.

5. With a slotted spoon, transfer the rabbit and the pepper strips to a platter and cover to keep warm. Strain the sauce, discarding the bouquet garni, cinnamon sticks, and onions, and wipe the casserole. Return the sauce to the casserole and boil over high heat until thick and glossy. Return the rabbit and peppers to the casserole, cover, and cook over low heat, turning once or twice, until heated through, about 5 minutes. Taste for seasoning. Serve immediately on warmed dinner plates, accompanied by Creamy Semolina with Bay Leaf & Parmesan (page 243).

FOUR TO SIX SERVINGS

WINE SUGGESTION: We sampled this with a local Barbaresco, a wine with a perfect acid balance, custom-made for a region such as the Piedmont in Italy, where food is earthy and plentiful.

CUTTING UP A RABBIT To cut up a whole rabbit for cooking: Place the rabbit, belly side down, on a clean work surface. Trim the flaps of skin, tops of forelegs, and any excess bone. Set aside. With a cleaver or a heavy-duty knife, divide the carcass into three sections crosswise: hind legs, saddle, and forelegs, including the rib cage. Cut between the hind legs to separate them into two pieces. Split the front carcass into two pieces to separate the forelegs. Split the saddle crosswise into three even pieces.

CREAMY SEMOLINA WITH BAY LEAF & PARMESAN

If you love polenta but don't love the labor-intensive, long stirring, then you'll love this creamy semolina, which cooks in less than five minutes. I cook it in whole milk scented with bay leaf, then flavor the delicate, creamy grains with a touch of freshly grated nutmeg and Parmesan cheese. I think of it as grown-ups' nursery food. I love to serve this with both *La Broufade:* Beef & White Wine Daube from Arles (page 256) and Pina's Braised Rabbit (page 241). Any leftover semolina can be smoothed into a gratin dish, dotted with butter and additional cheese, then placed under a grill to brown. In this recipe, either fine semolina or what is sold as semolina flour for preparing pasta can be used.

    1 quart (1 l) whole milk
    2 fresh bay leaves or dried imported bay leaves
    2 teaspoons fine sea salt
    1 cup (170 g) fine semolina
    ½ cup (2 ounces; 60 g) freshly grated Parmigiano-Reggiano cheese
    Freshly grated nutmeg

1. In a large saucepan, combine the milk and bay leaves, and bring to a boil over moderate heat. Remove from the heat, cover, and let steep for 1 hour (see Note).
2. Bring the milk back to a simmer over moderate heat. Add the salt and very slowly add the semolina in a thin, steady stream, stirring constantly with a wooden spoon to prevent lumping. (Should any lumps form, press them against the side of the pot and they will disappear.) Once all the semolina has been added, adjust the heat so that the mixture bubbles. Stir constantly until the mixture forms a mass that cleanly pulls away from the sides of the pan, 3 to 5 minutes. (The mixture should resemble a very elegant potato puree.) Add the cheese and a sprinkling of nutmeg, and stir to blend. Remove the bay leaves, taste for seasoning, and serve. (The mixture will harden as it cools, but it can be softened by reheating.)

SIX TO EIGHT SERVINGS

NOTE: If you can't spare the extra moments to infuse the milk with bay leaf, simply add the bay leaf to the milk as it is simmering and remove the bay leaf once the semolina is cooked.

*In my experience it is the countryman who is the real gourmet and
for good reason: It is he who has cultivated, raised, hunted, or fished
the raw materials and has made the wine himself.*

PENELOPE GRAY

CHANTEDUC RABBIT
WITH GARLIC & PRESERVED LEMONS

Rabbits have long been a part of the culture at Chanteduc. Through the years, successive generations of farmers who lived on the property raised rabbits, walking down the hill once a week to sell them at the Tuesday market. When we moved to the farm in 1984, the farmer's son, Yves Reynaud, regularly came around, hunting the rabbits and wild hare that raced through the vineyards, or the ducks, geese, and wild boar found in the woodland. Yves always shared his bounty, and so Walter and I were well supplied with wild game for our table. One fall he presented me with a rabbit the day before I was leaving to return to Paris. There wasn't going to be time to prepare or eat it, so I cut it up to freeze. I was alone in the house on that rainy evening, and just as I was preparing the rabbit, a mouse appeared from behind a shelf. I nearly lost my cool that evening. That was a lot more of the rustic life than I had bargained for!

I created this recipe as a special springtime dish, designed for when the season's first garlic shows up in the market around the middle of April. The garlic is cooked whole—just the very top third of the head is trimmed off and discarded. As the garlic cooks, cut side down, in an aromatic blend of white wine, rabbit braising liquid, preserved lemons, and the juice in which they are preserved, it takes on a biting, deep flavor. The rabbit itself stays decidedly tender as the preserved lemons blend completely into the sauce. I like to accompany it with Couscous My Way (page 247) or Creamy Semolina with Bay Leaf & Parmesan (page 243).

6 plump, fresh whole heads of garlic

3 tablespoons extra-virgin olive oil

1 whole fresh rabbit (about 3 pounds; 1.5 kg), cut into serving pieces, or substitute chicken

Bouquet garni: 2 fresh bay leaves and a large bunch of thyme, fastened with household twine

12 slices Preserved Lemons (page 319), plus 4 tablespoons liquid from the jar of preserved lemons

1 cup (25 cl) dry white wine (see Wine Suggestions)

(continued on next page)

1. Trim and discard the top third of each head of garlic. Set aside.

2. In a large, covered casserole, heat the olive oil over moderately high heat. When the oil is hot but not smoking, add the rabbit. Turn the heat immediately to low (to keep the rabbit meat from drying out), cover, and cook gently but shake the pan from time to time, until the rabbit is tender but still moist, about 5 minutes per side. This may have to be done in batches. (Cooking time will vary according to the size of the pieces.) As each rabbit piece is cooked, transfer it to a platter and season lightly with salt and pepper.

3. In the fat that remains in the casserole, brown the trimmed heads of garlic, cut side down, until they are toasty brown, 2 to 3 minutes. Return the rabbit to the casserole along with the bouquet garni, preserved lemons and their liquid, and the wine. Cover and turn heat to very low, allowing the liquid to simmer very gently. Stir from time to time. Braise until the rabbit is cooked through but still soft and moist, about 1 hour. The sauce should be thick and glossy. Taste for seasoning.

4. To serve, arrange portions of rabbit and garlic on warmed individual dinner plates, spooning the sauce over it all.

FOUR TO SIX SERVINGS

WINE SUGGESTIONS: Serve this with a gentle white. I like it with a floral white from the Rhône, such as a Sablet blanc de blanc. Other worthy contenders include a young Italian white, Pinot Bianco, with its flowery fragrance and crisp acidity, or a California Sauvignon Blanc, a wine grape that loves garlic.

COUSCOUS MY WAY

I prepare couscous almost as often as rice or pasta since it's a quick, ideal accompaniment to some of my favorite poultry and fish dishes. This is my favorite way to prepare couscous. It is all but foolproof, demands little time, and results in a perfectly seasoned couscous that is ultimately fine, with no lumps. The secret is the microwave oven, which steams the grain to perfection. Serve this with Chanteduc Rabbit with Garlic & Preserved Lemons (page 245).

> 1 cup (175 g) quick-cooking couscous
> 3 tablespoons extra-virgin olive oil
> ¾ teaspoon fine sea salt
> 1¼ cups (31 cl) water

In a large, shallow bowl, combine the cousous and salt, and toss with a large two-pronged carving fork to blend. Add the oil and fluff until the grains are evenly separated and coated with oil. Add the water and continue to fluff. Set aside and occasionally fluff and toss the grains until all the liquid has been absorbed, 10 to 15 minutes. Cover with plastic wrap, place in the center of a microwave oven, and cook for 2 minutes on high. Remove from the oven, fluff once more, and serve immediately. (Leftover couscous can easily be reheated in the microwave. Just be sure to continue to fluff the grains to avoid lumps.)

FOUR TO SIX SERVINGS

᠅ **WHAT IS THIS THING CALLED COUSCOUS?** ᠊ Couscous is often mistakenly called a pasta, but it is actually a refreshingly light and crunchy meal of coarsely ground hard, durum wheat. It is packaged in both traditional and precooked varieties. Couscous is the traditional dish of the North African countries of Morocco, Algeria, and Tunisia, where it is eaten almost daily in some form. A nutritional powerhouse, couscous contains 13 percent vegetable protein and is highly digestible.

The Chanteduc dining room, ready for a feast.

9

MEAT

EVER SINCE MY EARLIEST DAYS IN PROVENCE, my local butcher, Roland Henny, has played a major role in our lives. The freshest local lamb, pedigreed beef from award-winning cattle in the Auvergne, deliciously moist pork, and delicate veal grace our table, thanks to his attention to quality and extraordinary skills. Ask for a leg of lamb, and out of the cooler comes an entire baby lamb, to be butchered with the skill of a surgeon. The pork roast doesn't come ready cut, but will be fashioned from just the right portion of the pig, then tied with the virtuosity of a fine craftsman. And along with each cut will come a recipe filled with invaluable tips. He'll share the secrets of a perfect Provencal beef daube (use several cuts of meat and lace it with strips of pork rind, or *couenne*). He'll decorate the leg of lamb with artistry and flourish, and even run to his *atelier* upstairs, to share his special curry when he hears that Curry d'Agneau is on the menu tonight.

Cookery means … English thoroughness, French art, and Arabian hospitality;
it means the knowledge of all fruits and herbs and balms and spices;
it means carefulness, inventiveness, and watchfulness.

JOHN RUSKIN

DAUBE OF VEAL, WINE & GREEN OLIVES

In France, one of the most popular cuts of veal for long, slow cooking is *tendron,* the portion of the breast that contains the cartilaginous riblike portions that visually resemble pork spare ribs when cooked. *Tendrons* are delicious, full of body and flavor, slightly gelatinous and chewy. For this recipe you can choose from any number of good cuts of stewing veal, including the breast, the short ribs, veal shoulder and shoulder chops, or the heel of round or shank. This is the sort of dish that reminds you that it is always better to cook meat, fish, or poultry on the bone, for it will always guarantee greater flavor. To prevent the dish from tasting fatty or greasy, be sure to trim as much fat as possible from the veal before cooking it.

> 4 tablespoons extra-virgin olive oil
> 3 pounds (1.5 kg) breast of veal with the bone (ask your butcher to cut across the lower breast portion to make several strips of equal width)
> 3 medium onions, halved and thinly sliced
> Fine sea salt and freshly ground black pepper to taste
> Bouquet garni: a large bunch of fresh thyme and several fresh bay leaves, tied in a bundle with household twine
> 2 cups (50 cl) white wine, such as Chardonnay
> 1 small can (14½ ounces; 400 g) imported whole tomatoes in juice, drained
> 1½ cups (10 ounces; 300 g) pitted green olives

1. In a large, covered casserole, heat 3 tablespoons of the oil over moderate heat. When the oil is hot, begin to brown the veal, carefully regulating the heat to avoid scorching the meat. Do not crowd the pan and be patient; good browning is essential so that the veal retains all of its flavor. The meat should be browned on all sides in several batches, taking about 10 minutes to brown each batch thoroughly. As each batch is browned, use tongs—to avoid piercing the meat—to transfer the veal to a platter. Immediately season generously with salt and pepper.

2. In the same casserole, with the remaining fat in the pan, use a spatula to scrape up any browned bits that stick to the bottom of the pan. (This will help enrich the final sauce.) Add the onions and a pinch of salt and cook over moderate heat until the onions are soft

and translucent, about 10 minutes. Add the bouquet garni, wine, tomatoes, and crush the tomatoes with a wooden spoon. Bring to a boil and cook for 2 to 3 minutes.

3. Return to the casserole all the veal and any juices the meat has released and bring just to a simmer over low heat. Cover and simmer gently, turning the veal to evenly coat it with the sauce, until the meat is very tender and almost falling off the bone, about 2 hours.

4. Meanwhile, bring a large pan of water to a boil. Add the olives and blanch them in the boiling water for 2 minutes. Drain well and add to the casserole. Taste the sauce for seasoning. Simmer over very low heat for 30 minutes more, for a total of 2½ hours cooking time.

5. Transfer the pieces of veal to warmed shallow soup bowls. Reduce the sauce over high heat until lightly thickened, then pour the sauce over the meat. Serve with Creamy Semolina with Bay Leaf & Parmesan (page 243). The daube can be prepared 1 to 2 days in advance. If prepared in advance, allow the daube to cool thoroughly at room temperature and then cover and refrigerate it until serving time. To serve, remove and discard any fat that has risen to the top of the daube and gently reheat.

SIX TO EIGHT SERVINGS

WINE SUGGESTION: This is a quiet, subtle dish, calling for a wine of like personality. I enjoy this with an older red that has toned down with age or a young Burgundy, such as a Savigny-lès-Beaune from the house of Tollot-Beaut.

ROASTING TIPS

- Place meat fat side up so that, as the fat melts, it bastes, seasons, and tenderizes the meat.
- Always be sure to remove the meat from the refrigerator several hours before roasting. Even an entire day is not too much. The meat must be at room temperature when placed in the oven; otherwise, it will steam and not roast evenly.
- Plan on 2 pounds (1 kg) of beef rib for four people. For a crowd, roast several steaks.
- Do not season meat before roasting. Salt tends to draw juices and flavor from the meat. Do season generously immediately after removing from the oven. This will give the steak a well-seasoned flavor.
- Let it rest. The meat continues to cook during the resting period. During this time, the juices retreat back into the meat, making for a juicy steak with richer flavor.

◡ **ON BLANCHING OLIVES** ◡ It's a tiny step but one that can make all the difference between a dish that's refined, elegant, and finished and one that is simply awkward. Green olives can impart a very strong, even sometimes bitter flavor when cooked. By blanching them for just one or two minutes in boiling water, you rid them of excess salt and potential bitterness.

MONSIEUR HENNY'S THREE-BEEF DAUBE

This is the richest, most sublime daube recipe I know. And one of the prettiest. During my earliest weeks of cooking school, our butcher, Roland Henny, put on a stunning show, demonstrating how to cut up rabbits, truss chickens, and select meat for a proper Provençal daube. He advises using at least three cuts of beef from different parts of the animal, thus some (such as short ribs or *plats de côtes*) enhance flavor with their cartilaginous bones, others (such as top round or *tende de tranche*) provide purer meat with little muscle separation, while still others (the shoulder blade or *paleron*) add both meat and muscle for added texture. The addition of both cloves and nutmeg here adds his small touch of genius: They serve to perfume the dish, but also bring out the sheer animal essence of the beef. Mr. Henny adds both marrow bones and thick strips of fatback or *couenne de porc* to his daube, ingredients that provide additional fragrance, texture, and flavor. He enhances the Provençal accent of the dish by embellishing it with the sweet and bitter touch of orange zest and the salty pungency of black olives. Mr. Henny's daube glistens like a jewel and the sauce has a hauntingly rich texture, so smooth you wanted to coat everything in sight with it—the meat, a slice of bread, toss it with pasta, spoon it into your mouth all on its own. The ideal vessel for preparing the daube is a pot-bellied earthenware *daubière,* a well-designed piece of kitchen equipment that reduces the amount of surface exposed, minimizing the evaporation of precious juices. The form also makes it easier to skim off any fat that rises to the surface.

6 medium onions, peeled

6 cloves

5 pounds (2 kg) stewing beef, preferably two or three different cuts, choosing from top or bottom round, heel of round, shoulder arm or shoulder blade, neck, or short ribs of beef

2 bottles (75 cl each) sturdy red wine, such as a Côtes du Rhône

A handful of fresh thyme

5 bay leaves, preferably fresh

1½ teaspoons freshly grated nutmeg

3 tablespoons extra-virgin olive oil

Sea salt and freshly ground black pepper

3 tablespoons tomato paste

2 pounds (1 kg) carrots, peeled and sliced into thin rounds

One 16-ounce (480-g) can peeled Italian plum tomatoes in juice

4 beef marrow bones, cut into 2-inch (5-cm) lengths

3 ounces (90 g) fresh fatback, cut into thin strips

Grated zest (orange peel) of 1 orange, preferably organic, or a strip of dried orange peel

4 ounces (125 g) imported black olives (such as French Nyons), pitted

(continued on next page)

1. Slice an onion in half lengthwise. Place it cut side down on a cutting board, and slice crosswise into very thin slices. Slice four more onions in this manner. Halve the remaining onion and insert three cloves into each half.

2. In a large nonreactive vessel, combine the meat, onions, wine, thyme, bay leaves, and nutmeg. Cover and set aside to marinate at room temperature for 24 hours.

3. The next day, strain out and separate the onions and meat. Reserve the marinade liquid. In a large, covered casserole, heat the oil over moderate heat until hot but not smoking. Add the onions, reduce heat to low, and gently brown the onions, 4 to 5 minutes. With a slotted spoon, transfer the onions to a platter. In the remaining fat, begin to brown the beef, carefully regulating the heat to avoid scorching the meat. Do not crowd the pan, and be patient: Good browning is essential, so the beef retains all of its flavor. The meat should be browned on all sides in several batches, taking about 10 minutes to thoroughly brown each batch. As each batch is browned, use tongs—to avoid piercing the meat—to transfer the beef to a platter. Immediately season generously with salt and freshly ground black pepper.

4. Once all the meat is browned, return it to the casserole, along with the browned onions, tomato paste, and marinade liquid. Season with salt and pepper. Bring to a bare simmer and cook, covered, for 1 hour. Add the carrots, tomatoes, marrow bones, and fat back and stir to evenly distribute the ingredients. Return to a bare simmer and cook, covered, for 2 hours more. Taste for seasoning. Test the meat for tenderness: If necessary, allow the daube to simmer for 1 hour more, or until the beef is fully tender. During the last 30 minutes of cooking, add the orange zest and black olives.

5. The daube will be more flavorful and less fatty if it is allowed to rest for 24 hours before serving. Allow the daube to cool thoroughly at room temperature, then cover and refrigerate until serving time. To serve, scrape off and discard all the fat that has solidified on the surface of the daube. Gently reheat and serve in warmed shallow soup bowls.

EIGHT TO TEN SERVINGS

WINE SUGGESTIONS: Any lusty, full-flavored red would be at home with this daube: Try a young Côtes du Rhône, a Corbières from France's Midi, a California Zinfandel, or an Australian Shiraz.

CITY STEAK

Côte de boeuf au gros sel, or a thick, single prime rib of beef, is one of France's favorite cuts of meat. Beautifully marbled, cooked to a rare tenderness, it is the quickest way I know to satisfy a craving for a pure, simple roast. Since I cook in the city as well as the country, I devised this "city steak" for those who don't have access to a real grill. The method is classically French: The beef rib is set atop a bed of salt (which serves as a flavorful cushion as well as delicate seasoning) and roasted in a very hot oven for about 18 minutes for a 2-pound (1-kg) steak. The resulting flavor is a cross between a roasted prime rib roast and a perfectly grilled steak. As a sauce, I simply serve the juices that drip from the beef as it rests, accompanied by Fake *Frites* (page 137) and Cheesemaker's Salad (page 75).

EQUIPMENT: An instant-read meat thermometer

12 ounces (375 g) coarse sea salt
1 prime rib of beef (about 2 pounds; 1 kg), at room temperature, trimmed of excess fat
1 teaspoon extra-virgin olive oil
Sea salt and coarsely ground black pepper to taste

1. Preheat the oven to 500°F (260°C; gas mark 9).
2. Place the salt in a thin, even layer on a baking sheet. Lightly brush the beef on both sides with oil. Place the beef, fattest side up, on the bed of salt. Place in the lower portion of the oven and roast until the skin is crackling and brown, and the meat begins to exude fat and juices, about 18 minutes. To test for doneness, insert an instant-read meat thermometer into the thickest part of the steak for at least 15 seconds. At 120°F (50°C) the steak is rare; at 125°F to 130°F (55°C) it is medium rare.
3. Remove from the oven and take the beef off the bed of salt. Season generously with salt and pepper on both sides. Place the beef on a rack set over a pan or a platter to catch the drippings. Loosely tent with foil and set aside to rest in a warm place to allow the meat to uniformly absorb the juices, at least 15 minutes.
4. To serve: With a large carving knife and fork, cut the meat away from the bone, following the contours of the bone. Slice the beef into thick diagonal slices and transfer to a warmed platter. Place the juices collected during the resting period in a sauce boat and serve.

FOUR SERVINGS

WINE SUGGESTION: The simplicity of this roast allows you to pull out a great bottle of red. I look for one of my oldest vintage Châteauneuf du Pape, preferably from Château du Beaucastel.

LA BROUFADE: BEEF *&* WHITE WINE DAUBE FROM ARLES

One cool but sunny afternoon in Arles, I sat on the narrow first-floor terrace of Les Vaccarès, overlooking the plane trees and an oversized statue of the Provençal poet Fréderic Mistral. It was the first time I had sampled this wonderfully fragrant and tender Provençal daube—thin slices of beef cooked with some of my favorite ingredients: white wine, capers, anchovies, garlic, onions, and tomatoes. The daube, also known as *broufaddo,* is an ancient one. It was a favorite with boatmen who worked on barges on the Rhône River, men who would be away from home for days at a time. It's a satisfying dish that takes well to reheating and tastes even better the second or third day.

2 whole anchovies in salt or 4 anchovy fillets in salt

4 tablespoons whole milk

2 tablespoon capers

2 medium onions

10 plump, fresh garlic cloves, peeled and halved

One 28-ounce (765-g) can peeled Italian plum tomatoes in juice, drained (the juice can be reserved for sauces, soups, or stocks)

6 small French pickles or cornichons, thinly sliced

Sea salt to taste

1 bottle (75 cl) white wine, preferably from the Rhône Valley

1 fresh bay leaf

Several sprigs of fresh thyme, wrapped and tied in a cheesecloth bundle

2 pounds (1 kg) boneless braising beef in a single piece (such as beef shoulder, chuck, blade, neck, rump, or brisket), cut against the grain into 6 slices 1½ inches (3 cm) thick and trimmed of most of its fat

1. Rinse the anchovies and fillet if necessary. Soak the anchovies in the milk for 10 minutes to soften and remove any excess salt.

2. Drain the capers, rinse well, and soak in cold water for 10 minutes to remove any excess salt.

3. Slice the onions in half lengthwise. Place them, cut side down, on a cutting board and cut crosswise into very thin slices. Place in a large bowl and add the garlic, drained tomatoes, and pickles. Drain the anchovies (discarding the milk), rinse, and add to the bowl. Drain the capers and add to the bowl. Add 1 teaspoon of salt and toss to blend, slightly breaking up the tomatoes with the back of a spoon.

4. Place the wine in a large saucepan, bring to a simmer, and simmer gently until no alcohol aroma wafts from the pan, about 10 minutes. Set aside.

5. In a large, heavy-bottomed casserole, place about ⅓ of the tomato-onion mixture on the bottom of the casserole. Add the bay leaf and thyme bundle. Top with a layer of beef, lightly seasoning each slice of beef with salt and pepper. Continue with 2 additional alter-

nating layers of the tomato-onion mixture and the beef. Add enough wine to just barely cover the mixture. Cover and bring just to a simmer over moderately low heat. Simmer gently until the meat is very tender, about 4 hours. There should be plenty of rosy, thick sauce. Check the daube from time to time, stirring the ingredients and making sure they are well distributed and the meat is largely submerged. Do not let the mixture boil. Taste for seasoning. Remove and discard the bay leaf and thyme.

6. The daube can be served immediately or may be prepared 1 to 2 days in advance. If prepared in advance, allow the daube to cool thoroughly at room temperature, then cover and refrigerate until serving time. To serve, scrape off and discard all the fat that has solidified on the surface of the daube. Gently reheat and serve in warmed shallow soup bowls. Serve with Brown Rice from the Camargue (page 272) or Creamy Semolina with Bay Leaf & Parmesan (page 243).

FOUR TO SIX SERVINGS

WINE SUGGESTIONS: Although one always thinks of red wine with beef, the white wine used to prepare this daube would be an ideal accompaniment. For a white wine, choose a Rhône or even an Hermitage. Otherwise, serve a young red, such as a Côtes du Rhône.

Clos Chanteduc, the wine from the Wells property.

WHAT'S IN A DAUBE? You could call it a stew, but that would only be half the story. The daube is one of many French dishes that fall into the category of *la cuisine mijotée*—earthy, soul-satisfying preparations that simmer slowly in a tightly enclosed vessel. Unlike other stews or one-dish meals that are bound with thickening agents—such as *boeuf bourguignon,* thickened with flour and butter, or a *blanquette,* thickened with egg yolks—a proper daube focuses not on the accompanying sauce or vegetables but on the meat, fish, or poultry that is slowly simmered to create a potful of complex, concentrated flavors. The most traditional daubes come from Provence, historically a region where meat, when it made its rare appearance, usually came in a dish prepared with the most inexpensive cuts, generally lamb, mutton, or beef. Cooked in a well-seasoned *daubière*—a large, rotund earthenware casserole, much like a bean pot with a long, narrow neck designed to minimize evaporation—the daube might be coaxed along over an open fire, in a brick oven, or on top of a stove.

BEEF DAUBE WITH MUSTARD, HERBS & WHITE WINE

I can guess why a daube might have earned a reputation as hearty, sometimes heavy fare. The wrong mix of hefty ingredients, and you have a dish that makes your cheeks bulge and your digestive system demand a rebate. After years of preparing these long-simmering favorites, I've developed a way to make a light, very digestible daube, essentially a dish that equals more than the sum of its parts. The key is a careful balance of flavors, of acids, of herbs. This recipe, to my mind, has it all. A rather tough cut of beef is teamed with light, acerbic ingredients such as white wine, mustard, and a tangy dose of herbs, all of which serve to tame, tenderize, and perfume the pieces of meat that are ready to absorb the pungent flavors. I think of this as a springtime daube, for days when you want the heartiness of beef and a warm bowl of stew but nothing overwhelming. Be sure to give the bouquet garni an extra little portion of tarragon; its flavor marries beautifully with the mustard and white wine. Incredibly simple and incredibly delicious, the daube is a perfect match for the gentle sweetness of the Onion-Parmesan Gratin (page 128). Note that the chunks of meat here may seem large at first, but the meat shrinks in size as it cooks.

> 3 medium onions, peeled
> 3 tablespoons extra-virgin olive oil
> 2 pounds (1 kg) boneless braising beef (such as beef shoulder, chuck, blade, neck, rump, or brisket), cut into 3-inch (7.5-cm) cubes
> Sea salt and freshly ground black pepper to taste
> 1 bottle (75 cl) dry white wine, such as a Chardonnay
> 2 tablespoons imported Dijon mustard
> One 16-ounce (480-g) can peeled Italian plum tomatoes in juice
> 3 plump, fresh garlic cloves, peeled and halved
> Bouquet garni: several sprigs of flat-leaf parsley, thyme, tarragon, and fresh bay leaves tied in a bundle with household twine

1. Slice the onions in half lengthwise. Place, cut side down, on a cutting board and slice crosswise into very thin slices. Set aside.

2. In a large covered casserole, heat 3 tablespoons of the oil over moderate heat. When the oil is hot, begin to brown the beef, carefully regulating the heat to avoid scorching the meat. Do not crowd the pan and be patient: Good browning is essential, so the beef retains all its flavor. The meat should be browned on all sides in several batches, taking about 10 minutes to brown each batch thoroughly. As each batch is browned, use tongs—to avoid piercing the meat—to transfer the beef to a platter. Immediately season generously with salt and pepper.

3. Only a thin film of fat should remain in the bottom of the casserole. (If there is excess fat, pour off and discard it.) Add the wine, pouring it all over the surface of the pan.

Scrape up any browned bits from the bottom of the casserole. Adjust the heat to bring the liquid to a gentle simmer and cook, uncovered, until most of the wine and alcohol have cooked off, about 7 minutes from the time the liquid comes to a simmer. Add the mustard and whisk to blend.

4. Return the beef, and any juices it has released, to the casserole. Add the tomatoes and their liquid, the onions, garlic, and bouquet garni. Cover and simmer over low heat until the beef is fork-tender, 2 to 3 hours. Remove and discard the bouquet garni. With a slotted spoon, transfer the beef, onions, and tomatoes to a platter. Boil the sauce over high heat until reduced by about one-third, about 10 minutes. Return the solids to the sauce, reheat gently, and serve in warmed shallow soup bowls. (The daube can be prepared 1 to 2 days in advance. If prepared in advance, allow the daube to cool thoroughly at room temperature, then cover and refrigerate until serving time. To serve, scrape off and discard all the fat that has solidified on the surface of the daube. Gently reheat and serve in warmed shallow soup bowls.)

FOUR TO SIX SERVINGS

WINE SUGGESTIONS: The last time I prepared this daube, I rummaged around in my wine cellar and came up with a 1982 white Hermitage from Gérard Chave. I was certain the wine would be past its prime, but it wasn't at all. Other favorite wines for this dish include a white Savennières from the Loire Valley or a Mâcon-Villages from Burgundy.

A WORD ON BRAISING What's the difference between a stew and a braise? When dealing with mental images, one imagines a stew as a hearty and substantial one-dish meal. Braising has a sexy quality to it, as if the meat is obligated to go through many rites of passage before it can be officially dubbed "braised." In reality, stewing usually means that the meat is cut into pieces and is completely submerged in liquid as it cooks. Braising usually calls for a whole piece of meat, and the quantity of cooking liquid is diminished considerably in relation to the meat. I love braising, for it coaxes the optimum flavor from the meat in two phases. Initially, the meat is colored on all sides, giving it a wonderful brown "crust" without allowing the flavor of the meat to escape. This step also creates pan juices that enrich the sauce. Before the meat can become any tougher, it is bathed in cooking liquid and cooked, with a cover. This second phase steams the meat and gradually tenderizes it, breaking down the tough and fibrous qualities characteristic of tastier but tough cuts of meat.

EAT YOUR CURRY, AND BE BRILLIANT!
Why should I make the effort to try something new when I already like the food I eat?
Part of the answer lies in the Indian belief that eating more complex and subtly flavored foods
exercises the brain, making it better at understanding and appreciating
and surviving the subtle complexities of life.
THE SPICE HOUSE CATALOG, ON CURRY POWDERS

SPICY LAMB CURRY WITH YOGURT & APPLES

Lamb curry, or *curry d'agneau,* is one of France's classic bistro dishes. I've always loved the idea of this spicy, warming dish, but in many bistros the curry is prepared with strong-flavored mutton rather than lamb, and the seasoning tends to be bland. So I make it at home with fresh spices from my own pantry. While a classical curry needs an acid base such as tomatoes to balance the dish, this version uses a touch of yogurt and grated apple, refreshing additions. Be certain to remove as much fat as possible from the lamb to make for a lighter, more flavorful dish. And don't rummage around your spice cabinet for old bottles of stale spices. Invest in a few new bottles, for I'm sure you'll make this often. The spice level suggested here makes for a fairly hot curry. If a more subtle flavor is desired, reduce or eliminate the cayenne pepper.

> 6 tablespoons extra-virgin olive oil
> 1 lamb shoulder, about 3 pounds (1.5 kg), bone reserved and meat cut into 2-inch
>   (5-cm) cubes, and excess fat removed
> Sea salt and freshly ground black pepper to taste
> 4 medium onions, halved lengthwise and thinly sliced
> One 2-ounce (60-g) piece fresh ginger, finely chopped
> 4 plump, fresh garlic cloves, peeled and minced
> 1 tablespoon freshly ground cumin seeds
> 2 tablespoons freshly ground coriander seeds
> 1 tablespoon ground turmeric
> 1 teaspoon ground cayenne pepper
> 1 cup (25 cl) whole-milk yogurt
> 1 firm, acidic apple, such as Granny Smith, grated

1. In a large covered casserole, heat 3 tablespoons of the oil over moderate heat. When the oil is hot, begin to brown the lamb, carefully regulating the heat to avoid scorching the meat. Do not crowd the pan, and be patient; good browning is essential, so that the

lamb retains all of its flavor. The meat should be browned on all sides in several batches, taking about 10 minutes to brown each batch thoroughly. As each batch is browned, use tongs—to avoid piercing the meat—to transfer the lamb to a platter. Immediately season generously with salt and pepper.

2. Leave the fat that remains in the casserole and use a spatula to scrape up any browned bits that stick to the bottom. (This will help enrich the final sauce.) Add the onions and a pinch of salt and cook over moderate heat until the onions are soft and golden brown, about 15 minutes. Add the ginger and garlic and cook 1 minute more. Add the ground cumin, coriander, turmeric, and cayenne, and cook until the spices are fragrant, about 15 seconds more. Add the lamb and any juices the meat has released, along with the yogurt, grated apple, and 1 cup (25 cl) of hot water. Stir to blend. The liquid should just barely cover the meat. Cover and simmer gently, turning the lamb regularly to coat it evenly with the sauce, until the meat is very tender, about 1½ hours. The sauce should be fragrant and fairly thick. Taste for seasoning. Remove and discard the bone. (The lamb can be prepared in advance. Cool in the casserole and refrigerate up to 1 day. If desired, scrape off any fat that has risen to the surface. At serving time, return to a simmer over low heat. Taste for seasoning.) To serve, transfer the lamb and curry to warmed dinner plates. Serve Basmati Rice (page 273) alongside.

FOUR TO SIX SERVINGS

WINE SUGGESTIONS: One can choose wines of two different kinds: A rich, round, tannic red wine, such as a well-aged Gigondas from the Côtes du Rhône region, would stand up well to the spice. Equally interesting and compatible would be a spicy white wine, such as a Gewürztraminer, a floral white such as a Viognier, or a Bandol rosé, filled with floral, spicy flavors.

There is no sight on Earth more appealing than
the sight of a woman making dinner for someone she loves.
THOMAS WOLFE

LEMON‑THYME LAMB CHOPS

Dry cooking over high heat produces meat with a crisply golden and crusty exterior and a tender melting interior. For this style of dry cooking you need tender meat, such as best-quality lamb chops or slices of leg of lamb. To keep the interior of the meat moist while cooking (and to keep it from sticking to the unoiled pan or grill), the meat is first marinated in a classic mixture of the very best olive oil and freshly squeezed lemon juice. Do not salt the meat, or it will draw out the flavorful juices. These thin and dainty lamb chops are meant to be eaten with one's fingers or, if you can find them, with special silver lamb-chop holders that are sold in some antique stores in France.

8 single-rib lamb chops about ½ inch (1 cm) thick, partially boned (6 to 9 ounces; 180 to 270 g, per chop)
3 tablespoons freshly squeezed lemon juice
¼ cup (6 cl) extra-virgin olive oil
1 teaspoon fresh lemon-thyme leaves or thyme leaves
Fine sea salt and freshly ground black pepper to taste

1. Place the lamb chops, lemon juice, oil, and thyme in a large, shallow dish. Cover with plastic wrap and marinate at room temperature for 20 minutes, turning them over once or twice.
2. Preheat a heavy-duty cast iron skillet or ridged pan over high heat for 5 minutes or prepare a wood or charcoal fire. The fire is ready when the coals glow red and are covered with ash.
3. If cooking in a skillet, lower the heat to moderate, add the lamb chops, and cook until nicely browned, about 2 minutes per side for rare. If cooking over a wood or charcoal fire, cook about 2 minutes per side for rare. Season each side with salt and pepper after cooking. To test for doneness, press the meat with the tip of your finger. If the meat is very soft, the lamb chops are rare. If the meat is medium-soft, the lamb chops are medium-rare. If the meat is very firm, the lamb chops well done.
4. To serve, pour the remaining marinade liquid over the lamb chops or use the liquid as a vinaigrette for an accompanying salad. Serve immediately.

FOUR SERVINGS

WINE SUGGESTION: Certainly the most traditional combination is lamb and a lovely red Bordeaux. Other choices are Cabernet equivalents from Australia, New Zealand, or California, or a fine Spanish Rioja Reserva.

SALT OF THE EARTH My favorite salt, the *sel gris de Guérande,* is a totally unrefined salt gathered along the Guérande peninsula of Brittany, near the villages of Batz-sur-Mer, Kervalet, Saillé, and Guérande. Working from May to September by hand, the salt workers, or *paludiers,* trap the seawater in shallow beds, allow it to evaporate in the sun and wind, and then rake the salt into gigantic mounds. This is why they like to call it "the fruit of the ocean, the sun, and the wind." The color is naturally a slight, pale gray, thus the name *sel gris.* Most of the salt is sold in this state with a bit of moisture still clinging to the grains. Other varieties are simply dried slightly with very faint electrical power, reducing the water content by about 8 percent. The salt is then ground with a stone mill for a finer grain.

On the very top of the evaporating beds, even finer salt casts a thin veil. This is called the *fleur de sel*—literally, the flower of the salt; it is the caviar of the sea salt world. With a very faint perfume of violets, this very fine grained salt is favored by bakers and chefs, and is used sparingly as a table salt and as a special final seasoning.

THOUGHTS ON LAMB The term "spring lamb" is often bandied about without much thought to its meaning. Originally, spring lamb described a young lamb, born in the early months of the year and slaughtered in the spring months. Since cross-breeding of different species enables the ewe to give birth year-round, the term in America has come to describe any tender lamb that is less than a year old and slaughtered in the spring or summer months. Other descriptive terms, such as hothouse or "Easter" lamb, generally mean the lamb has been fed on nothing but mother's milk (as opposed to a regular grain-and-grass diet) and is sold under the age of ten weeks. Since these lambs are so young, they are smaller in size, weighing anywhere from twenty to thirty pounds (10 to 15 kg). Even as the lamb gets older, to approximately six months, and is fifty to sixty pounds in weight (25 to 30 kg), it can still be considered young lamb.

LEG OF LAMB ON A BED OF ARTICHOKES,
POTATOES & HERBS

This recipe originated one Christmas week when we had a houseful of guests begging for lamb. Potatoes and artichokes are a brilliant combination, especially when enhanced by the drippings from roasting lamb. The final touch of fresh herbs from a bouquet garni perfume both your kitchen and the dish as the lamb roasts.

EQUIPMENT: One oval baking dish just slightly larger than the lamb (about 9 x 13 inches; 23 x 33 cm)

4 artichokes, 8 baby artichokes (see Note, page 95), or two 9-ounce (270-g) packages of frozen artichoke hearts, thawed
2 pounds (1 kg) medium-size yellow-fleshed potatoes (such as Yukon Gold), peeled and quartered
1 tablespoon fresh thyme leaves, carefully destemmed
2 plump, fresh heads of garlic, cloves peeled but left whole
3 tablespoons extra-virgin olive oil
2 tablespoons freshly squeezed lemon juice
4 large bouquet garni: each made up of several sprigs of parsley, several sprigs of thyme, summer savory, rosemary, and several fresh bay leaves, securely fastened with household twine
Sea salt and freshly ground black pepper to taste
1 leg of lamb, with bone (about 5 pounds; 2.5 kg), carefully trimmed of fat and tied (ask your butcher to do this for you)

1. Preheat the oven to 425°F (220°C; gas mark 7/8).
2. Thoroughly drain the artichoke slices. In a large bowl, combine the artichokes, potatoes, thyme leaves, garlic, 2 tablespoons of oil, and lemon juice. Toss to coat evenly with the oil. Arrange 2 bouquet garni on the bottom of the baking dish. Add the artichoke-potato mixture and season generously with salt and pepper. Top with the remaining 2 bouquet garni.
3. Place a small metal roasting rack crosswise on top of the baking dish. Rub the lamb all over with the remaining tablespoon of oil. Season the lamb generously on all sides with salt and pepper. Place it on top of the rack so it will roast evenly and not steam. Place the baking dish in the oven and roast, allowing 10 to 12 minutes per pound (500 g) for medium rare, 15 minutes for medium. Turn the lamb several times during cooking and baste occasionally.
4. Remove the lamb from the oven and, once again, season generously on all sides with salt and pepper. On a large carving board, place a salad plate upside down on a dinner

plate. Transfer the lamb, exposed bone in the air, at an angle on the upside-down plate. Cover loosely with foil. Let rest for at least 25 minutes and up to 1 hour.

5. Meanwhile, test the vegetables in the roasting pan for doneness. Continue roasting if necessary. Once completely roasted, taste for seasoning. Discard the bouquet garni. Transfer the vegetables to a large platter, leaving the juices in the pan. Cover and keep warm in a low oven until the lamb is ready.

6. Place the roasting pan with cooking juices over moderate heat and cook to caramelize the juices, 2 to 3 minutes. Be careful not to burn them. Spoon off any excess fat and add several tablespoons of cold water to deglaze the pan, scraping up any bits that cling to the bottom. Turn the heat to low and simmer until reduced by half, 5 to 7 minutes. Strain through a fine-mesh sieve. Taste for seasoning and pour into a warmed sauce boat. Set aside and keep warm.

7. To serve, carve the lamb in very thin slices. Add any juices the meat releases to the sauce boat. Arrange the lamb alongside the vegetables on the platter. Serve, passing the sauce.

TEN TO TWELVE SERVINGS

WINE SUGGESTIONS: While a Cabernet is traditional with lamb, the acidity of the potato-artichoke mixture calls for a more acidic, floral white. I enjoy a white Côtes du Rhône or, if I'm feeling in a festive mood, a white Châteauneuf du Pape or Hermitage. For a red, I would pick Côtes du Rhône.

It is not really an exaggeration to say that peace and happiness begin,
geographically, where garlic is used in cooking.
MARCEL BOULESTIN

GIGOT PROVENÇAL: OVEN-ROASTED LEG OF LAMB

Our Provençal butcher, Roland Henny, sells the finest local lamb; it has a mild, delicate flavor, just faintly perfumed with wild thyme and rosemary from the land on which the animals graze. I roast it ever so simply and add a healthy touch of garlic, roasted whole in its skin, making for a meltingly tender dish.

EQUIPMENT: One oval baking dish just slightly larger than the lamb
(about 9 x 13 inches; 23 x 33 cm)

6 plump, fresh whole heads of garlic
2 large bouquet garni: each made up of several sprigs of parsley, several sprigs of
    thyme, summer savory, rosemary, and several fresh bay leaves, securely fastened
    with household twine
About 2 tablespoons extra-virgin olive oil
Sea salt and freshly ground black pepper to taste
1 leg of lamb, with bone (about 5 pounds; 2.5 kg), carefully trimmed of fat and tied (ask
    your butcher to do this for you)
Several large sprigs of rosemary (optional)

1. Preheat the oven to 425°F (220°C; gas mark 7/8).
2. Trim and discard the top third of each head of garlic. Place on the baking dish, cut side up, and drizzle with oil. Arrange the bouquet garni around the garlic. Place a small metal roasting rack on top of the baking dish. (Alternatively, place meat on a bed of rosemary.) Rub the lamb all over with olive oil. Season the lamb generously with salt and pepper. Place the lamb on top of the rack or bed of herbs so it will roast evenly, not steam. Place the baking dish in the oven and roast, allowing 10 to 12 minutes per pound (500 g) for medium rare, 15 minutes for medium. Turn the lamb several times during cooking and baste occasionally.
3. Remove the lamb from the oven and, once again, season generously. On a large carving board, place a salad plate upside down on a dinner plate. Transfer the lamb, exposed bone in the air, at an angle on the upside-down plate. Tent with foil and let rest for at least 25 minutes and up to 1 hour.

(continued on next page)

LEFT: *Patricia removes the lamb from the bread oven before letting it rest.*
RIGHT: *Walter, the family meat carver, at work on a freshly roasted leg of lamb.*

4. Transfer the garlic to a large platter, leaving the juices in the pan. Cover and keep warm in a low oven until the lamb is ready.

5. Meanwhile, prepare the sauce: Place the roasting pan over moderate heat and scrape up any bits that cling to the bottom. Cook for 2 to 3 minutes, scraping and stirring until the liquid is almost caramelized. Do not let it burn. Spoon off and discard any excess fat. Add several tablespoons of cold water to deglaze (hot water would cloud the sauce). Bring to a boil, turn the heat to low, and simmer until thickened, about 5 minutes.

6. Strain the sauce through a fine-mesh sieve and pour into a sauce boat. Carve the lamb in very thin slices. Arrange on a large warmed serving platter, surrounded by the garlic.

TEN TO FIFTEEN SERVINGS

WINE SUGGESTION: A good Bordeaux, preferably from the Paulliac region, is the most classic French choice. In our region we are more likely to drink a peppery, full-bodied red, such as one from the village of Gigondas.

I pray that death may strike me in the middle of a large meal.
I wish to be buried under the tablecloth between four large dishes.

SPIT-ROASTED BRINE-CURED PORK

George Germon and Johanne Killeen are neighbors of ours in Provence, and besides sharing a passion for cooking and hearty eating, we also share a love for cooking over an open fire. George is particularly adept at fire-building and rotisserie cooking. When an entree such as this Spit-Roasted Brine-Cured Pork is on the menu, I let him take charge, and he fires up the waist-high fireplace we installed as a centerpiece of our kitchen. George's special cure uses many of the herbs and spices found on our property, including the juniper berries that grow wild in the oak and pine woods and the fennel grains we gather from plants once they have gone to seed. Be sure to choose a pork roast that is not completely devoid of fat. The fat will melt and circle the pork as it roasts, keeping the pork moist and delicious. Excess fat will fall into the drip pan to season vegetables resting below. For those who do not have access to a rotisserie, oven directions are included.

⅔ cup (100 g) sugar
⅓ cup (150 g) coarse sea salt
15 peppercorns
8 juniper berries
2 tablespoons fennel seeds
10 sprigs of fresh rosemary
10 sprigs of fresh thyme
6 fresh bay leaves
3 to 4 pounds (1.5 to 2 kg) boneless pork loin, rolled and tied with string at 1½-inch (3-cm) intervals

GARNISH
8 carrots, trimmed and peeled
4 plump, fresh heads of garlic, with the top third of each trimmed and discarded

1. In a large, nonmetallic container, combine the sugar, salt, peppercorns, juniper berries, fennel seeds, 5 sprigs of rosemary, 5 sprigs of thyme, and bay leaves. Add 1 quart (1 l) of boiling water and stir to dissolve the sugar and salt completely. Add 3 quarts (3 l) of cold water to cool the brine.

2. Place the pork in the brine, making sure it is completely submerged. If the meat floats to the surface, weight it down with a plate. Cover and refrigerate. Allow the pork to cure

(continued on next page)

for at least 24 hours and up to 48 hours, depending on how much of a cured flavor you want the meat to acquire. The brine will draw out moisture from the meat and accentuate its natural, sweet flavor. A longer curing process will produce a saltier and more pronounced taste from the brine.

3. Several hours before roasting, remove the pork from the brine and place it on a rack to drain. Allow the meat to come to room temperature. Remember to reserve some of the brine for basting the meat.

4. With paper towels, completely dry the pork. Lace the remaining sprigs of rosemary and thyme under the string.

5. For open-fire roasting: Build a hot fire with aromatic woods. Place a rotisserie in front of the fire with a drip pan underneath. Place the carrots and garlic in the roasting pan. Make certain your spit is either chrome-plated or made of stainless steel. Other metals could taint the flavor of the meat. Put the spit through the center of the roast so it will be properly balanced as it turns. Take your time doing this: If the spit does not turn smoothly, excess strain will be put on the rotisserie, and the meat may cook unevenly. The distance between the fire and the rotisserie will determine the intensity of the heat.

Place the spit on its rack, with the meat about 6 inches (15 cm) in front of the fire. After about 20 minutes, the fat on the outside of the pork should melt and begin to self-baste the meat. If this has not happened after 30 minutes, move the spit closer to the fire. But if the roast begins to brown too quickly, move the spit farther from the heat. Keep in mind that although you are cooking with a live fire, the heat should not be extreme. It is the residual heat of the flame that will slow-roast the pork, and it should take about the same time as conventional oven roasting. Do not worry if the herbs singe and smoke a bit. This is how they impart their heady fragrance to the meat. Maintain the heat of the fire by adding logs as necessary.

Cook the pork until it reaches an internal temperature of 150°F (65°C). Pork is safe to eat at 140°F (60°C). Total roasting time should be 1 to 2 hours, depending on the intensity of the fire. Remove the spit from its rack and then from the roast. See Step 7.

6. For oven roasting: Preheat the oven to 500°F (260°C; gas mark 9). Place the pork on a roasting rack in a roasting pan. Arrange the carrots and garlic around the pork. (The rack will prevent the pork from sticking to the pan and will allow it to roast more evenly.) Place in the center of the oven and roast until the skin is crackling and brown and the meat begins to exude fat and juices, 20 to 30 minutes.

Lower heat to 350°F (175°C; gas mark 4/5) and baste with the juices from the pan, adding brine liquid if necessary—about ½ cup (12.5 cl) at a time—to maintain a thin layer of liquid in the pan at all times. Baste at 20-minute intervals.

Roast for about 25 minutes per pound (500 g), or until the pork reaches an internal temperature of 150°F (65°C). Remove from the oven.

7. Place the roast on a cooling rack over a pan or plate to catch the drippings. Loosely tent with foil and set aside in a warm place to rest about 20 minutes. To serve, remove and discard the string and the herbs. Cut the pork into thick slices and place on a warmed platter, along with the carrots and garlic. Drizzle with drippings collected during the resting period and serve.

TWELVE SERVINGS

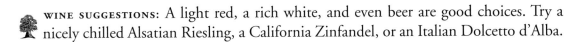 **WINE SUGGESTIONS:** A light red, a rich white, and even beer are good choices. Try a nicely chilled Alsatian Riesling, a California Zinfandel, or an Italian Dolcetto d'Alba.

BROWN RICE FROM THE CAMARGUE

The Camargue is France's marshy rice-growing region just south of Arles, the city made famous by Van Gogh. Here farmers produce a uniquely nutty, fragrant brown rice known as *ris de camargue*. The grains, so the growers claim, take on a special richness because they're air-dried by the mighty Provençal wind, the mistral. But there's more than folklore to the flavor! Any excellent brown rice can be used here. In this recipe the rice is "toasted" in the oil before the liquid is added, to intensify the nutty essence of the grain.

> 2 tablespoons extra-virgin olive oil
> 1 cup (195 g) best-quality brown rice
> 1 teaspoon fine sea salt
> Bouquet garni: a generous bunch of parsley stems, fresh bay leaves, basil leaves, rosemary leaves, celery leaves, and sprigs of thyme, wrapped in the green part of a leek and securely fastened
> 2 cups (50 cl) water, Potager Stock (page 321), or homemade Chicken Stock (page 322)

In a large, heavy-duty saucepan, combine the oil and rice, and toss to coat. Cook over low heat, stirring with a wooden spoon, until the rice begins to crackle and a lightly toasted aroma wafts through the kitchen, 2 to 3 minutes. Add the salt, bouquet garni, and water. Stir and bring to the boil over high heat. Cover, turn the heat to low, and cook without stirring for 30 to 35 minutes. Once cooked, the rice should be firm to the bite and not mushy. Remove and discard the bouquet garni and serve.

SIX SERVINGS

◡: **ON STORING RICE** :◞   Remember that rice can turn rancid over time and should not be considered a "for life" pantry item. Buy in small quantities and date your packages. Try to keep grains such as brown rice in the refrigerator, and store for no more than six months.

◡: **THE BOUQUET GARNI** :◞   A bouquet garni is a simple way to infuse almost any soup, stock, or grain with the subtle perfumes of herbs and spices. The classic bouquet garni consists of parsley, thyme, bay leaf, and a few peppercorns, but use your imagination. Rice is particularly happy with basil, juniper berries, rosemary, and thyme.

BASMATI RICE

Indian basmati rice, which translates as "queen of fragrance," wins me over on aroma alone. Grown in the foothills of the Himalayas, basmati is a long-grain rice that I think of as feminine, almost flirtatious in its delicacy and tenderness. If you have a choice of varieties, select the highest grade Dehradun. In this recipe I don't embellish the rice at all but simply boil it in the traditional manner, in lightly salted water. For a fluffier, more tender result, the rice can be soaked in cold water for 1 hour to soften the grains. When pressed for time, I simply give it a quick wash in cold water. Because the grains of basmati rice are small and light, they cook quickly, an additional plus when time is of the essence. Note that cooking times for rice are not constant; the time will vary according to the freshness of the rice, the pan in which it is cooked, and the exact degree of heat.

1 cup (175 g) basmati rice
1⅓ cups (33 cl) water
¾ teaspoon fine sea salt

1. Pour the rice in a large bowl and cover with cold water. Swish the grains around with your fingers to allow any impurities to float to the top. Carefully pour off and discard the water. Set the rice aside.
2. In a medium-size saucepan with a tight-fitting lid, bring the water to a roiling boil over high heat. Add the rice and salt, and stir. Once the water boils, stir again, to make sure the rice does not stick to the bottom of the pan. Turn the heat to very low, cover, and cook until the rice is tender and has absorbed all the water, 10 to 15 minutes. Do not stir. Remove the pan from the heat and allow the rice to relax, covered, for up to 15 minutes. Fluff the rice with 2 forks, and serve.

FOUR SERVINGS

10
DESSERTS

WITH ORCHARDS OF CHERRIES, WILD as well as greengage plums, green and purple figs, three varieties of pears, one wild peach, a trio of apricots, a pair of almond trees, and a fledgling hazelnut, it's no wonder that fruit and nut desserts feature prominently on the Chanteduc dessert menu. From May to December the harvest supplies the makings of Cherry-Almond Tart, Cherry & Goat Cheese Gratin, Provençal Honey-Almond Cookies, and our ever-favorite Apricot-Honey-Almond Tart. Come fall, the last grapes on the vines star in the Winemaker's Grape Cake, while our single wild apple tree supplies fruit for Eli's Apple Crisp. Even the herb garden plays a role, flavoring the delicate Fresh Lemon Verbena Ice Cream, and come fall, I gather every bit of fruit I can to create our bread oven favorite, Baked Fruit & Honey with Beaumes de Venise.

FACING PHOTOGRAPH: *A view from the courtyard at Chanteduc, looking up to the windows of the Pigeonnier, where the farmers once raised pigeons. Below, Walter carved a heart into a door leading to a storage area for clay garden pots and tools.*

WINEMAKER'S GRAPE CAKE

Come September, I prepare this cake often, taking advantage of whatever clusters of grapes I can find on our vines after harvesting. At Chanteduc, we grow a mixture of Grenache, Syrah, and Morvèdre grapes, each of which contributes its own personality to the wine and to this cake. I love the rustic crunch that seeded grapes impart, and so I also recommend trying Zinfandel, Cornith, and Cabernet grapes. For seedless grapes, try Red Flame. The original recipe was given to me by Rolando Beramendi at Italy's fine Tuscan estate Capezzana, where this intriguing not-too-sweet cake appears frequently at the table during the fall harvest. Note that the cake is prepared with half butter and half olive oil, producing an unusually light and moist cake.

EQUIPMENT: One 9-inch (23-cm) springform pan

Butter and flour for preparing the cake pan
2 large eggs, at room temperature
⅔ cup (135 g) sugar
4 tablespoons (2 ounces; 60 g) unsalted butter, melted
¼ cup (6 cl) extra-virgin olive oil
⅓ cup (8 cl) whole milk
½ teaspoon pure vanilla extract
1½ cups (200 g) unbleached all-purpose flour
¾ teaspoon baking powder
A pinch of sea salt
Grated zest (yellow peel) of 1 lemon
Grated zest (orange peel) of 1 orange
10 ounces (300 g) small, fresh purple grapes (see above for varieties)
Confectioners' sugar, for garnish

1. Preheat the oven to 350°F (175°C; gas mark 4/5).
2. Generously butter and flour the springform pan, tapping out any excess flour. Set aside.
3. In the bowl of an electric mixer fitted with a whisk, beat the eggs and sugar until thick and lemon-colored, about 3 minutes. Add the butter, oil, milk, and vanilla extract, and mix until blended.
4. Sift the flour, baking powder, and salt into a large bowl. Add the lemon zest and orange zest, and toss to coat the zest with flour. Spoon the mixture into the bowl of batter and stir with a wooden spoon until thoroughly blended. Scrape down the sides of the bowl and mix once more. Set aside for 10 minutes to allow the flour to absorb the liquids.
5. Stir about ¾ of the grapes into the batter. Spoon the batter into the prepared cake pan and smooth out the top with a spatula.

(continued on next page)

6. Place the pan in the center of the oven. Bake for 15 minutes, then sprinkle the top of the cake with the remaining grapes. Bake until the top is a deep golden brown and the cake feels quite firm when pressed with a fingertip, about 40 minutes more, for a total baking time of 55 minutes. Remove to a rack to cool. After 10 minutes, run a knife along the sides of the pan. Release and remove the side of the springform pan, leaving the cake on the pan base. Sprinkle with confectioners' sugar just before serving. Serve at room temperature, cut into thin wedges.

EIGHT TO TWELVE SERVINGS

WINE SUGGESTIONS: Grape cake is an ideal match for *vin santo,* the rich, smooth, aromatic sweet wine prepared in small quantities on many Italian estates.

❧ **IN A PURPLE HAZE** ❧ Over time, I have identified the mystery that discourages many shoppers from buying grapes: the inevitable hazy white film. Though one might understandably assume it's due to a spray of pesticide, the film is in fact a natural substance produced by the grape. It acts as a protective covering to prevent moisture from penetrating the fruit. It also keeps the skin from cracking when the grape loses moisture. Even better, the film contains nothing toxic! You will find the same harmless film on plums.

A selection of grapes from the Vaison market.

LAVENDER HONEY ICE CREAM

Honey-making is a thriving cottage industry in my corner of Provence, where independent honey makers are about as numerous as independent cheese makers. I have a favorite, sold at the stand right in front of the post office. Since adding local honey to my pantry, I find I often substitute it for sugar in any recipe where it makes sense. This one was inspired by chef-proprietor Charles Mouret of the family-run restaurant Saint-Hubert in the nearby village of Entrechaux. One evening when I declined dessert, Mme. Mouret insisted I try their lavender honey ice cream. I never regretted it! If you can't find lavender honey, choose a first-rate fresh raw honey with a strong bouquet, preferably one that is not more than a year old. It should still be fragrant, and it should not be too dark. You want the ice cream to turn the color of a pale eggshell.

EQUIPMENT: One ice-cream maker with a 1 quart (1-l) capacity

2 teaspoons best-quality pure vanilla extract
6 large egg yolks
¾ cup (650 g) creamy lavender honey or other good, fresh raw honey
2 cups (50 cl) whole milk
1 cup (25 cl) heavy cream

1. In the bowl of an electric mixer, beat the vanilla extract, egg yolks, and honey at high speed until thick and lemon-colored, about 1 minute. Set aside.
2. In a large saucepan, heat the milk over moderate heat just until tiny bubbles form around the edges of the pan. Gradually pour ⅓ of the boiling milk into the egg yolk mixture, whisking constantly. Return the milk and egg yolk mixture to the remaining milk in the saucepan. Turn the heat to low and, keeping the custard below the simmering point, stir constantly with a wooden spoon in a figure-8 motion until the mixture reaches the thickness of heavy cream, or 165°F (75°C) on a candy thermometer. Do not let it boil. For a visual test, run your finger down the back of the spoon; if the mark holds, the mixture is sufficiently cooked. The whole process should take about 5 minutes.
3. Remove the custard from the heat and immediately stir in the cream to stop the cooking. To achieve a perfectly smooth texture, strain the mixture through a fine-mesh sieve. Cool completely before placing the mixture in an ice cream maker. To speed cooling, transfer the cream to a large chilled bowl. Place the bowl inside a slightly larger bowl filled with ice cubes and water. Stir occasionally. To test the temperature, dip your fingers into the mixture. The cream should feel cold to the touch. The process should take about 30 minutes.
4. When thoroughly cooled, transfer to an ice-cream maker and freeze according to the manufacturer's instructions.

ONE QUART (1 L) ICE CREAM

APRICOT≠HONEY≠ALMOND TART

For the past ten years, this has been my most successful dessert, hands down. I love to make it and I love to eat it. It is so dazzling to look at that your guests will be incredulous, exclaiming "*You* made that?" when you bring it to the table. And the recipe, from start to finish, is child's play. The pastry is simply patted into the pan. It's so foolproof that during the sizzling summer months I often get up very early and bake the tart first thing, before the idea of lighting an oven strikes me as a criminal act.

The purely Provençal combination of apricots, almonds, and honey seems to have been made in heaven, for when apricots are at their peak, the fruit truly tastes as though it has been infused with the flavors of honey and of almonds. When apricots are out of season, I use fresh purple figs, plums, or a combination of fruits such as peaches, apricots, and nectarines. Whenever pitted fruits are used, be sure to cut them in half and bake them cut side up, so the juices will reduce and intensify during baking. Baked this way, there is also less of a tendency for the juices to leak into the crust.

EQUIPMENT: One 9-inch (23-cm) fluted tart pan with removable bottom

THE CRUST

    Unsalted butter for preparing the tart pan
    8 tablespoons (4 ounces; 120 g) unsalted butter, melted and cooled
    ½ cup (100 g) sugar
    ⅛ teaspoon pure almond extract
    ⅛ teaspoon pure vanilla extract
    A pinch of fine sea salt
    1¼ cups plus 1 tablespoon (180 g) unbleached all-purpose flour

    2 tablespoons finely ground unblanched almonds

THE CREAM

    ½ cup (12.5 cl) heavy cream
    1 large egg, lightly beaten
    ½ teaspoon pure almond extract
    ½ teaspoon pure vanilla extract
    2 tablespoons raw full-flavored honey, such as lavender
    1 tablespoon superfine flour, such as Wondra

    About 1½ pounds (750 g) fresh apricots, pitted and halved (do not peel)
    Confectioners' sugar, for garnish

(continued on next page)

FACING PHOTOGRAPH: *Variations on a theme: Raspberry Tart and Apricot-Honey-Almond Tart.*

1. Preheat the oven to 375°F (190°C; gas mark 5).

2. Butter the bottom and sides of the tart pan and set aside.

3. In a large bowl, combine the butter and sugar and, with a wooden spoon, stir to blend. Add the almond and vanilla extracts, salt, and flour, and stir to form a soft, cookielike dough. Do not let it form a ball. Transfer the dough to the center of the buttered pan. Using the tips of your fingers, evenly press the pastry onto the bottom and sides of the pan. The dough will be quite thin.

4. Place the pan in the center of the oven and bake until the dough is slightly puffy and set, about 12 to 15 minutes. Sprinkle the almonds on the crust. (This will prevent the crust from becoming soggy.)

5. Meanwhile, prepare the cream: In a medium-size bowl, combine the cream, egg, almond and vanilla extracts, and honey, and whisk to blend. Whisk in the flour.

6. Starting just inside the edge of the prebaked pastry pan, neatly overlap the halved apricots, cut side up, at a slight angle. Make 2 or 3 concentric circles, working toward the center. Fill the center with the remaining apricots.

7. Pour the cream evenly over the fruit. Place in the center of the oven and bake until the filling is firm and the pastry is a deep golden brown, 50 to 60 minutes. The apricots will shrivel slightly. Remove to a rack to cool. Sprinkle with confectioners' sugar just before serving.

EIGHT SERVINGS

VARIATION: To prepare this tart with fresh raspberries, prebake the dough as directed. Add the cream and bake until the filling is firm and the pastry is a deep golden brown, about 10 minutes. Remove from the oven and allow to cool. At serving time, arrange a single layer of raspberries (about 12 ounces; 375 g) on top of the filling. Sprinkle with confectioners' sugar just before serving.

A tart variation prepared with fresh purple figs.

FIADONE: CORSICAN CHEESECAKE

Light, fluffy, with a tinge of lemon, this cheesecake might well be considered Corsica's flagship dessert. It would be hard to spend a day on this sunny Mediterranean island without encountering some version of what the Corsicans call *fiadone.* I first sampled these tiny individual cheesecakes at a village café deep in the center of the island, where they served individual lemony cheesecakes along with a zesty lemon soda, perfect for a blazing hot July afternoon. You will find this cake much lighter than a traditional cheesecake, and far more delicate.

EQUIPMENT: One 9-inch (23-cm) springform pan

Unsalted butter and flour for preparing the cake pan
2 teaspoons pure vanilla extract
6 large eggs, separated
⅔ cup (130 g) sugar
2 pounds (1 kg) whole-milk ricotta (or two 15-ounce containers)
Grated zest (yellow peel) of 2 lemons, blanched and refreshed
Confectioners' sugar, for garnish

1. Preheat the oven to 325°F (165°C; gas mark 4).
2. Generously butter and flour the pan, tapping out any excess flour. Set aside.
3. In the bowl of an electric mixer fitted with a whisk, beat the vanilla extract, egg yolks, and sugar at high speed until thick and lemon-colored, about 3 minutes. At low speed, gradually incorporate the ricotta and lemon zest. Beat until smooth.
4. In the bowl of an electric mixer fitted with a whisk, beat the egg whites at top speed until stiff but not dry. Whisk ⅓ of the egg whites into the cheese mixture and combine thoroughly. With a rubber spatula, gently fold in the remaining egg whites. Do this slowly and patiently. Do not overmix, but be sure that the mixture is well blended and no streaks of white remain.
5. Pour the batter into the prepared cake pan. Place the pan in the center of the oven and bake until the cheesecake is a deep golden brown, is fairly firm in the center, pulls away from the sides of the pan, and a toothpick inserted in the center comes out clean, about 1 hour and 30 minutes. Transfer to a baking rack to cool. Once cooled, cover the cheesecake with plastic wrap and refrigerate until serving time. (The cake can be made 1 day in advance.) To serve, release the sides of the springform pan, leaving the cheesecake on the pan base. Sprinkle the top generously with confectioners' sugar and serve, cut into very thin wedges.

SIXTEEN TO TWENTY SERVINGS

CROQUETTES: PROVENÇAL HONEY-ALMOND COOKIES

Croquettes, or firm, dry cookies perfumed with the almonds and honey of Provence, can be found at nearly every pastry shop in the region. Recipes vary from baker to baker, but these crunchy cookies, which closely resemble the Italian *biscotti,* are dear to the Provençal heart. I consider my friend Rita Kramer the ultimate cookie sleuth. She will spend days perusing pastry windows, examining displays, and sampling sweets before delivering her careful judgment. These are my interpretation of the honey *croquettes* she judged best in our village, those found at a small bakery off Place Montfort. Like many bakers, I often add a touch of fragrant orange flower water to the dough, though it is optional. When *croquettes* are carefully stored in an airtight container, they remain fresh for weeks. They are a fine accompaniment to a cup of coffee or tea and are ideal with Lavender Honey Ice Cream (page 279) or for dipping into homemade orange liqueur, "44" (page 337).

Almonds in many stages: fresh from the tree,
dried in their shells, and freshly cracked.

3 large eggs

6 ounces (180 g) raw honey

1 cup (200 g) sugar

½ teaspoon pure vanilla extract

½ teaspoon pure almond extract

2 teaspoons orange flower water (optional) (see Note, page 168)

A pinch of salt

10 ounces (300 g) whole unblanched almonds

2¼ to 2½ cups (300 to 335 g) unbleached all-purpose flour

1. Preheat the oven to 350°F (175°C; gas mark 4/5).

2. In the bowl of an electric mixer fitted with a whisk, whisk the eggs, honey, sugar, vanilla and almond extracts, orange flower water, and salt at medium speed until thoroughly blended, about 2 minutes. With a wooden spoon, stir in the almonds. Gradually incorporate the flour, spoonful by spoonful, enough to form a soft dough.

3. Flour your hands thoroughly and divide the dough into 4 pieces. The dough will be very soft and sticky. With your hands, form each piece of dough into a log about 3 inches (7.5 cm) wide and 11 inches (27.5 cm) long. Place on a nonstick baking sheet.

4. Place the baking sheet in the center of the oven and bake until the dough is an even, light golden brown, 25 to 30 minutes. Remove the baking sheet from the oven and transfer the logs to a rack to cool for about 10 minutes. Do not turn off the oven.

5. Transfer each log to a cutting board and cut with a sharp knife into diagonal slices ½ inch (1 cm) thick. Stand the slices upright on the baking sheet. Return the baking sheet to the center of the oven and bake until the cookies are a deep golden brown, 10 to 15 minutes more. Remove from the oven and transfer the cookies to a rack to cool. They should be dry and crisp. Once cooled, the cookies can be stored in an airtight container for up to 1 month.

ABOUT 60 COOKIES

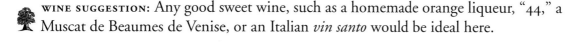 WINE SUGGESTION: Any good sweet wine, such as a homemade orange liqueur, "44," a Muscat de Beaumes de Venise, or an Italian *vin santo* would be ideal here.

TIP: When using honey in place of sugar in a recipe, the ratio of the substitution is 1 to 1.

What is a roofless cathedral compared to a well-built pie?
WILLIAM MAGINN

CHERRY⸗ALMOND TART

Cherries and almonds are natural partners, and this is one dish that heads my hit parade of desserts in May and June when there is an abundance of the fruit on our trees and at the market. Serve this with fresh Vanilla-Bean Ice Cream (page 289) and watch your guests swoon.

EQUIPMENT: One 9-inch (23-cm) fluted tart pan with removable bottom

THE PASTRY

    8 tablespoons (4 ounces; 120 g) unsalted butter, melted and cooled, plus additional
        for preparing the tart pan
    ½ cup (100 g) sugar
    A pinch of fine sea salt
    ⅛ teaspoon pure almond extract
    ⅛ teaspoon pure vanilla extract
    2 tablespoons finely ground blanched almonds
    1¼ cups plus 1 tablespoon (180 g) all-purpose flour

THE FILLING

    5 tablespoons heavy cream
    1 large egg, lightly beaten
    ½ teaspoon pure almond extract
    ½ teaspoon pure vanilla extract
    ¼ cup (50 g) sugar
    1 tablespoon all-purpose flour
    2 tablespoons finely ground blanched almonds
    1 tablespoon kirsch (cherry eau-de-vie)

    4 tablespoons finely ground blanched almonds
    1 pound (500 g) fresh cherries, pitted
    Confectioners' sugar, for garnish

(continued on next page)

1. Preheat the oven to 350°F (175°C; gas mark 4/5).
2. Butter the bottom and sides of the tart pan. Set aside.
3. In a medium-size bowl, combine the butter, sugar, salt, almond and vanilla extracts, and almonds. Stir with a spoon to blend. Gradually incorporate enough flour to form a smooth, soft dough. (The dough should resemble soft cookie dough.) Place the dough in the center of the buttered pan. With the tips of your fingers, press the pastry evenly on the bottom and sides of the pan. The dough will be quite thin. (You do not need to weight or prick the shell.)
4. Place the lined tart pan in the center of the oven and bake until the dough is just slightly puffy and turns a very pale brown, about 10 minutes. Remove from the oven and set aside. Do not turn off the oven.
5. Meanwhile, make the filling: In a small bowl, combine the cream, egg, and almond and vanilla extracts, and whisk to blend. Stir in the sugar, flour, ground almonds, and kirsch.
6. Sprinkle 2 tablespoons of ground almonds on top of the prebaked pastry shell. (They will prevent the crust from becoming soggy.)
7. Arrange the cherries in a single layer in the pastry shell. Pour the filling over the cherries. Sprinkle with the remaining 2 tablespoons of ground almonds. Place in the center of the oven and bake until the filling is firm and the pastry is a deep golden brown, about 45 minutes. Remove to a rack to cool. Sprinkle with confectioners' sugar just before serving.

EIGHT SERVINGS

❧ ON ALMONDS ☙ The almond is actually a close relative of the peach, plum, and apricot, so it is no surprise that the trees grow harmoniously in our small orchard. The almond belongs to the rose family, and the nut is actually the seed of a fruit that has both a sweet edible layer and a hard stony layer. Essentially, almonds fall into two categories: bitter almonds, which can be toxic if eaten in quantities and are primarily reserved for the production of almond extract; and the other type, the one we enjoy in tarts, pastries, and savory dishes. As far back as the Middle Ages, almonds were in great demand for making such stylish foods as marzipan and "almond milk," a mixture of water and ground almonds. The most delicate variety of almonds sold for eating are Jordan almonds. Long and thin in shape, the name is a variation of the French word *jardin,* or garden.

VANILLA-BEAN ICE CREAM WITH FRESH CHERRIES

When it comes to cooking, sometimes it's fun to gild the lily. This is that leaf of gold created to stand on its own or to embellish a fresh Cherry-Almond Tart (page 287). I love replacing regular cream with thick crème fraîche, making for a tart, puckery ice cream—a dramatic match with cherries.

EQUIPMENT: One ice-cream maker with a 1-quart (1-l) capacity

4 plump, moist vanilla beans
2 cups (50 cl) whole milk
6 large egg yolks
¾ cup (150 cl) crème fraîche
2 cups (8 ounces; 250 g) fresh cherries, pitted and quartered

1. Flatten the vanilla beans and cut them in half lengthwise. With a demitasse spoon or small knife, scrape out the seeds and place them in a bowl. Reserve the pods.
2. In a large saucepan, combine the milk and vanilla pods over high heat. Bring just to a boil, remove from the heat, cover, and set aside to infuse for 15 minutes.
3. In the bowl of an electric mixer fitted with a whisk, beat the vanilla seeds, egg yolks, and sugar until thick and lemon-colored, about 3 minutes. Set aside.
4. Strain the milk with the vanilla pods through a fine-mesh sieve into a large saucepan. Pour the milk into another saucepan and place over moderate heat just until tiny bubbles form around the edges of the pan. Pour ⅓ of the milk into the egg yolk mixture, whisking constantly. Return this milk and egg yolk mixture to the remaining milk in the saucepan. Turn the heat to low and, keeping the custard below the simmering point, stir constantly with a wooden spoon in a figure-8 motion until the mixture reaches the thickness of heavy cream, or 165°F (75°C) on a candy thermometer. Do not let it boil. For a visual test, run your finger down the back of the spoon; if the mark holds, the mixture is sufficiently cooked. The whole process should take about 5 minutes.
5. Remove the custard from the heat and immediately stir in the cream to stop the cooking. To achieve a perfectly smooth texture, strain the mixture through a fine-mesh sieve. Cool completely before placing the mixture in an ice cream maker. To speed cooling, transfer the cream to a large chilled bowl. Place that bowl inside a slightly larger bowl filled with ice cubes and water. Stir occasionally. To test the temperature, dip your fingers into the mixture. The cream should feel cold to the touch. The process should take about 30 minutes.
6. When thoroughly cooled, stir in the cherries. Transfer to an ice-cream maker and freeze according to the manufacturer's instructions.

ONE QUART (1 L) ICE CREAM

CHERRY & GOAT CHEESE GRATIN

The old saying, "Necessity is the mother of invention," proved true with this recipe. One afternoon I was "trapped" at home, waiting for a delivery man to show up. I'd intended to make this gratin with fresh cream but discovered I had none on hand. The only possible substitutes were yogurt and a very fresh young goat cheese. I gambled on the goat cheese and won. My guests were delighted, and so was I, for I had a new creation with a myriad of possibilities. Try this with cherries, a mix of berries, peaches, or raspberries, or with apricots, a personal favorite. The slight tartness of the goat cheese goes well with this, as does the flavor surprise once cooked. And while some cooks commonly think of a gratin as something with a cheese topping, in French cooking a gratin can be anything baked in a round vessel or gratin dish.

EQUIPMENT: One 10½-inch (27-cm) round porcelain baking dish

Unsalted butter for preparing the baking dish
1½ pounds (750 g) cherries, pitted
½ cup (4 ounces; 125 g) very fresh, moist goat cheese
⅓ cup (65 g) sugar
2 large eggs
½ cup (90 g) finely ground blanched almonds
A pinch of fine sea salt
½ teaspoon pure vanilla extract
½ teaspoon pure almond extract
Confectioners' sugar, for dusting the gratin

1. Preheat the oven to 375°F (190°C; gas mark 5).
2. Butter the baking dish. Arrange the cherries in a single layer.
3. In the bowl of a food processor, combine the remaining ingredients except the confectioners' sugar and process to blend. Pour the mixture over the cherries.
4. Place the baking dish in the center of the oven. Bake until the gratin is firm and a deep golden brown, about 30 minutes. Remove to a rack to cool. Dust lightly with confectioners' sugar, and serve in wedges.

SIX TO EIGHT SERVINGS

CHANTEDUC CLAFOUTIS

In the summer months, our property in Provence, as well as the market, is alive with a great mix of last-of-season cherries with first-of-season fresh raspberries, red currants, blueberries from the Auvergne, and wild blackberries from our fields. The more berries you mix here, the more complex the flavors you will achieve and the more potential applause! When preparing this with mixed fruits, I do pit the cherries for a more elegant—and less dangerous—dessert. This clafoutis should be served at room temperature, but serve it the same day you prepare it for maximum flavor.

EQUIPMENT: One 10½-inch (27-cm) round porcelain baking dish

2 tablespoons kirsch (cherry eau-de-vie)
½ cup (100 g) plus 2 tablespoons sugar
2 pounds (1 kg) mixed berries and fruit, such as pitted cherries, raspberries, blackberries, blueberries, and currants
2 large eggs
6 tablespoons heavy cream
6 tablespoons whole milk
Confectioners' sugar, for garnish

1. Preheat the oven to 425°F (220°C; gas mark 7/8).
2. In a small bowl, combine the kirsch and 2 tablespoons of sugar, and stir to dissolve the sugar. Add the berries and toss to blend. Transfer the mixture to the baking dish. Place in the center of the oven and bake until the fruit is hot and steaming, about 10 minutes. (The pre-baking will help the fruits give up the excess liquid that might make the clafoutis watery.)
3. Transfer the fruits to a colander to drain. (Reserve the juice to flavor the baked clafoutis, whipped cream, iced teas, or mineral water.) Set aside to cool, about 5 minutes. Reserve the baking dish.
4. Lower the oven temperature to 350°F (175°C; gas mark 4/5).
5. In the bowl of an electric mixer, whisk the eggs at high speed until frothy, 1 to 2 minutes. Add the remaining sugar and whisk until well blended, 1 to 2 minutes more. Add the cream, milk, and the remaining tablespoon of kirsch. Beat until well blended and set aside.
6. Transfer the drained fruits to the baking dish, arranging them in a single layer. Carefully pour the batter over the fruits, filling just to the top. (You may have an excess of batter. If so, fill to the top, place the pan in the center of the oven, and bake for 5 minutes. Then add the remaining batter. This will avoid the problem of the batter spilling over onto the floor of the oven.) Continue baking until the batter is golden and set, 35 to 40 minutes. Transfer to a rack to cool.

(continued on next page)

7. Preheat the oven broiler.

8. When the clafoutis is cool, place on a baking sheet. Sprinkle the top evenly and gener-ously with confectioners' sugar. Place under the broiler, about 1 inch (2.5 cm) from the heat. Broil until the sugar is caramelized and golden, about 1 minute. Transfer to a rack to cool.

9. Serve at room temperature, with whipped cream flavored with a touch of kirsch, with the berry cooking juices, or with Vanilla-Bean Ice Cream (page 289).

EIGHT SERVINGS

 WINE SUGGESTION: A festive aperitif, such as a champagne rosé.

⌇ CLAFOUTIS ⌇   The classical definition of a *clafoutis* is a flan or thick crêpe baked in the oven with dark cherries. The cherry stones are left intact to add flavor to the thick batter as it bakes. A dish native to the Limousin region of France, it is a rustic desert shared at the family table as a simple yet hearty and fulfilling end to a meal.

LEMON LOVER'S TART

In Provence, the lemon is considered the fruit that gives you the energy of the sun. Some even believe that when you eat a lemon, your body discharges an electric, positive force. Maybe that's why we always feel good after a healthy dose of citrus, as in this rich, creamy tart. Lemon curd—a puckery blend of eggs, butter, sugar, and lemon that thickens slowly on top of the stove—offers an incomparably pure lemon flavor and a silky smooth texture. This is a cold-weather recipe, for days when you might welcome the warmth of steam and the stove. You may initially find the long hand-beating a bit tedious, but once you sample the results, you will not be disappointed. The tart can be prepared several hours in advance and requires no last-minute preparation, making it ideal for entertaining.

> 1 recipe for a Lemon Pastry Shell (page 296)
> 2 large eggs, at room temperature
> 3 large egg yolks, at room temperature
> 1 cup (200 g) sugar
> 8 tablespoons (4 ounces; 120 g) unsalted butter, at room temperature, cut into 8 pieces
> Grated zest (yellow peel) of 2 lemons, preferably organic, blanched and refreshed
> ½ cup (12.5 cl) freshly squeezed lemon juice, strained

1. Prepare the lemon pastry shell according to the recipe directions.
2. In the top of a double boiler set over, but not touching, simmering water, combine the eggs, egg yolks, and sugar. Whisk frequently until the curd is thick and pale lemon colored, 8 to 10 minutes.
3. Add the butter, tablespoon by tablespoon, allowing each spoonful to melt before adding the next. Add the zest and lemon juice, whisking frequently over simmering water, until thick and custardlike and the first bubbles appear on the surface, about 4 minutes. The mixture should not boil. Pour the curd into the prebaked and cooled pastry shell. Smooth with the spatula and set aside until set, about 30 minutes. To serve, cut into thin wedges.

EIGHT SERVINGS

LEMON PASTRY SHELL

Pat-in-the-pan pastry shells are quick, easy, and foolproof. They have long been a part of my everyday repertoire. This one, lightened with confectioners' sugar and touched with a hint of lemon, is delicious as the base of my Lemon Lover's Tart. The dough is delicate and fragile, so be cautious once the shell is baked.

EQUIPMENT: One 9-inch (23-cm) fluted tart pan with removable bottom

8 tablespoons (4 ounces; 120 g) unsalted butter, melted and cooled, plus additional
    for buttering the tart pan
¼ teaspoon pure vanilla extract
⅛ teaspoon pure almond extract
Grated zest (yellow peel) of 1 lemon, blanched and refreshed
¼ cup (30 g) confectioners' sugar
A pinch of fine sea salt
1¼ cups plus 1 tablespoon (180 g) unbleached all-purpose flour

1. Preheat the oven to 350°F (175°C; gas mark 4/5).
2. Butter the bottom and sides of the tart pan. Set aside.
3. In a medium-size bowl, combine the butter, vanilla and almond extracts, grated zest, sugar and salt, and stir with a spoon to blend. Gradually incorporate enough flour to form a smooth, soft dough. (The dough should resemble soft cookie dough.) Place the dough in the center of the buttered pan. With the tips of your fingers, press the pastry evenly on the bottom and sides of the pan. The dough will be quite thin. (You do not need to weight or prick the shell).
4. Place the shell in the center of the oven and bake just until the dough is firm and lightly browned, 12 to 15 minutes. Remove from the oven and set aside to cool for at least 10 minutes before filling. Do not remove from the pan.

ONE 9-INCH (23-CM) PASTRY SHELL

Food is, delightfully, an area of licensed sensuality, of physical delight which will,
with luck and enduring taste buds, last our life long.

ANTONIA TILL

LEMON *POTS DE CRÈME*

S mooth, airy, with a gentle pucker of lemon, these individual golden lemon creams
make a delightfully light dessert. They are delicious with crunchy *Croquettes:* Provençal
Honey-Almond Cookies (page 284).

EQUIPMENT: Eight ½-cup (12.5-cl) ovenproof ramekins, custard cups, or *petit pots*

½ cup (12.5 cl) lemon juice (about 4 lemons)
½ cup (100 g) sugar
6 large egg yolks
1½ cups (37.5 cl) heavy cream

1. Preheat the oven to 325°F (165°C; gas mark 4).
2. In a small bowl, combine the lemon juice and sugar, and stir to dissolve thoroughly. In
a large bowl, gently whisk the egg yolks, then whisk in the cream. Whisk in the lemon
juice and sugar, combining thoroughly. Strain through a fine-mesh sieve or several layers
of cheesecloth. Let stand for 2 to 3 minutes, then remove any foam that rises to the top.
3. Place the ramekins in a baking pan large enough to hold them generously. Divide the
cream evenly among the ramekins, filling each about half full. Add enough hot tap water
to the baking pan to reach about halfway up the ramekins. Cover the pan loosely with aluminum foil to prevent a skin from forming. Place in the center of the oven and bake until
the creams are just set around the edges but still trembling in the center, 30 to 35 minutes.
4. Remove the pan from the oven and carefully remove the ramekins from the water.
Refrigerate, loosely covered, for at least 2 hours and up to 24 hours. Serve the *pots de
crème* chilled, without unmolding.

EIGHT SERVINGS

WINE SUGGESTION: A lemony Gewürztraminer *sélection de grains noble,* served lightly
chilled.

SCHAUM TORTE: MERINGUES FOR THE MONTH OF MAY

These individual meringue shells are one of the fondest memories of my Wisconsin upbringing. *Schaum Torte* is a Memorial Day specialty created to greet the season's first crop of strawberries. This torte is really a series of individual meringue kisses. Slice off the top, fill the meringue with strawberries and cream, replace the top, and dig in! My recipe is lighter than the traditional version, which includes a layer of ice cream between the layers of meringue. I prefer the simplicity of a meringue, fresh fruit, and a dollop of freshly whipped cream.

Schaum Torte: *Meringues for the Month of May.*

4 large egg whites, at room temperature
½ teaspoon cream of tartar (optional)
1 teaspoon pure vanilla extract
1 cup (200 g) superfine sugar
1 quart (1 l) fresh strawberries or mixed berries
1 tablespoon sugar
¾ cup (18.5 cl) heavy cream

1. Preheat the oven to 200°F (90°C; gas mark 1). Line a baking sheet with aluminum foil or a nonstick liner. (Do not use parchment paper or a greased-and-floured baking sheet, for meringues tend to stick to them.)

2. In a heavy-duty mixer fitted with a whisk, beat the egg whites, cream of tartar, and vanilla extract at medium-low speed until small bubbles appear and the surface is frothy, about 45 seconds. Increase the speed to medium and gradually add half of the superfine sugar, whisking until soft peaks form, about 45 seconds. Increase the speed to high and whisk until thick, stiff, glossy white peaks form, about 2 minutes more. Remove the bowl from the mixer. Sprinkle the remaining superfine sugar over the mixture and, with a large spatula, quickly and gently fold it in, working the egg whites as little as possible.

3. Using a large serving spoon, ladle 6 large, round dollops of meringue on the prepared baking sheet. Work as quickly as possible so as not to deflate the whites. Place the baking sheet in the center of the oven and bake until crisp and dry but not yet beginning to color, about 2 hours. (If the meringues begin to brown, lower the oven temperature to 150°F [65°C] or the lowest possible setting.)

4. Remove the baking sheet from the oven and, with a spatula, carefully transfer the meringues to a wire rack to cool. If they stick to the foil, they haven't sufficiently dried out; return them to the oven to dry thoroughly. (The meringues can be prepared several days in advance and stored, fully cooled, in a dry airtight container.)

5. About 2 hours before serving the meringues, rinse and stem the strawberries. Cut lengthwise into thin slices. Toss with the sugar and set aside at room temperature.

6. In a heavy-duty mixer fitted with a whisk, beat the cream until it forms soft peaks.

7. Using a sharp serrated knife, slice the top quarter off each meringue. (The meringues may chip or break off, but try to avoid transforming them to bits.) Place each meringue on a dessert plate. Spoon the strawberries into the shell, allowing the fruit to overflow onto the plate. Top the berries with the whipped cream. Place the meringue caps on top of the whipped cream and serve immediately.

SIX SERVINGS

 WINE SUGGESTION: Try this with a young Sauternes or a sweet Vouvray Moelleux from the Loire.

CHOCOLATE GOURMANDISE

When one food trend fades from fashion, the void is always filled by a slight variation. You may have ended your love affair with chocolate soufflés, but this creamy, warm chocolate dessert—a cross between a soufflé and chocolate mousse—will step in to steal your heart away. The recipe comes from Claude Udron, former chef and co-owner of the Paris restaurant Pile ou Face. It was the finale to nearly every meal I savored in that extraordinary restaurant. While the dessert must be baked at the very last minute, it can be prepared several hours in advance, making for minimal last-minute work.

EQUIPMENT: Four 1-cup (25-ml) ovenproof ramekins

Butter and flour for preparing ramekins
4 ounces (120 g) bittersweet chocolate, preferably Lindt Excellence, grated or finely chopped
8 tablespoons (4 ounces; 120 g) unsalted butter
3 large eggs
¾ cup (150 g) sugar
¼ cup (35 g) bleached all-purpose flour

1. In the top of a double boiler set over, but not touching, simmering water, combine the chocolate and butter. Whisk until melted. Set aside.
2. In the bowl of an electric mixer fitted with a whisk, gently whisk together the eggs, sugar, and flour, mixing just to blend. Gradually whisk in the chocolate-butter mixture. Set aside to rest for 1 hour, to allow the flavors to mellow.
3. Preheat the oven to 400°F (200°C; gas mark 6/7).
4. Generously butter and flour the ramekins. Place on a baking sheet. Carefully pour the mixture into the ramekins. Place the baking sheet in the center of the oven and bake just until the edges are set and the interior is still a bit liquid, 10 to 12 minutes. Transfer the ramekins to 4 dessert plates and serve immediately. (Like individual soufflés, the dessert is eaten directly from the baking dish.)

FOUR SERVINGS

WINE SUGGESTIONS: Chocolate and certain sweet wines are perfect partners. I enjoy this with a slightly chilled red Rasteau *vin doux naturel* from neighbor André Romero at the Domaine de la Soumade; the intensely fruity, cherrylike wine cries out for a match with chocolate. Other good choices are a Muscat de Beaumes de Venise, Maury Vintage from Mas Amiel in the Roussillon, a California Muscat, or a sip of good rum.

CHOCOLATE-HONEY MOUSSE

In the winter months, when most of the best fruits are out of season, I turn to chocolate for solace. This is a variation on a chocolate mousse created at the El Olivo restaurant in Madrid, where it was served rather festively and generously from a large bowl. Each guest was handed a silver spoon and encouraged to help himself. The dessert is a cinch to make and should be prepared ahead of time. I often serve it in antique footed champagne glasses, or *coupes,* making for a dramatic, old-fashioned presentation.

2 cups (50 cl) heavy cream
8 ounces (250 g) bittersweet chocolate, preferably Lindt Excellence, finely chopped
1 tablespoon raw honey, such as lavender
4 large egg whites

1. Pour half the cream into a medium-size saucepan and bring to a simmer over moderate heat. Remove the pan from the heat, add the chocolate, and stir until the chocolate is thoroughly melted and the mixture is well blended. Transfer to a large bowl. Add the honey and stir to blend. Set aside to cool to lukewarm.
2. In the bowl of a heavy-duty mixer fitted with a whisk, whisk the egg whites until stiff but not dry. Set aside.
3. In another bowl of the heavy-duty mixer fitted with a whisk, beat the remaining cream. Whisk at medium speed, gradually increasing to high speed, until the cream is lightly whipped and stiff peaks form when the whisk is lifted. Set aside.
4. Add ⅓ of the beaten egg whites to the chocolate mixture. Mix vigorously. With a large spatula, gently fold in the remaining whites. Do this slowly and patiently. Do not overmix, but be sure that the mixture is well blended and that no streaks of white remain. Fold the whipped cream into the egg and chocolate mixture.
5. Spoon the mousse into a large soufflé dish or attractive serving bowl, individual ramekins, or small bowls. Cover with plastic wrap and refrigerate until firm, about 4 hours. Serve chilled with *Croquettes:* Provençal Honey-Almond Cookies (page 284).

SIX TO EIGHT SERVINGS

WINE SUGGESTION: Try this with a distinctive sweet dessert wine, such as a well-aged Spanish Málaga.

GINGERED CONFIT OF APPLES & PEARS

I have always had a fascination for espaliered fruit trees. So once we began expanding the orchard at Chanteduc, I added a trio of espaliered pear trees, each shaped into a compact, well-trained W. The three French varieties—Comice, Poire William's, and Beurre Hardy—ripen at different times and in good years provide plenty of fruit for the table and for cooking. One of my preferred ways to use them is in this old-fashioned confit, a golden dessert of soft pears and apples bathed in a thick, transparent syrup. It's great served warm with a dollop of cream or at room temperature as a sweet end to a meal. The cooking procedure is typical of all confits: The juices of the fruits are first released, then gradually reabsorbed by the fruit, which plump up during the long, slow cooking process.

> 1⅓ cups (230 g) sugar
> Grated zest (yellow peel) of 2 lemons, blanched and refreshed
> Grated zest (orange peel) of 2 oranges, blanched and refreshed
> 1 pound (500 g) cooking pears, preferably a range of varieties
> 5 pounds (2.5 kg) cooking apples, preferably a range of varieties
> A walnut-sized knob of ginger and 10 cloves wrapped in a cheesecloth bag
> 1 teaspoon pure vanilla extract
> 3 tablespoons Poire William's (pear eau-de-vie)

1. Place the sugar, lemon zest, and orange zest in a large shallow bowl. Peel, quarter, and core the fruit, adding each piece of fruit to the mixture in the bowl as it is prepared. With your fingers, toss to coat the fruit evenly with the sugar mixture.

2. Transfer the coated fruits, sugar, and zest to a large, heavy-bottomed saucepan. Cook over the lowest heat possible until the sugar is dissolved to a clear liquid, about 20 minutes. Stir from time to time. Add the cheesecloth bag with ginger and cloves. Cook, uncovered, over the lowest heat possible until the liquid is very thick and syrupy, but the fruit still holds its form, about 3 hours. (The fruit will first release a great deal of liquid. The long, slow cooking process is necessary to permit the juices to reduce, intensify, and thicken.) Stir from time to time and keep the heat low to avoid scorching the fruit. Remove and discard the cheesecloth. Stir in the vanilla extract and pear eau-de-vie. Serve warm, with a touch of fresh cream. (The compote may be stored up to 1 month, covered and refrigerated.)

TEN TO TWELVE SERVINGS

Local pears, ready for preserving or for eating out of hand.

⌁ PLANT PEARS FOR YOUR HEIRS ∽ The expression refers to the fact that it can take a pear tree up to nine years to bear fruit. Patience, patience!

⌁ ON APPLES AND PEARS ∽ Once you come to know the different varieties of apples and pears, you will have a sense of how they behave when cooked. Golden Delicious, Granny Smith, and Northern Spy are firm-fleshed varieties that offer intense apple flavor and a pleasant tang. They also hold their shape when cooked. Mcintosh tend to fall apart, but a few can be tossed into a mixture of firm-fleshed varieties to add dimension to the flavor. For pears, the Bartlett and Bosc are the most versatile. They not only hold their shape during cooking, they impart a distinct flavor. The Anjou, though less firm, provides plenty of sweet juice for pies and tarts.

⌁ A TEST FOR RIPENESS ∽ What's the best way to tell if a pear is ripe? We tend to poke at the fruit, seeking in the flesh a tender spot, a softness. This softness, however, can also mean that it's already too late. Instead, pull on the stem of the pear. When ripe, the stem should provide little resistance to pressure.

ELI'S APPLE CRISP

Early one November my friend Eli Zabar brought over a crateful of different varieties of apples from his orchard in Provence. The sky that day was a brilliant blue, a few golden leaves were still clinging to the vines in our vineyards, and the scent of a warming apple dessert wafting through my kitchen seemed like an ideal way to end a perfect autumn Saturday. Prepare this with a good, tangy cooking apple and, if possible, combine several varieties—such as Granny Smith, Rome, Mcintosh, and Fuju—for a more complex depth of flavor and texture. This is a quick, easy, appealing, inexpensive dessert, and you don't have to make a crust!

EQUIPMENT: One 10½-inch (26.5-cm) baking dish

Unsalted butter for preparing the baking dish
3 tablespoons (1½ ounces; 45 g) unsalted butter
2 pounds (1 kg) cooking apples, peeled, cored, and cut lengthwise into 8 even wedges
2 tablespoons freshly squeezed lemon juice
½ teaspoon ground cinnamon
1½ teaspoons pure vanilla extract
2 large eggs, at room temperature
6 tablespoons sugar
1 cup (25 cl) heavy cream

1. Preheat the oven to 400°F (200°C; gas mark 6/7).
2. Generously butter the bottom and sides of the baking dish. Set aside.
3. In a large skillet, combine the butter, apples, lemon juice, and ¼ teaspoon cinnamon, and cook just until soft, about 7 minutes. Stir in ½ teaspoon of vanilla extract.
4. Transfer the apples to the baking dish, smoothing them in a single layer with a spatula.
5. In a large bowl, combine the eggs and sugar, and whisk until well blended. Add the cream, the remaining vanilla extract and cinnamon, and whisk to blend. Pour over the apples in the baking dish.
6. Place the baking dish in the center of the oven and bake until the top is a deep golden brown, 30 to 45 minutes. Do not underbake, or the results will be soggy rather than crispy. Serve in wedges, accompanied by a dollop of crème fraîche. The dessert is best served the day it is made, for the delicate flavors will fade.

EIGHT SERVINGS

*A gap in the hedge gave a view into the gardens: a border of jasmine, pansies,
and verbena which ran along the wide path was interplanted with fragrant wallflowers
the faded rose of old Cordoba leather. A long green hole snaking across the gravel drive
sent up every few yards a vertical, prismatic fan, and the multicolored drops
showered over the flowers in a perfumed cloud.*

MARCEL PROUST

*I doubt the world holds for anyone a more soul-stirring surprise
than the first adventure with ice cream.*

HEYWOOD BROUN

FRESH LEMON VERBENA ICE CREAM

One of the earliest signs of spring at Chanteduc is the sight of the first bright green shoots of lemon verbena—or *verveine*—sprouting from this hearty perennial's stalky frame. Within weeks they grow into long, pointed, rough-textured leaves with an intense lemony perfume. Throughout the spring and summer I use lemon verbena leaves liberally, preparing refreshing and lightly sedative herbal teas, or infusions, as well as this popular summer ice cream. The dessert is also delicious prepared with fresh mint or with less traditional "sweet" herbs, such as thyme or rosemary.

EQUIPMENT: One ice-cream maker with a 1-quart (1-l) capacity

2 cups (50 cl) heavy cream
1 cup (25 cl) whole milk
⅔ cup (135 g) sugar
60 fresh lemon verbena leaves

In a large saucepan, combine the cream, milk, sugar, and verbena leaves, and heat over moderate heat just until tiny bubbles form around the edges of the pan. Remove from the heat, cover, and let steep for 1 hour. Strain through a fine-mesh sieve, discarding the verbena. Refrigerate until thoroughly chilled. Transfer to an ice-cream maker and freeze according to the manufacturer's instructions. Serve with *Croquettes:* Provençal Honey-Almond Cookies (page 284).

FOUR SERVINGS

FRESH CHEESE WITH PINE NUTS & HONEY

Soft, fresh cheese drizzled with honey and sprinkled with pine nuts creates a popular Mediterranean dessert. The sweet honey counters the saltiness of cheese, and the meaty flavor and crunch of pine nuts add depth and texture. At Chanteduc I always have a variety of honeys on hand, and the market provides fresh goat's and sheep's milk cheese year-round. While our giant umbrella pines could supply us with tiny, meaty pine nuts, I gave up after one laborious attempt to extract the tiny nuts from the cones. I decided it was a lot less bothersome to purchase pine nuts in town! If you don't have time to make the cheese, buy a fresh ricotta or a fresh mild goat's cheese.

THE CHEESE

    2 cups (50 cl) small-cured whole-milk cottage cheese

    2 cups (50 cl) whole-milk yogurt

THE GARNISH

    About ½ cup (12.5 cl) strong-flavored raw honey, such as chestnut or buckwheat

    4 tablespoons pine nuts, lightly toasted and cooled

1. The day before, or the morning of the day you plan to serve the dessert, combine the cottage cheese and yogurt in the bowl of a food processor. Puree until completely smooth. Scoop the mixture into a 6-cup (1.5-l) cheesecloth-lined, perforated mold such as a porcelain *coeur à la crème* mold or a cheesecloth-lined large sieve set over a bowl. Cover loosely with a cloth. Set aside to drain at room temperature until the cheese becomes dry and firm, about 12 hours. (Do not be surprised at the quantity of liquid the cheese releases.) It is ready when no more liquid drips from it. With the back of a spoon, carefully smooth the top of the cheese. Cover and refrigerate until ready to use. (The cheese will benefit from a day's curing, to allow the flavors to meld and mellow.)

2. To serve: If you made the cheese in a perforated mold, unmold it onto a chilled serving platter. If you prepared it in a cheesecloth-lined sieve, spoon the cheese into a decorative bowl. Pass the honey and pine nuts, letting your guests drizzle their own toppings.

SIX TO EIGHT SERVINGS

Beekeeper and honey maker Christine Poquet at her stand outside the post office at the Vaison market.

◡: **A TASTE OF HONEY** :◡ I grew up on thin, runny, supermarket honey, often a not-too-fragrant blend of clover, lemon, orange, and wild flowers. So the sweet spread never intrigued me—until I discovered the thick, creamy raw honey of Provence.

I use distinctly flavored single-flower honeys such as lavender, rosemary, orange blossom, clover, and acacia for flavoring teas, on toast with butter, or simply eaten from the spoon by themselves.

For cooking, I reach for the stronger varieties, such as buckwheat and chestnut. Thyme and rosemary honeys are also excellent for recipes that rely heavily on the juxtaposition of sweet and salty, for example, with pork or ham.

To restore creamy honey to its liquid state for easier measuring and cooking, simply place the jar in tepid water. Avoid hot water because the exposure to extreme temperature can ruin the composition and flavor. Like most fine food, honey does not remain at its peak forever. Buy it in small jars and use within a year for best flavor and fragrance.

I feel a recipe is only a theme,
which an intelligent cook can play each time with a variation.
MADAME BENOIT

BAKED FRUIT & HONEY WITH BEAUMES DE VENISE

This is a favorite summer dessert at our house in Provence. When I fire up my wood-burning oven to make dinner, I frequently slip in some fresh fruit to bake in the residual heat while I serve the main course. Sometimes I use only fresh purple figs; other times I use a combination of pitted summer fruits, such as sliced peaches, apricots, nectarines, and plums, with a few raspberries and blueberries added for color and texture. Here, the sweet, honeylike flavor of Muscat de Beaumes de Venise—a rich, fortified wine—is the perfect foil for summer fruits and honey.

EQUIPMENT: One 10½-inch (27-cm) round porcelain baking dish

1 tablespoon unsalted butter, at room temperature, for preparing the baking dish
3 pounds (1.5 kg) mixed fresh fruits, such as figs, peaches, nectarines, apricots, plums, blueberries, and raspberries
2 tablespoons raw honey, heated gently to soften
4 tablespoons Muscat de Beaumes de Venise (or see Wine Suggestions for variations)

1. Preheat the oven to 375°F (190°C; gas mark 5).
2. Generously butter the baking dish. If using a mixture of pitted fruits, halve them and layer them in the dish, slightly overlapping and cut side up. Scatter the mixed berries on top. Drizzle with the honey and some of the Muscat de Beaumes de Venise. Place in the center of the oven and bake until the fruits are soft, plump, and tender, about 30 minutes. Remove from the oven, drizzle with the remaining Muscat de Beaumes de Venise, and serve, accompanied by Lavender Honey Ice Cream (page 279).

FOUR TO SIX SERVINGS

WINE SUGGESTIONS: My favorite muscats come from the vineyards of Domaine de Coyeaux and Domaine Durban in the nearby village of Beaumes de Venise. Varied sweet fortified wines can be served here, including a French Banuyls, an Italian Moscato, or a dark Spanish sherry such as a Gonzalez Byass Oloroso Dulce, Soldera 1847.

CHUNKY PEACH ICE CREAM

Peach trees are plentiful in Provence but difficult to grow on our land. We have a single wild peach called *pêche de vigne* since it traditionally sprouted up between the vines. Every peach tree at Chanteduc has been short-lived but dearly loved. One September when I was in Paris, a friend staying at the house faxed me daily "peach reports." She spoke lovingly to the ripening fruit on the beautiful white-fleshed *pêche blanche* tree, begging it not to fall until I arrived. That year we had a bumper crop! When peaches are in season, this is a sublime way to enjoy them. This ice cream is light and makes best use of the fragile, fleeting peach flavor by using chunks of the fruit rather than turning it into a puree.

EQUIPMENT: One ice-cream maker with a 1-quart (1-l) capacity

2 pounds (1 kg) ripe peaches (6 to 8)
2 tablespoons fresh lemon juice
¼ cup (50 g) sugar
1 cup (25 cl) heavy cream

1. In a large pot of boiling water, blanch the peaches for several seconds. Transfer to a colander to drain. Rinse quickly with cold water to stop the cooking and make the fruit easier to peel. Peel, halve, and pit the peaches. Place the peach halves in a bowl and crush them with your hands until no large clumps remain; do not puree. You should have about 4 cups (1 l) of pulp. Add the lemon juice and sugar, and stir to blend and dissolve the sugar. Taste for sweetness. Cover with plastic wrap and refrigerate until well chilled, several hours or overnight.
2. When the peach mixture is thoroughly chilled, stir in the heavy cream. Transfer to an ice-cream maker and freeze according to the manufacturer's instructions.

ONE QUART (1 L) ICE CREAM

⌣ **A PEACHY STORY** ~ My favorite peach story involves a Madame Recamier, a renowned beauty who hosted one of Paris's most fashionable salons. She was depicted by the likes of such celebrated painters as Jacques Louis David and Ingres in the beginning of the nineteenth century. She fell sick and refused to eat anything. Anything? When she was offered peaches drizzled with syrup and cream, she apparently ate every last bite and regained her strength and appetite soon after.

*Chanteduc's "sunset terrace" was designed to capture the cool of the day
and the glorious evening sunsets to the west.*

11

PANTRY

O NE SIMPLY CAN'T HAVE AN ACTIVE COUN-
try house without a successful personal
pantry, there to draw upon throughout the
year, to season, to flavor, to embellish. Always, we
have on hand huge crocks filled with our home-
grown ripe olives, some cured simply with salt and
herbs, others immersed in brine, for longer keeping.
Preserved lemons—cured in salt, bay leaves, and
olive oil—are a newer entry, a result of the Moroccan influence on French cuisine. Salt-cured
anchovies rest secure in huge glass jars, and will be
used to flavor appetizers, soups, daubes of tuna as
well as beef. There's the Italian-inspired Mostarda:
Fig & Prune Chutney—designed for the cheese
course, and our favorite *Pili Pili:* Spicy Herb Oil for
anointing pasta, breads, soups, and vegetables.
Chantal's Bachelor's Confiture—pitted fruits preserved in syrup and alcohol—saves the day when we
haven't had time to prepare a serious dessert but want
to end the evening with a sweet finale. And, of
course, there's a selection of homemade liqueurs,
with Fresh Cherry Wine leading the pack.

PILI PILI: SPICY HERB OIL

Just about every pizzeria table in Provence features a huge bottle of spicy oil, a popular condiment known as *pili pili.* Seasoned with a variety of herbs and hot pepper, the oil is used to add a touch of fire to pizzas. At home I also drizzle it over platters of fresh tomatoes and herbs. When preparing the oil in Provence we use little *piments langue d'oiseau,* or bird's tongue peppers, tiny peppers that grow in the tropics. They're fiery hot, much like the *tien tsin* chile peppers used in Asian cooking. Crushed red peppers are the most available substitute. Since the oil is going to be overwhelmed by the spice, there is no need to use extra-virgin olive oil here. The word *pili pili* actually comes from the Swahili for "hot pepper," though the African-Provençal connection is not an obvious one.

> 1 tablespoon dried leaf oregano
> 2 teaspoons crushed red peppers (hot red pepper flakes) or substitute about 12 of
>   your favorite dried red peppers, or to taste
> 1 teaspoon fennel seeds
> 4 sprigs of fresh thyme
> 4 sprigs of fresh rosemary
> 4 fresh bay leaves
> 1 cup (25 cl) olive oil

In a sterilized bottle (preferably one that you can discard once you use up the oil), layer the oregano, peppers, and fennel seeds. Put the sprigs of herbs and the bay leaves into the bottle. Cover with oil and close securely. Set aside to mature for at least 1 week. Taste and add additional peppers, if desired. Drizzle on pizzas, fresh or grilled vegetables, grilled meats, vegetables, or poultry.

ONE CUP (25 CL) SPICY OIL

VARIATION: The same seasoning mixture can be added to red wine vinegar to make a perky vinegar for dressing raw sliced tomatoes or cucumbers, or for deglazing Provençal Roast Tomatoes (page 113).

FACING PHOTOGRAPH: Pili Pili *is the spicy herbal oil used to season pizzas, meats, pastas, and cheese.*

There is no such thing as a little garlic.
ALFRED BAER

AÏOLI: GARLIC MAYONNAISE

Aïoli is a staple of Provençal cuisine. This golden sauce is used to enrich a fish soup, enliven boiled vegetables, replace classic mayonnaise on sandwiches, or flavor toast to accompany a green salad.

Preferably, garlic mayonnaise should be made by hand with a mortar and pestle. Aïoli made with a blender or a food processor will be gluelike. Alternatively, you can mash the garlic and salt together to a paste with the flat side of a knife, then prepare the mayonnaise with a whisk or an electric hand mixer. For best results, be sure that all ingredients are at room temperature.

EQUIPMENT: A mortar and pestle

6 plump, fresh garlic cloves, peeled and minced
½ teaspoon fine sea salt
2 large egg yolks, at room temperature
1 cup (25 cl) extra-virgin olive oil

1. Pour boiling water into a large mortar to warm it; discard the water and dry the mortar. Place the garlic and salt in the mortar and mash together with a pestle to form as smooth a paste as possible. The fresher the garlic, the easier it will be to crush.
2. Add the egg yolks. Stir, pressing slowly and evenly with the pestle, always in the same direction, to thoroughly blend the garlic and yolks. Continue stirring and gradually add just a few drops of the oil. Whisk until thoroughly incorporated. Do not add too much oil in the beginning, or the mixture will not emulsify. As soon as the mixture begins to thicken, add the remaining oil in a slow, steady stream, whisking constantly. Taste for seasoning. Transfer to a bowl and serve immediately. The sauce can be refrigerated, well sealed, for up to 2 days. To serve, bring to room temperature and stir once again.

ABOUT ONE CUP (25 CL) SAUCE

Garlic is the ketchup of intellectuals.
UNKNOWN

ROUILLE: GARLIC, SAFFRON & RED PEPPER MAYONNAISE

Rouille is simply a spicy sibling of aïoli, or garlic mayonnaise. Most of us first tasted this saffron-red sauce as an accompaniment to bouillabaisse, the classic fish soup of the Mediterranean. There are many versions of rouille; some include potato or bread as a thickener, some add white wine for a tangy tartness, but my favorite is a classic aïoli embellished with a hint of saffron and a generous hit of spicy red pepper. Stir a spoonful of this into Monsieur Henny's Rabbit Bouillabaisse (page 239), and you're firmly on the soil of Provence.

EQUIPMENT: A mortar and pestle

6 plump, fresh garlic cloves, peeled and minced
½ teaspoon sea salt
2 large egg yolks, at room temperature
1 cup (25 cl) extra-virgin olive oil
¼ teaspoon saffron threads
¼ teaspoon ground cayenne pepper, or to taste

1. Pour boiling water into a large mortar to warm it. Discard the water and dry the mortar. Place the garlic and salt in the mortar and mash with a pestle to form as smooth a paste as possible. The fresher the garlic, the easier it will be to crush.
2. Add the egg yolks. Stir, pressing slowly and evenly with the pestle, always in the same direction, to thoroughly blend the garlic and yolk.
3. Very slowly add a few tablespoons of oil, drop by drop, stirring until the mixture thickens. This forms the base of the emulsion. Stir in the saffron threads and cayenne pepper. Once this mixture has thickened, you can add the remaining oil in a slow, thin stream with less fear of the emulsion breaking. Continue stirring until the sauce is thickened to a mayonnaise consistency. Taste for seasoning. The sauce can be refrigerated, well sealed, for up to 2 days. Bring to room temperature to serve.

ABOUT ONE CUP (25 CL) SAUCE

PISTOU: OLIVE OIL, BASIL & GARLIC SAUCE

Pistou comes from the Provençal word *pista,* which means to grind, pound, and crush, which is what one does with this universally loved garden-fresh sauce. Pistou is an essential accompaniment to the Provençal vegetable soup of the same name and does double duty as a perfect sauce for homemade fettucine or as a sauce for flavoring whole roasted fish. Unlike the Italian pesto, this sauce does not contain pine nuts or cheese. Each summer I make sure that my garden's basil crop is abundant, and to bottle that summertime flavor, I always keep small containers of this simple sauce in the freezer. Pistou can be prepared in the food processor, but the sauce will be superior in texture and flavor if prepared by hand.

EQUIPMENT: A mortar and pestle

4 plump, fresh garlic cloves, peeled and minced
Fine sea salt to taste
2 cups (50 cl) loosely packed fresh basil leaves and flowers
½ cup (12.5 cl) extra-virgin olive oil

1. By hand: Place the garlic and salt in a mortar and mash with a pestle to form a paste. Add the basil, little by little, pounding and turning the pestle with a grinding motion to form a paste. Slowly add the oil, drop by drop, until all the oil has been used and the paste is homogenous. Taste for seasoning. Stir again before serving.
2. In a food processor: Place the minced garlic, salt, and basil in the bowl of a food processor and process to a paste. Add the oil and process again. Taste for seasoning. Stir again before serving.
3. Transfer to a small bowl. Serve immediately. The sauce can be stored, covered and refrigerated, for 1 day, or frozen for up to 6 months. Bring to room temperature and stir again before serving.

ABOUT ONE CUP (25 CL) SAUCE

*I used to love the way everyone talked about food as if it were
one of the most important things in life. And, of course, it is. Without it we would die.
Each of us eats about one thousand meals a year. It is my belief that we should try
and make as many of these meals as we can truly memorable.*

ROBERT CARRIER

FRESH HERB SAUCE FOR
MEATS, POULTRY, FISH *&* VEGETABLES

Fresh herb sauce, or *sauce verte,* is a versatile blend of fresh herbs enhanced with the tang of capers, vinegar, mustard, and the lemony fresh flavor of extra-virgin olive oil. For oil I prefer one of the fine offerings from the region of Les Baux, near Arles, such as the incomparable oil from the Coopérative Oleicole de la Vallée des Baux in Mausanne-les-Alpilles. I use *sauce verte* as I would mayonnaise, on poached or roasted fish and on leftover roast chicken, lamb, or beef.

> 2 tablespoons sherry wine vinegar
> Fine sea salt to taste
> 2 tablespoons imported Dijon mustard
> Small handful of mixed fresh herbs and greens, such as sorrel, parsley, arugula, mint, and tarragon, carefully destemmed
> 6 tablespoons extra-virgin olive oil
> 2 tablespoons minced capers

1. In a small bowl, whisk together the vinegar, salt, and mustard. Set aside.
2. Using a sharp scissors or a large chef's knife, finely chop the leaves of the herbs. Set aside.
3. In the bowl of a food processor, combine all the ingredients and process until well blended. Taste for seasoning.
4. Transfer to a small bowl. Serve immediately. The sauce can be refrigerated, well sealed, for up to 2 days. To serve, bring to room temperature and stir once again.

ONE CUP (25 CL) SAUCE

DOUBLE VINEGAR VINAIGRETTE

Few sauces I make inspire more compliments than my vinaigrette, a recipe which certainly proves that less is more. The use of two different kinds of vinegar produces a rich, well-rounded flavor. Red wine vinegar contributes color and robustness. Sherry wine vinegar adds finesse, perfume, and a certain lightness. A vinaigrette of one part vinegar and four parts olive oil, seasoned judiciously with salt and pepper, works magic.

2 tablespoons best-quality red wine vinegar
2 tablespoons best-quality sherry wine vinegar
Fine sea salt to taste
1 cup (25 cl) extra-virgin olive oil
Freshly ground black pepper to taste

Place the red wine and sherry wine vinegars and salt in a bottle. Cover and shake to blend. Add the oil and shake to blend. Taste for seasoning. The vinaigrette can be stored at room temperature or in the refrigerator up to one week. Shake again at serving time.

ABOUT 1 CUP (24 CL) VINAIGRETTE

AS OIL AND VINEGAR BATTLE IT OUT A vinaigrette is actually a "short-term" emulsion and hence a cousin of such celebrated sauces as béarnaise, hollandaise, and its counterpart, mayonnaise, which is always served cold. It is short-term because if left to stand for a while, the oil and vinegar will separate. That's logical since the basic principle linking these sauces is their dependence on a chemical reaction that blends substances which normally repel one another. The easiest example, in the case of the vinaigrette, is oil and water (the vinegar). Even the expression, "They go together like oil and water," to denote two people or things that don't go well together, gives an idea of what kind of relationship must be established.

Classically, the ratios for vinaigrette are comparable to that of mayonnaise, meaning one part vinegar to three parts oil. When the oil and vinegar are shaken together, the emulsion holds, but only temporarily. But it does not result in a thick vinaigrette that bathes salad greens in flavor and glossy shine. In fact, it is the addition of other ingredients to the equation, namely garlic or other onion flavorings or mustard, that creates a thicker vinaigrette. Chemically, the onions separate the oil and make it a weaker opponent for the vinegar. This leaves more freedom in deciding the ratio of oil to vinegar that makes the most agreeable-tasting vinaigrette. I've created a special vinaigrette of equal parts of oil and lemon to be blended in a salad of endive and Parmesan. I especially like the tanginess of lemon to balance the creamy smoothness of the olive oil.

PRESERVED LEMONS

Preserved lemons are a staple of North African cuisine, where cooks from Morocco, Tunisia, and Algeria use the soft, tangy fruit in local stews, or lamb and chicken *tagines.* In Provence, where the North African population is substantial, everything from preserved lemons to couscous to giant bundles of fresh coriander can readily be found at local markets.

The process of preserving a lemon transforms the texture so that it is soft and yielding. Even more amazing is the change in taste to pure lemon, removed of any bitter or acrid flavoring, with the added dimension of a pickled flavor. Probably the most vital aspect of properly preserving lemons is to take care to fully submerge them in the oil before storing. Though the initial week of marinating in salt and juices does radically transform the lemon, the period afterward mellows and defines the final result.

I keep the lemons on hand to mince and toss with couscous, to slip inside a whole roasted fish, and to flavor Chanteduc Rabbit with Garlic & Preserved Lemons (page 245). Any of the distinctive, full-flavored preserving liquid that remains in the jar can be used to flavor olives, to add sparingly to vinaigrettes, or in place of oil in seasoning fish or poultry.

> 2 lemons, preferably organic
> ⅓ cup (70 g) coarse sea salt
> ½ cup (12.5 cl) freshly squeezed lemon juice
> About ½ cup (12.5 cl) extra-virgin olive oil

Scrub the lemons and dry them well. Cut each lemon lengthwise into 8 wedges. In a bowl, toss the lemon wedges, salt, and lemon juice to coat the fruit evenly. Transfer to a 2-cup (50-cl) glass container with a non-metal lid. Close the container tightly and let the lemons ripen at room temperature for 7 days. Shake daily to evenly distribute the salt and juices. To store, add olive oil to cover and refrigerate for up to 6 months. To use, bring to room temperature.

TWO CUPS (50 CL) PRESERVED LEMONS

HARISSA: SPICY RED PEPPER SAUCE

Very spicy and highly aromatic, *harissa* is a popular North African relish that is used to season olives, can be thinned with olive oil and lemon juice to flavor couscous, or can be used to brush on meats or poultry for grilling. Today, *harissa* shows up on some of the finest menus in France: Parisian chef Joël Robuchon prepares a spicy coating for roast lamb, while chef Alain Passard serves a dab of it with his roasted baby pig. In Provence, *harissa* appears everywhere: Markets sell as particularly spicy cayenne pepper *piment pour harissa* and the relish can easily be found in supermarkets sold by the tube, much like tomato concentrate. Recipes for *harissa* vary from country to country—some add coriander or caraway, others create a blend of garlic, red pepper, basil, and oil. Some mix only coriander and cumin. My favorite is a simple blend of chili peppers, cumin, oil, and a touch of salt. I don't store it as a relish, but prepare it fresh each time I serve it.

EQUIPMENT: An electric spice mill

3 tablespoons cumin seeds
2 tablespoons ground cayenne red pepper
Fine sea salt to taste
2 tablespoons extra-virgin olive oil

Place the cumin in a spice mill and grind to a fine powder. In a small bowl combine the cumin, cayenne, and a pinch of salt. Toss to blend evenly. Slowly add the olive oil and whisk to blend. Taste for seasoning. Use to season couscous, brush on grilled meats or poultry, or use to season olives.

ABOUT 6 TABLESPOONS SAUCE

POTAGER STOCK

While I always have chicken stock on hand, I also like to make an herbal stock from the garden during the warmer months. The stock is lighter than chicken stock and full of the varied, herbal flavors of the garden. I use it as I would any poultry stock: as an ideal base for soups.

4 leeks, cleaned and chopped

4 carrots, scrubbed and chopped

4 turnips, scrubbed and chopped

4 ribs celery, cleaned and chopped

4 onions, halved but not peeled

1 head of garlic, halved but not peeled

2 tomatoes, halved and seeded

2 large bunches of flat-leaf parsley

1 large bunch of thyme

1 large bunch of rosemary

2 bay leaves

6 black peppercorns

4 quarts (4 l) water

In an 8-quart (8-l) stockpot, combine all the ingredients. Bring to a boil, lower the heat, and simmer, uncovered, for 1½ hours. Strain the stock, pressing out as much moisture as possible from the vegetables. Discard the vegetables and herbs. The stock may be refrigerated, covered, for 2 to 3 days or frozen up to 2 months.

ABOUT TWO AND A HALF QUARTS (2.5 L) STOCK

∾ **KEEP THE SKIN ON!** ∾ When I saw my first batch of stock bubbling away in one of Paris's finer restaurants, I was shocked to see a few onion halves floating on the top. Actually, it wasn't the onions that shocked me—any good stock has to begin with an array of fresh aromatic vegetables and flavorings. What surprised me was that the skin was still intact on the onions. Thinking it impossible that a French cook would have accidentally or, God forbid, carelessly thrown the onions in with the stock, I had to ask. It was explained to me that the skin imparts its color to the stock as it cooks without adding any bitterness. The purpose of the onion, therefore, is actually twofold: The flesh perfumes the stock while the skin adds richness to the color. To make a stock that has a lighter flavor of onion, halve the onions (skin and all) and sweat them before adding to the stock. Precooking them will remove some of the strong flavor.

CHICKEN STOCK

This is my light, freshly flavored chicken stock, which I always have on hand in the freezer. It's a way to cut down on cooking time and enrich my larder, and it enlarges my repertoire on days I don't have much time to cook. And I adore the way my house smells when the stock is simmering away. Remember not to peel the onion; the onion skin will impart a pleasant color to the stock.

4 pounds (2 kg) chicken parts (necks, wings, and feet), rinsed
Sea salt to taste
1 large onion, unpeeled but halved, each half stuck with a clove
3 plump, fresh garlic cloves, peeled
Bouquet garni: several parsley stems, celery leaves, bay leaves, and sprigs of thyme, wrapped in the green part of a leek and tied in a bundle with household twine
4 large carrots, peeled
4 leeks, white and tender green part, trimmed and well rinsed
4 whole black peppercorns

1. In the bottom of a large pasta pot with a built-in colander, combine the chicken parts, 1 tablespoon of salt, and cold water to cover. Bring to a boil over high heat, skimming off any impurities that rise to the surface. With a slotted spoon, transfer the chicken to a large sieve. Rinse, drain, and set aside. Discard the blanching liquid.

2. Rinse out the pot. Place the colander in the pot. Add the blanched chicken and all the remaining ingredients. Add cold water to cover and, uncovered, bring just to a simmer over moderately high heat. Skim off any impurities that rise to the surface. Cook at the gentlest possible simmer for 3 hours, skimming as necessary.

3. If using a pot with a built-in colander, lift out the colander and discard the solids. If not using a built-in colander, line a fine-mesh sieve with dampened cheesecloth and set over a large bowl. Ladle the liquid into the bowl. Do not pour because all the impurities remain at the bottom and make for a cloudy stock. Measure. If the stock exceeds 3 quarts (3 l), return it to moderate heat and reduce.

Bouquet garni is an essential ingredient in the Provençal kitchen.

ABOUT TWO QUARTS (2 L) STOCK

⌁ TIPS FOR FINER STOCK ∿ A few tips on how to make a clear, full-flavored stock:

- Do not cover the stockpot. Impurities will continue to rise to the surface as it cooks and should be skimmed off regularly.
- Once the stock is cooked, strain before cooling. Allowing to cool with vegetables and herbs may darken and cloud the stock.

⌁ STRAINING TIP ∿ I always make my stocks in a large stainless pasta cooking pot with a built-in colander. When it comes time to strain the stock, you simply lift out the strainer, and much of the straining has been done for you. I then pass this liquid through cheesecloth and allow the stock to cool overnight so it can be fully defatted.

⌁ THOUGHTS ON BLANCHING CHICKEN ∿ When preparing any poultry stock, I always blanch the chicken parts first in boiling water. This rids the chicken of excess fat and, more important, helps the stock begin with very clean ingredients.

RAS AL HANOUT

Ras al Hanout, which translates as "best in the shop," is a popular Middle Eastern blend of spices traditionally used to flavor soups, couscous, and stewlike *tagines*. In France, the spice is usually found ready ground. But one Sunday while visiting the food and flea market in the nearby village of Jonquières, I found a marvelous whole-spice mix at a colorful Moroccan food stand, ready for grinding at home. It's a heady, deliciously perfumed mix, one that I use readily to season rabbit stews, sprinkle on couscous, or add a dash to olives tossed with spicy *Harissa* (page 320).

EQUIPMENT: A spice grinder

½ cinnamon stick
Small piece dried ginger, about the size of a fingernail
1 teaspoon ground turmeric
1 teaspoon whole grain coriander
1 teaspoon allspice
1 teaspoon cumin seeds
1 teaspoon caraway seeds
1 teaspoon fennel seeds
1 teaspoon whole black peppercorns
1 teaspoon whole white peppercorns
1 teaspoon whole cloves

Combine the ingredients in a spice grinder and grind to a fine powder. (This may have to be done in batches.) Transfer the ground spices to an airtight spice jar. Store in a cool, dry, dark spot for up to six months.

ABOUT 3 TABLESPOONS

TOMATO SAUCE

This is my idea of what a homemade tomato sauce should be: rich, elegant, smooth, and tasting of fresh herbs. I sometimes double the recipe, so there's always some in my freezer for those days I don't have time to cook.

2 tablespoons extra-virgin olive oil
1 small onion, minced
3 plump, fresh garlic cloves, peeled and minced
Sea salt to taste
One 28-ounce (765-g) can peeled Italian plum tomatoes in juice, or one 28-ounce
    (765-g) can crushed tomatoes in puree
Bouquet garni: several sprigs of fresh parsley, bay leaves, and celery leaves, tied in a
    bundle with household twine

In a large unheated saucepan, combine the oil, onion, garlic, and salt, and stir to coat with oil. Cook over moderate heat just until the garlic turns golden but does not brown, 2 to 3 minutes. If using whole canned tomatoes, place a food mill over the skillet and puree the tomatoes directly into it. Crushed tomatoes can be added directly from the can. Add the bouquet garni, stir to blend, and simmer, uncovered, until the sauce begins to thicken, about 15 minutes. For a thicker sauce, for pizzas and toppings, cook for 5 minutes more. Taste for seasoning. Remove and discard the bouquet garni. The sauce may be used immediately, stored in the refrigerator up to 2 days, or frozen up to 2 months. If small quantities of sauce will be needed for pizzas or other toppings, freeze in ice cube trays.

ABOUT THREE CUPS (75 CL) SAUCE

SALT‑CURED BLACK OLIVES

In Provence, salt-cured olives are known as *olives piquées* because the cure consists of pricking the olives with a small fork to allow the salt to penetrate the fruit quickly and rid it of its natural bitterness. We pick our ripe, wrinkled black olives—of the tanche variety—at Christmas time, which usually coincides with the first freeze. I never quite understood the necessity of the "first freeze" until a farmer suggested that I place the olives in the freezer so they would cure more quickly. Only then did I realize that the freezing speeded up the ripening process of the fruit, which then speeded up the curing of the olive. That year we had newly cured olives within just three or four days!

The first year that I prepared these I was told by everyone, "These don't keep long." But no one would tell me how long was long. After preparing them, I soon discovered that salt-cured olives don't spoil. Their fresh, vibrant olive flavor simply fades in about 6 months. Not coincidentally, this coincides with the time that the brine-cured olives are just about ready for eating. Smart, clever folks, those farmers of days past!

Now I generally store a portion of my uncured crop in the freezer and pull the olives out whenever my salt-cured stock runs out. Geographically, our olive trees lie in the government-defined zone for *Olives de Nyons*. Nyons olives were recently awarded an Appellation d'Origine Contrôlée, the only olive in France to boast of that honor. The AOC—much like the regulations concerning wine—serves as a standard of excellence for French agriculture.

> 2 pounds (1 kg) ripe, uncured black olives
> 3½ ounces (100 g) coarse sea salt
> 6 sprigs of fresh thyme
> 6 sprigs of fresh rosemary
> 6 fresh or dried bay leaves
> Several teaspoons extra-virgin olive oil
>
> OPTIONAL FLAVORINGS
> Fresh thyme
> Fresh rosemary
> Fresh bay leaves
> Extra-virgin olive oil
> Whole black peppercorns
> Red wine vinegar
> Freshly minced garlic
> Grated zest (yellow peel) of 1 lemon
> Grated zest (orange peel) of 1 orange
> Hot red chile peppers

1. Do not wash the olives. If there are any leaves or stems still attached, remove and discard them. With a small seafood fork or a toothpick, prick the olives 3 or 4 times all over, piercing all the way to the center. (The pricking allows the fruit to absorb the salt quickly all the way to the pit.) Place in a large shallow bowl and add the salt. Toss with your hands to coat with salt. Add the thyme, rosemary, and bay leaves, and toss again.

2. Leave the olives uncovered, at room temperature, tossing them once or twice a day. After 3 or 4 days, sample one. If it tastes bitter, cure for several more days. By this time the olives should have absorbed much of the salt. A small bit of clear brine may form at the bottom of the bowl. Leave it there, for the olives will eventually absorb the brine. Transfer the olives and any brine to small glass jars. Sprinkle with a teaspoon or so of olive oil, just enough to moisten the olives. Seal. (Do not add additional flavorings at this time. They will mask the olives' fresh, vibrant flavor.) Cover the jars and store in a dark place, at room temperature, for up to 6 months.

3. At serving time, season to taste with any of the optional flavorings. Toss to distribute the flavors, and serve.

TWO POUNDS (1 KG) OLIVES

THE MASON'S BRINE-CURED BLACK OLIVES

Ahuge jar of brine-cured black olives sits on the counter in my kitchen in Provence year-round, curing away in an inky brine that is filled with history. Our mason, Jean-Claude Tricart, and his wife, Colette, were the first of our friends to serve us their own cured olives.

When it came time to cure my own ripe olives, the Tricarts kindly gave me a wine bottle filled with brine that had been in their family for years. I now proudly pass a bit of my brine on—much like a "mother" of vinegar—to anyone who asks.

Actually, you can begin with a simple brine of water and 10 percent salt, which is the standard Provençal recipe for curing the olives we harvest in December. The ripe olives are placed in brine until they are edible, a curing process that takes several weeks to several months depending on the ripeness and size of the olives. Unlike salt-cured olives, which are pricked with a fork to allow the salt to penetrate the meat of the olive, brine-cured olives are cured by being submerged in brine. Once cured, the olives can be kept for about one year. Longer than that, they begin to lose flavor and vitality. This is similar to the curing process used in the tiny Niçoise olives from Nice.

About 2 pounds (1 kg) ripe, uncured black olives
About 3½ ounces (100 g) fine sea salt
1 quart (1 l) water

OPTIONAL FLAVORINGS
Fresh thyme
Fresh rosemary
Fresh bay leaves
Extra-virgin olive oil
Whole black peppercorns
Red wine vinegar
Freshly minced garlic
Grated zest (yellow peel) of 1 lemon
Grated zest (orange peel) of 1 orange
Hot red chile peppers

1. Do not wash the olives. If there are any leaves or stems still attached, remove and discard them. In a large crock, combine the salt and water, and stir to dissolve. Add the olives, cover, and set aside in a cool spot for several months, stirring from time to time. They can be covered with a small plate to keep them all immersed in the brine. A scum will form on top, but it is harmless. (Do not discard the scum. It is the sign of a healthy curing process.) When starting with a fresh brine, the fruit will take 3 to 4 months of cur-

ing before they are edible. Once cured, they can be kept indefinitely. Never discard the salt brine, which will become black and inky. It can be used indefinitely, year after year. Do not add any seasonings other than salt and water to the brine. Add specific flavorings at serving time.

2. To serve, remove the olives from the brine with a slotted spoon or a specially designed perforated wooden ladle. Taste the olives. If they are excessively salty, they can be rinsed or soaked in cold water to remove some of the saltiness. Serve as they are or season with any of the optional flavorings noted above.

TWO POUNDS (1 KG) OLIVES

Petite olives à piquer, *tiny fresh ripe olives, ready for curing in salt.*

SALT-CURED ANCHOVIES

Pungent, with the rich, salty flavors of the sea, salt-cured anchovies are essential to my family's larder. Anchovies deepen the flavor of pasta sauces, provide an essential taste to La Broufade: Beef & White Wine Daube from Arles (page 256), and are delicious on their own, on top of a slice of freshly grilled bread.

  2 pounds (1 kg) very fresh anchovies
  2 pounds (1 kg) coarse sea salt
  Several bay leaves, preferably fresh
  Several sprigs of fresh thyme

Quickly rinse (do not wash or soak) the anchovies. Remove the head and gut the fish by holding it firmly just beneath the head. Discard the head and entrails. Place a thick layer of salt on the bottom of a large canning jar. Place a layer of anchovies, side by side, on top of the salt. Place a thin layer of salt on top. Continue until all the anchovies and salt have been used. Every layer or so, add several sprigs of fresh thyme and bay leaf. Cover securely. A brine will form as the anchovies absorb the salt and are cured. The anchovies are ready to eat in about 2 weeks and can be stored indefinitely in a cool, dark spot. Properly cured anchovies are a deep mahogany color, much like ham. To eat, simply fillet the anchovies and use in any dish calling for cured anchovies.

TWO QUARTS (2 L) CURED ANCHOVIES

MOSTARDA: FIG & PRUNE CHUTNEY

Mostarda is an Italian fruit chutney, often pickled fruit spiced with hot mustard oil, thus the name. Traditionally, it is served as an accompaniment to soft cheese, such as a mascarpone. One of the best versions I ever sampled was at Pina Bongiovanni's Osteria dell'Unione in the Piedmont, where she served a thick slice of firm toma cheese (made from a blend of goat's and sheep's milk) with a puckery, sweet-and-sour fruit mostarda. This is my version, one I serve with roast pork, goose, or duck, or with a tray of Oatmeal Biscuits (page 173) and Roquefort cheese.

> 1 pound (500 g) pitted prunes, quartered
> 1 pound (500 g) dried figs, quartered, or dried apricots, pitted and quartered
> 2 cups (50 cl) best-quality red wine vinegar
> 2 tablespoons creamy rosemary or thyme honey, or to taste
> 2 sticks whole cinnamon

In a large saucepan, combine all the ingredients. Stir to blend, cover, and cook over the lowest possible heat until most of the liquid has been absorbed, the fruit is soft and almost falling apart, a thin veil of liquid still remains, 45 minutes to 1 hour. Do not allow the mixture to reduce to a thick puree. Stir frequently to blend and break down the fruits and to avoid scorching the pan. Remove and discard the cinnamon stick. Cool thoroughly. Store in a covered container in the refrigerator for up to 1 month. Remove from the refrigerator about 30 minutes before serving.

ONE QUART (1 L) MOSTARDA

CHANTAL'S BACHELOR'S CONFITURE

The "bachelor's confiture" is a blend of fruits that ripen over time in a mixture of sugar, alcohol, and water. It is sampled either as dessert itself or, much like a liqueur, after a meal. Our winemaker's wife, Chantal Combe, makes one of the best versions I've ever tasted. She limits her choice of fruits to those with pits, which tend to be a bit firmer and break down less than softer fruits such as strawberries and raspberries. The pits also impart a wonderful nutty flavor. You can make the confiture all at once or add fruits as they come into season. Chantal prepares hers with sugar syrup, producing an even distribution of sugar and a clear, unclouded liquid.

> 2 pounds (1 kg) of mixed fresh fruits with pits, preferably a colorful mixture of
>   cherries, plums, peaches, nectarines, apricots, and grapes
> About 1 quart (1 l) Classic Sugar Syrup (recipe below), cooled
> About 1 quart (1 l) clear eau-de-vie or vodka

In a large widemouthed jar, begin layering the fruit in a colorful pattern. Leave cherries and grapes whole, and halve or quarter the other fruits. Do not peel the fruits and do not discard the pits. If, in halving or quartering the fruit, any pits detach from the fruit, simply arrange them along with the fruit in the jar. Pour equal portions of the cooled sugar syrup and alcohol over the fruit. Cover securely with plastic wrap and weight so the fruit is totally immersed in liquid. Set aside in a cool, dry place for at least 2 months. As the confiture ripens, the liquid will change from a clear to a rose color. Additional fruit can be added as they come into season. To serve as an after-dinner drink, ladle a few fruits into a small bowl along with a little bit of liquid. Or serve over ice cream, sorbet, or cake.

ABOUT TWO POUNDS (1 KG) CONFITURE

CLASSIC SUGAR SYRUP

> 2 pounds (1 kg) sugar
> 1 quart (1 l) water

In a large saucepan combine the sugar and water. Bring to a boil over high heat, stirring with a wooden spoon until all the sugar is dissolved. Set aside to cool. The sugar syrup can be stored, carefully sealed and refrigerated, for up to two weeks.

FRESH CHERRY WINE

Come May, our five cherry trees produce more cherries than we know what to do with. So I spend hours turning the fresh, plump vermilion fruit into cherry wine, pickled cherries, and, of course, cherry jam, plus a few batches for the freezer. This is an easy homemade liqueur, filled with the vibrant, dense flavor of cherries. Serve it in tiny glasses at the end of a meal, ideally with a cherry dessert alongside.

2 pounds (1 kg) ripe sweet cherries
1 cup (200 g) sugar
1 plump, moist vanilla bean, halved
Clear eau-de-vie or vodka
Red wine

1. Pit the cherries, reserving the pits. Combine the cherries, pits, vanilla bean, and sugar in a 3-quart (3-l) heavy-bottomed saucepan. Simmer over moderate heat, stirring from time to time, for 30 minutes. The mixture will be dark and syrupy.
2. Place a large sieve over a bowl and line the sieve with dampened cheesecloth. Pour the cherries and syrup into the sieve to strain the juice. Press down on the cherries to extract every bit of the juice you can. (The quantity of juice will vary according to the size and ripeness of the cherries.) Discard the cherries, cherry pits and vanilla bean. Measure the strained liquid into a dry, sterilized bottle. For each cup (125 ml) of juice, add 1 cup (125 ml) of eau-de-vie or vodka. Cork and set aside to macerate for 1 week. For each cup (125 ml) of liquid, add 2 cups (250 ml) of red wine, such as a simple Côtes du Rhône. Cork and allow to age for 2 months before sampling. Use within 1 year. After that time, the delicate cherry flavor will fade.

ABOUT ONE QUART (1 L) CHERRY WINE

FACING PHOTOGRAPH: *A variation of Chantal's Bachelor's Confiture, prepared with wild cherry plums.*

"44" — HOMEMADE ORANGE LIQUEUR

Orange liqueur, or "44," is one of the most traditional European homemade aperitifs. You'll find versions in Spain, Italy, and France, some made with cloves, cinnamon, some with a mix of oranges, bitter oranges, and lemons, some flavored with coffee beans, and those sweetened with honey. The original recipe given to me called for a single orange studded with 44 coffee beans, mixed with 44 sugar cubes and a bottle of clear eau-de-vie. The mixture is then set aside for 44 days. The result is a fragrant, fruity drink, which can mixed with a bit of white white as an aperitif or served "as is" with dessert or as an after-meal liqueur. I found the original version too sweet for my taste, so have cut the amount of sugar in half.

EQUIPMENT: 1½-quart canning jar with lid, thoroughly washed and dried

1 large orange, preferably organic
44 coffee beans
22 sugar cubes (or 6 tablespoons granulated sugar)
1 quart (1 l) clear eau-de-vie or vodka

Thoroughly scrub and dry the orange. With the end of a sharp knife, pierce the orange all over, and insert the 44 coffee beans into the skin, embedding each bean in the orange. Place the orange in a canning jar. Add the sugar cubes and the eau-de-vie. Cover securely. Turn the jar upside down and shake to help dissolve the sugar. Place in a cool, dry, dark spot. Shake the jar daily, until the sugar is completely dissolved. Set aside for 44 days. During this time, the liquid will turn from clear to a pale orange and will take on a lovely coffee-orange fragrance. The "44" can be stored indefinitely as is, or the liquid can be filtered and transferred to an attractive liqueur bottle. The orange and coffee beans are not consumed, and should be discarded once they lose their vigor. The "44" can be served chilled or at room temperature, added to white wine or served in tiny liqueur glasses as an accompaniment to fruit desserts or as an after-dinner drink.

ONE QUART (1 L) LIQUEUR

VARIATION: In Provence, many cooks prepare their orange liqueur by piercing the orange with cloves, tying the fruit with string, then suspending it in clear glass jar partially filled with clear eau-de-vie. (The orange should never touch the alcohol.) The jar is sealed, and the aromatic oils of the orange infuse the alcohol with their fruity essence, turning the eau-de-vie a pale, glistening orange. After about one month, the orange is discarded, the aperitif is sweetened to taste and transferred to a sealed bottle.

FACING PHOTOGRAPH: *The makings of "44"—Homemade Orange Liquor, and a suspended orange variation prepared with cloves and eau-de-vie.*

GRAPES IN EAU-DE-VIE

In Provence, homemakers preserve all manner of fruits in eau-de-vie, the powerful, colorless alcohol obtained by distilling the grape skins, seeds, and stems that are left over from winemaking. In the past, almost every winemaker made his own alcohol, but now the government strictly controls its distillation. So now I preserve my fruits in good-quality marc, grappa, or a clear, flavorless alcohol such as vodka.

1 pound (500 g) Muscat grapes (or use fresh, stemmed cherries)
1 quart (1 l) marc, grappa, or vodka

Rinse and dry the fruit. Place in a sterilized 1½-quart (1.5-l) jar. Pour the alcohol over it. Seal the jar and allow the fruit to macerate in the liquid at least 6 weeks. During this time, turn the jar upside down from time to time to redistribute the alcohol and the natural sugars in the fruit. To serve, place several pieces of fruit in a small stemmed glass and add a few tablespoons of the fruity liquid. The infused eau-de-vie can also be served as an after-dinner *digestif.* Use within 1 year. After that time, the fruity flavors will fade.

ABOUT ONE AND A HALF QUARTS (1.5 L)

RASPBERRIES IN EAU-DE-VIE

Raspberries are one of the world's most sumptuous fruits. Nothing is more luxurious than your own raspberries floating in a raspberry eau-de-vie, a way to double the flavor and pleasure of a fruit liqueur.

1 pound (500 g) fresh raspberries
2 raspberry leaves, if available
1 cup (200 g) sugar
2 cups (50 cl) framboise (raspberry eau-de-vie)

Rinse and dry the raspberries. Layer the fruit and sugar in a sterilized 1½-quart (1.5-l) jar. Pour the alcohol over the fruit. Seal the jar and allow the fruit to macerate at least 1 month in a dark, cool spot. During this time, turn the jar upside down from time to time to redistribute the alcohol and the sugars in the fruit. To serve, place several pieces of fruit in a small stemmed glass and add a few tablespoons of alcohol. Or dribble the liquid over fresh raspberry sorbet or homemade Vanilla-Bean Ice Cream (page 291), then spoon a few preserved berries over it all.

ONE AND A HALF QUARTS (1.5 L)

INDEX

(Page numbers in *italic* refer to illustrations.)

Accompaniments, *see* Side dishes
Aïoli (garlic mayonnaise), *83,* 314
　Catalan fried noodles with, 155
　monkfish bouillabaisse with, *80,*
　　81–82
Al Forno (Providence, R.I.), 154
All-star herb salad, 54
Almond(s), *284*
　apricot-honey tart, *280,* 281–82
　cherry tart, *286,* 287–88
　crust, 281, 282
　honey cookies, Provençal (*cro-*
　　quettes), 284–85
　toasted, Porquerolles Island, 30
　types of, 288
Amazing sorrel soup, *90,* 91
L'Ambroisie (Paris), 124
Anchovy(ies):
　garlic crisps, 45
　salt-cured, 330
　scrubbed toast, 31
　-stuffed olives, lemon-flecked,
　　46, *48*
Anne's goat cheese gratin, *20,* 21
Appellation d'Origine Contrôlée
　(AOC), 51, 326
Appetizers, 19–51
　anchovy-garlic crisps, 45
　Anne's goat cheese gratin, *20,* 21
　artichoke and basil ragout, 110
　Barcelona grilled artichokes, *106,*
　　107
　cachat (Provençal cheese spread),
　　41
　Chanteduc black olives, *48,* 51
　crustless onion quiche, 34–35
　curried zucchini blossoms, *28,*
　　28–29
　ginger and lime scallop seviche,
　　215
　harissa-seasoned black olives, 47,
　　48
　herb cheese Lyonnais, 36
　herb-cured filet of beef (carpac-
　　cio), 23

herbed green olives, 49
JR's shrimp with basil, 26–27
lemon-flecked olives, 46, *48*
Lou Canestéou's cheese chips, 25
Marie-Claude's Armagnac
　chèvre, 40
onion caraway bread tart, *190,* 191
petite friture (fried baby fish),
　209–10, *210*
Porquerolles Island toasted
　almonds, 30
Roquefort dip, 39
Rue de Lévis "caviar," 44
scrubbed toast, 31
Sheila and Julian's quick foie
　gras, 32–33
smoked trout tartare, 22
tomato clafoutis, 38
tuna tapenade, 43
Apple(s), 303
　crisp, Eli's, 304
　gingered confit of pears and, 302
　spicy lamb curry with yogurt
　　and, 260–61
　Toutoune's winter salad, 70
Apricot(s), 282
　fig, walnut, and raisin rye, *182,*
　　183–84
　honey-almond tart, *280,* 281–82
Arab parsley, 63
Arles, beef and white wine daube
　from (*la broufade*), 256–57
Armagnac chèvre, Marie-Claude's,
　40
Arpège (Paris), 54, 128
Artichoke(s), 77
　Barcelona grilled, *106,* 107
　and basil ragout, 110
　June vegetable ragout with herb
　　garden pistou, 115
　leg of lamb on bed of potatoes,
　　herbs and, 264–65
　Parmesan, and black truffle soup,
　　94–95
　sliced, and prosciutto salad, 76

storing, 77
trimming and preparing, 77, 95
the winemaker's chicken with
　olives and, *30,* 231–32
Arugula:
　and Parmesan salad, *58,* 59
　sliced artichoke and prosciutto
　　salad, 76
Asparagus:
　braised, *142,* 143
　June vegetable ragout with herb
　　garden pistou, 115

Baby chocolate brioche, 170–71
Bachelor's confiture, Chantal's, *332,*
　333
Baer, Alfred, 314
Baked fruit and honey with
　Beaumes de Venise, 308
Baking soda, 174
Banon, *24*
Barcelona grilled artichokes, *106,* 107
Bar Pinochio (Barcelona), 107
Basil, *102,* 272
　and artichoke ragout, 110
　cold tomato soup with, 92
　JR's shrimp with, 26–27
　olive oil, and garlic sauce (pis-
　　tou), 316
　puree, 26
Basmati rice, 273
Bass, *see* Sea bass
La Bastide de Moustiers (Provence),
　150
Bay leaf, *102,* 272
　creamy semolina with Parmesan
　　and, 243
Beal, Gillian, 239
Bean(s):
　fresh, with garlic and herbs, 127
　June vegetable ragout with herb
　　garden pistou, 115
　summer pistou, *84,* 85–87, *86*
　winter pistou, 97
Beard, James, 124

Beaumes de Venise, baked fruit and honey with, 308
Beef:
    braising vs. stewing, 259
    city steak, 255
    daube with mustard, herbs, and white wine, 258–59
    herb-cured filet of (carpaccio), 23
    pairing herbs with, 55
    roasting tips for, 251
    salad, Saturday, 74
    three-, daube, Monsieur Henny's, 252, 253–54
    and white wine daube from Arles (la broufade), 256–57
Beet(s), 61
    grated, salad, 61
    storing, 61
Beet tops, 61
    the true salad fan's salad, 57
Belgian endive, 70
    Chanteduc winter salad, 56
    French café salad, 71
    salad of Roquefort, walnuts, lamb's lettuce and, 68, 69
    Toutoune's winter salad, 70
La Belle Gasconne (Poudenas), 40
Belvedere (Serravalle Laghe), 67
Benoit, Madame, 308
Beramendi, Rolando, 277
Berenger, Aymar, 205
Berenger, Eliane, 81, 195, 205
Bernalardi, Carolyn, 62
Berry(ies):
    Chanteduc clafoutis, 292, 293–94
    schaum torte (meringues for month of May), 298, 298–99
    see also Raspberry(ies)
Biscuits, oatmeal, 172, 173–74
Bistro fare:
    salad of Roquefort, walnuts, Belgian endive, and lamb's lettuce, 68, 69
    spicy lamb curry with yogurt and apples, 260–61
    Toutoune's winter salad, 70
Blanc, Georges, 228
Blenders, adding hot ingredients to, 157
Blue cheeses, 172
Bluefish, 205
Boiling, hot vs. cold water for, 151
Bongiovanni, Pina, 241, 331
Le Bouchon de François Clerc (Paris), 44
Bouillabaisse:
    monkfish, with aïoli, 80, 81–82
    rabbit, Monsieur Henny's, 239–40

Boulestin, Marcel, 267
Bouquet garni, 272, 322
Braised:
    asparagus, 142, 143
    and gratinéed fennel, 122–23
    rabbit, Pina's, 241–42
    red onions, 106, 130
    whole garlic, 106, 130
Braising, 259
Bread, 44, 165–93, 187
    baby chocolate brioche, 170–71
    caraway corn-rye, 188–89
    crusty wheat and polenta, 178–79
    dough, 185
    expressions surrounding, 168
    fig, apricot, walnut, and raisin rye, 182, 183–84
    fougasse, 192, 192–93, 193
    golden Parmesan-pepper loaf, 175
    oatmeal biscuits, 172, 173–74
    onion caraway, tart, 190, 191
    pine nut rolls, 169
    pompe à l'huile (Provençal olive oil brioche), 166, 167–68
    Rita's rye, 186–87
    sesame, flax, and sunflower seed, 176–77
    walnut, rye, and currant loaf, 180–81
Bresse, chicken with tarragon and sherry vinegar from, 226–27
Brine-cured:
    black olives, the mason's, 48, 328–29
    pork, spit-roasted, 269–71, 270
Brioche:
    additional sweet and savory fillings for, 171
    baby chocolate, 170–71
    Provençal olive oil (pompe à l'huile), 166, 167–68
La broufade (beef and white wine daube from Arles), 256–57
Broun, Heywood, 305
Brown rice from the Camargue, 272
Brusco, Laura, 67
Butter:
    -roasted herbed chicken (poulet aux fines herbes), 222, 222–24
    truffle, pasta, Hervé's, 158–59

Cabbage, French country guinea hen and, 225
Cachat (Provençal cheese spread), 41
Café salad, French, 71
Cake, winemaker's grape, 277–78
Camargue, brown rice from the, 272
Caramelized fennel soup, 98

Caraway (seeds), 189
    corn-rye bread, 188–89
    onion bread tart, 190, 191
Carbonara, Checchino dal 1887's spaghetti alla, 160
Carpaccio (herb-cured filet of beef), 23
    legend behind word, 201
"Carpaccio," monkfish, 200–201
Carrier, Robert, 120, 317
Carrots:
    Maggie's vegetable potage, 100
    pairing herbs with, 55
    Provençal, 132
    summer pistou, 84, 85–87, 86
    winter pistou, 97
Casseroles:
    the Vaison fishmonger's fresh tuna, 218
    Walter's Thanksgiving oyster, 219–20
Catalan cuisine:
    fried noodles, 155
    scrubbed toast, 31
    tuna daube, 216–17
Cauliflower soup, curried, 89
"Caviar," Rue de Lévis, 44
Celery:
    Parmesan gratin, 131
    and Parmesan salad, 67
    as supposed cure for hangovers, 67
Celery root, 125
    lasagne, 124–25
Chantal's bachelor's confiture, 332, 333
Chanteduc:
    black olives, 48, 51
    clafoutis, 292, 293–94
    rabbit with garlic and preserved lemons, 244, 245–46
    winter salad, 56
Charleston Receipts, 219
Château Eza (Eza), 169
Checchino dal 1887's spaghetti alla carbonara, 160
Cheese:
    chips, Lou Canestéou's, 25
    fresh, with pine nuts and honey, 306
    herb, Lyonnais, 36
    spread, Provençal (cachat), 41
    truffle "sandwich," 158
    see also Goat cheese; Gruyère; Parmesan; Roquefort
Cheesecake, Corsican (fiadone), 283
Cheese course:
    cachat (Provençal cheese spread), 41

cheesemaker's salad as accompaniment for, 75
crusty wheat and polenta bread as accompaniment for, 178–79
oatmeal biscuits as accompaniment for, *172*, 173–74
Rita's rye as accompaniment for, 186–87
pear and watercress salad as accompaniment for, 66
Cheesemaker's salad, 75
Cherry(ies):
    almond tart, *286*, 287–88
    Chanteduc clafoutis, *292*, 293–94
    fresh, vanilla-bean ice cream with, 289
    fresh, wine, *334*, 335
    and goat cheese gratin, 291
Chesterton, G. K., 41
Chèvre, *see* Goat cheese
Chez Toutoune (Paris), 70
Chicken:
    blanching, for stock, 323
    butter-roasted herbed (*poulet aux fines herbes*), 222, *222*–24
    cooking rabbit vs., 240
    herb roasting rack for, 227
    lemon soup, quick, 99
    with shallots, lemon, and thyme, 228–29
    stock, 322–23
    with tarragon and sherry vinegar, 226–27
    trussing, 235
Chickpea salad, Daniel's, 72–73
Child, Julia, 85
Chilled cream of pea soup, 93
Chinese parsley, 63
Chips, Lou Canestéou's cheese, 25
Chives, 55
    growing, 71
Chocolate:
    baby brioche, 170–71
    gourmandise, 300
    honey mousse, 301
Christmas, brioche served at, 168
Chunky peach ice cream, 309
Chutney, fig and prune, 331
Cilantro, 63
Cipriani, Giuseppe, 201
City steak, 255
Clafoutis, 294
    Chanteduc, *292*, 293–94
    tomato, 38
Clams, 163
    spaghetti with, Patricia's, 162–63
Classic sugar syrup, 333
Clos Chanteduc, *257*

Cloves, 129
Cod, seared pancetta-wrapped, 211
Cold tomato soup with basil, 92
Combe, Chantal, 333
Combe, Daniel, 72, 231
Condiments:
    the mason's brine-cured black olives, *48*, 328–29
    mostarda (fig and prune chutney), 331
    pili pili (spicy herb oil), *312*, 313
    pure tomato confit (oven-roasted tomatoes), *118*, 119
    ras al hanout, 324
    salt-cured anchovies, 330
    salt-cured black olives, 326–27
    see also Sauces; Vinaigrettes
Confits:
    of apples and pears, gingered, 302
    pure tomato (oven-roasted tomatoes), *118*, 119
Confiture, Chantal's bachelor's, *332*, 333
Cookies, Provençal honey-almond (*croquettes*), 284–85
Coopérative Oleicole de la Vallée des Baux, 317
Coriander, 63
Cornmeal, 179
Corn-rye bread, caraway, 188–89
Corsican cheesecake (*fiadone*), 283
Courtine, Robert J., 128
Couscous, 247
    my way, 247
Crabmeat salad, minted, 207
Cream of pea soup, chilled, 93
Creamy:
    olive oil and Parmesan potato puree, 141
    semolina with bay leaf and Parmesan, 243
Crisp (dessert), Eli's apple, 304
Crisps (toasts), anchovy-garlic, 45
Croquettes (Provençal honey-almond cookies), 284–85
Crustless onion quiche, 34–35
Crusty wheat and polenta bread, 178–79
Cumin (seeds):
    roasting, 236–37
    -rubbed grilled quail, 236–37
    and turnip puree, 117
Curnonsky, 130
Currant(s), *108*
    history of, 181
    walnut, and rye loaf, 180–81
Curry(ied), 260
    cauliflower soup, 89

spicy lamb, with yogurt and apples, 260–61
yogurt green bean salad, 65
zucchini blossoms, *28*, 28–29

Dairy products, nutmeg and, 35
Daniel's chickpea salad, 72–73
D'Artagnan, Inc., 33
Daubes, 257
    beef, with mustard, herbs, and white wine, 258–59
    beef and white wine, from Arles (*la broufade*), 256–57
    Catalan tuna, 216–17
    Monsieur Henny's three-beef, *252*, 253–54
    of veal, wine, and green olives, 250–51
Daubières, 253, 257
Daudet, Leon, 49
Deal, Christian and Josiane, 13
Depardieu, Gérard, 162
Deshpande, Shashi, 207
Desserts, 275–309
    apricot-honey-almond tart, *280*, 281–82
    baked fruit and honey with Beaumes de Venise, 308
    Chantal's bachelor's confiture, *332*, 333
    Chanteduc clafoutis, *292*, 293–94
    cherry-almond tart, *286*, 287–88
    cherry and goat cheese gratin, 291
    chocolate gourmandise, 300
    chocolate-honey mousse, 301
    chunky peach ice cream, 309
    croquettes (Provençal honey-almond cookies), 284–85
    Eli's apple crisp, 304
    fiadone (Corsican cheesecake), 283
    fig tart, 281, *282*
    fresh cheese with pine nuts and honey, 306
    fresh lemon verbena ice cream, 305
    gingered confit of apples and pears, 302
    grapes in eau-de-vie, 338
    lavender honey ice cream, 279
    lemon lover's tart, 295
    lemon *pots de crème*, 297
    raspberries in eau-de-vie, 338
    raspberry tart, *280*, 282
    schaum torte (meringues for month of May), *298*, 298–99
    vanilla-bean ice cream with fresh cherries, 289
    winemaker's grape cake, 277–78

Desuagiers, Marc, 269
Diables, 135
Digestifs:
    Chantal's bachelor's confiture,
        332, 333
    "44" (homemade orange
        liqueur), *336, 337*
    fresh cherry wine, *334, 335*
    grapes in eau-de-vie, 338
    raspberries in eau-de-vie, 338
Dill, 55
Dips:
    Roquefort, 39
    tuna tapenade, 43
El Dorado Petit (Barcelona), 155
Double vinegar vinaigrette, 318
Dry cooking, 262
Ducasse, Alain, 150
Duck:
    carving, 235
    with lime and honey, 233–35
    with olives and artichokes, the
        winemaker's, *230,* 231–32
    trussing, 235
Durrell, Lawrence, 32
Dutrery, Raymond, 75

Eau-de-vie:
    grapes in, 338
    raspberries in, 338
Egg(s):
    Checchino dal 1887's spaghetti
        alla carbonara, 160
    crustless onion quiche, 34–35
    infusing with essence of truffles,
        159, *159*
Eggplant, 121
    gratin, Monsieur Henny's,
        120–21
Eli's apple crisp, 304
Endive, *see* Belgian endive
Entrées, *see* Main dishes

Fake *frites,* 137
Fava beans, in June vegetable ragout
    with herb garden pistou, 115
Fennel, 123
    braised and gratinéed, 122–23
    caramelized, soup, 98
    cleaning of outer skin, 98
    fusili with sausage, red wine and,
        148, 148–49
    Provençal penne, 161
Fettucine with Roquefort, lemon
    zest, and rosemary, 147
Fiadone (Corsican cheesecake), 283
Fideos, in Catalan fried noodles,
    155

Fig:
    apricot, walnut, and raisin rye,
        182, 183–84
    and prune chutney, 331
    tart, 281, *282*
Fines herbes, 224
Finger bowls, 237
First courses, *see* Appetizers; Pasta;
    Salads; Soups
Fish, 195
    Catalan tuna daube, 216–17
    fresh herb sauce for, 317
    fried baby (*petite friture*), 209–10,
        210
    monkfish bouillabaisse with aïoli,
        80, 81–82
    monkfish "carpaccio," 200–201
    pairing herbs with, 55
    removing skin from, 204–5
    salt-cured anchovies, 330
    sea bass in parchment with warm
        pistou, *202,* 203–4
    seared pancetta-wrapped cod,
        211
    smoked trout tartare, 22
    steamed salmon with warm
        lemon vinaigrette, 206
    tuna tapenade, 43
    the Vaison fishmonger's fresh
        tuna casserole, 218
    whole, roasted in crust of sea salt,
        212, 213–14, *214*
    whole baked, filleting, 204
    see also Shellfish
Fisher, M. F. K., 176
Flax (seed), 177
    sesame, and sunflower seed
        bread, 176–77
Fleur de sel, 263
Floyd, Keith, 122
Foie gras:
    Sheila and Julian's quick,
        32–33
    the true salad fan's salad as
        accompaniment for, 57
Food processors, adding hot ingredi-
    ents to, 157
"44" (homemade orange liqueur),
    336, 337
Fougasse, *192,* 192–93, *193*
French café salad, 71
French country guinea hen and cab-
    bage, 225
Fried:
    baby fish (*petite friture*), 209–10,
        210
    noodles, Catalan, 155
Frites, fake, 137

Fruit:
    Chantal's bachelor's confiture,
        332, 333
    Chanteduc clafoutis, *292,* 293–94
    and honey with Beaumes de
        Venise, baked, 308
    see also specific fruits
Frying, skimmer use in, 27
Fusili with sausage, fennel, and red
    wine, *148,* 148–49

Game, 221, 236–46
    cumin-rubbed grilled quail,
        236–37
    see also Rabbit
Garlic, *102*
    anchovy crisps, 45
    Chanteduc rabbit with preserved
        lemons and, *244,* 245–46
    family soup, 103
    fresh beans with herbs and, 127
    mayonnaise (aïoli), *83,* 314
    olive oil, and basil sauce (pistou),
        316
    saffron, and red pepper mayon-
        naise (rouille), 315
    smashed potatoes with, 136
    whole, braised, *106,* 130
Germon, George, 154, 269
Giaccone, Caesar, 67
Giacomo, Giuseppina, 145, 159
Gigot Provençal (oven-roasted leg of
    lamb), *266,* 267–68
Ginger(ed):
    confit of apples and pears, 302
    and lime scallop seviche, 215
    and sherry lobster, *197,* 197–99
    shrimp, Maria's, 196
Girardet, Fredy, 221, 233
Goat cheese (chèvre), *24*
    Armagnac, Marie-Claude's, 40
    and cherry gratin, 291
    gratin, Anne's, *20,* 21
Golden Parmesan-pepper loaf, 175
Gourmandise, chocolate, 300
Gracia, Marie-Claude, 40
Grains:
    basmati rice, 273
    brown rice from the Camargue,
        272
    couscous my way, 247
    creamy semolina with bay leaf
        and Parmesan, 243
Grape(s), *278*
    cake, winemaker's, 277–78
    in eau-de-vie, 338
    white film on, 278
Grated beet salad, 61

Gratinéed and braised fennel, 122–23
Gratins:
    celery-Parmesan, 131
    cherry and goat cheese, 291
    dauphinois, *138*, 139
    dauphinois, JR's, 140
    eggplant, Monsieur Henny's, 120–21
    goat cheese, Anne's, *20*, 21
    onion-Parmesan, 128–29
    semolina, 243
Gray, Penelope, 245
Grayson, David, 178
Green bean(s):
    red and green salad, 62–63
    summer pistou, *84*, 85–87, *86*
    tarragon, salad, 64
    yogurt salad, 65
Grilled:
    artichokes, Barcelona, *106*, 107
    cumin-rubbed quail, 236–37
    monkfish "carpaccio," 200–201
    mushrooms, meaty, 108–9
Gruyère:
    gratin dauphinois, *138*, 139
    JR's gratin dauphinois, 140
Guarnaschelli, Alexandra, 94
Guarnaschelli, Maria, 196
Guichard, Benoit, 109
Guinea hen, French country cabbage and, 225
Guy Savoy (Paris), 94

Hammond, Jane Christie, 219
Harissa (spicy red pepper sauce), 320
    -seasoned black olives, 47, *48*
Harry's Bar (Venice), 201
Henny, Roland, 13, 120, 221, *238*, *239*, 249, 253, 267
Herb(ed)(s):
    beef daube with mustard, white wine and, 258–59
    bouquet garni, 272, *322*
    butter-roasted chicken (*poulet aux fines herbes*), *222*, 222–24
    cheese Lyonnais, 36
    -cured filet of beef (carpaccio), 23
    fresh, sauce for meats, poultry, fish, and vegetables, 317
    fresh beans with garlic and, 127
    green olives, 49
    herbes de Provence vs. *fines herbes*, 224
    leg of lamb on bed of artichokes, potatoes and, 264–65
    Monday night spaghetti, 152

oil, spicy (*pili pili*), *312*, 313
pairing foods with, 55
potager stock, 321
roasting racks, 227
salad, all-star, 54
see also specific herbs
Herbes de Provence, 224
Hervé's truffle butter pasta, 158–59
Honey, 307
    almond cookies, Provençal (*croquettes*), 284–85
    apricot-almond tart, *280*, 281–82
    baked fruit with Beaumes de Venise and, 308
    chocolate mousse, 301
    duck with lime and, 233–35
    fresh cheese with pine nuts and, 306
    lavender, ice cream, 279
    substituting for sugar, 285
Hosain, Attia, 186

Ice cream:
    chunky peach, 309
    fresh lemon verbena, 305
    lavender honey, 279
    vanilla-bean, with fresh cherries, 289
Individual zucchini lasagne with spicy pizza sauce, 154
Italian:
    mostarda (fig and prune chutney), 331
    Parmesan and celery salad, 67
    Pina's braised rabbit, 241–42

JR's gratin dauphinois, 140
JR's shrimp with basil, 26–27
June vegetable ragout with herb garden pistou, 115
Juniper berries, 272

Killeen, Johanne, 154, 269
King Arthur's Flour Baker's Catalog, 168
Kramer, Rita, 85, 186, 284
Kramer, Yale, 85, 186

Lamb:
    chops, lemon-thyme, 262–63
    curry, spicy, with yogurt and apples, 260–61
    descriptive terms for, 263
    leg of, on bed of artichokes, potatoes, and herbs, 264–65
    oven-roasted leg of (*gigot Provençal*), *266*, 267–68
    pairing herbs with, 55

Lamb's lettuce, 69
    salad of Roquefort, walnuts, Belgian endive and, *68*, 69
Lasagne:
    celery root, 124–25
    individual zucchini, with spicy pizza sauce, 154
Lavender honey ice cream, 279
Lawson, William, 38
Lee, Sonja, 150
Leeks, in garlic family soup, 103
Leg of lamb on bed of artichokes, potatoes, and herbs, 264–65
Leibling, A. J., 231
Leibowitz, Fran, 132
Lemon(s):
    chicken soup, quick, 99
    chicken with shallots, thyme and, 228–29
    -flecked olives, 46, *48*
    lover's tart, 295
    pastry shell, 296
    pots de crème, 297
    preserved, *48*, 319
    preserved, Chanteduc rabbit with garlic and, *244*, 245–46
    thyme lamb chops, 262–63
    vinaigrette, warm, steamed salmon with, 206
    zest, fettucine with Roquefort, rosemary and, 147
Lemon verbena ice cream, fresh, 305
Lenôtre, Gaston, 219
Lime:
    duck with honey and, 233–35
    and ginger scallop seviche, 215
Lin Yutang, 216
Liqueurs:
    Chantal's bachelor's confiture, *332*, 333
    fresh cherry wine, *334*, 335
    homemade orange ("44"), *336*, 337
Little, Alastair, 211
Livers:
    the true salad fan's salad as accompaniment for, 57
    see also Foie gras
Lobster, sherry and ginger, *197*, 197–99
Lou Canestéou (Vaison-la-Romaine), *24*, 25, *25*
Lou Canestéou's cheese chips, 25
Lyonnais herb cheese, 36

McCrae, Anne, 21
Maggie's vegetable potage, 100
Maginn, William, 287

Main dishes:
 Barcelona grilled artichokes, *106,
  107*
 beef daube with mustard, herbs,
  and white wine, 258–59
 braised and gratinéed fennel,
  122–23
 la broufade (beef and white wine
  daube from Arles), 256–57
 Catalan tuna daube, 216–17
 celery root lasagne, 124–25
 Chanteduc rabbit with garlic and
  preserved lemons, *244,
  245–46*
 chicken with shallots, lemon, and
  thyme, 228–29
 chicken with tarragon and sherry
  vinegar, 226–27
 city steak, 255
 crustless onion quiche, 34–35
 cumin-rubbed grilled quail,
  236–37
 daube of veal, wine, and green
  olives, 250–51
 duck with lime and honey,
  233–35
 French café salad, 71
 French country guinea hen and
  cabbage, 225
 gigot Provençal (oven-roasted leg
  of lamb), *266,* 267–68
 ginger and lime scallop seviche,
  215
 June vegetable ragout with herb
  garden pistou, 115
 leg of lamb on bed of artichokes,
  potatoes, and herbs, 264–65
 lemon-thyme lamb chops,
  262–63
 Maria's ginger shrimp, 196
 minted crabmeat salad, 207
 monkfish "carpaccio," 200–201
 Monsieur Henny's eggplant
  gratin, 120–21
 Monsieur Henny's rabbit bouillabaisse, 239–40
 Monsieur Henny's three-beef
  daube, *252,* 253–54
 onion caraway bread tart, *190,
  191*
 Pina's braised rabbit, 241–42
 poulet aux fines herbes (butter-
  roasted herbed chicken), *222,
  222–24*
 Saturday beef salad, 74
 sea bass in parchment with warm
  pistou, *202,* 203–4
 seared pancetta-wrapped cod, 211

sherry and ginger lobster, *197,
  197–99*
 spicy lamb curry with yogurt and
  apples, 260–61
 spit-roasted brine-cured pork,
  269–71, *270*
 steamed salmon with warm
  lemon vinaigrette, 206
 the Vaison fishmonger's fresh
  tuna casserole, 218
 whole fish roasted in crust of sea
  salt, *212,* 213–14, *214*
 the winemaker's duck with olives
  and artichokes, *230,* 231–32
 see also Pasta
Maria's ginger shrimp, 196
Marie-Claude's Armagnac chèvre, 40
Mascaré, *24*
The mason's brine-cured black
 olives, *48,* 328–29
Mayonnaise:
 garlic (aïoli), *83,* 314
 garlic, saffron, and red pepper
  (rouille), 315
Meat, 249–71
 braising vs. stewing, 259
 daube of veal, wine, and green
  olives, 250–51
 dry cooking, 262
 fresh herb sauce for, 317
 herb roasting rack for, 227
 roasting tips for, 251
 see also Beef; Lamb; Pork
Meaty grilled mushrooms, 108–9
Meliani, Corine and Josiane, *133*
Meringues for month of May
 (*schaum torte*), *298,* 298–99
Milne, A. A., 140
Minchelli, Paul, 200
Mint(ed), 55
 crabmeat salad, 207
Mocenigo, Nagi, 201
Monday night spaghetti, 152
Monkfish bouillabaisse with aïoli,
 80, 81–82
Monkfish "carpaccio," 200–201
Monsieur Henny's eggplant gratin,
 120–21
Monsieur Henny's rabbit bouill-
 abaisse, 239–40
Monsieur Henny's three-beef daube,
 252, 253–54
More, Sheila and Julian, 32
Morley, Christopher, 156
Mostarda (fig and prune chutney),
 331
Mouret, Charles, 279
Mousse, chocolate-honey, 301

Müller, Dieter, 91
Mushrooms:
 grilled meaty, 108–9
 saungines, 108
Mustard, beef daube with herbs,
 white wine and, 258–59

Noodles, Catalan fried, 155
North African cuisine:
 harissa (spicy red pepper sauce),
  320
 preserved lemons, 319
Nutmeg, 35
Nyons olives, *50, 51,* 326

Oatmeal, 174
 biscuits, *172,* 173–74
Olive oil:
 basil, and garlic sauce (pistou),
  316
 brioche, Provençal (*pompe à
  l'huile*), *166,* 167–68
 from Les Baux, 317
 and Parmesan potato puree,
  creamy, 141
 spicy herb (*pili pili*), *312, 313*
Olives, black, *42, 44, 46,* 329
 Anne's goat cheese gratin, *20, 21*
 arugula, and Parmesan salad, *58,
  59*
 carrots Provençal, 132
 Chanteduc, *48, 51*
 green olives vs., 47
 harissa-seasoned, 47, *48*
 the mason's brine-cured, *48,*
  328–29
 de Nyons, *50, 51,* 326
 Rue de Lévis "caviar," 44
 salt-cured, 326–27
 storing, 47
 the winemaker's chicken with
  artichokes and, *230,* 231–32
Olives, green, *42, 46, 48*
 black olives vs., 47
 blanching, 251
 daube of veal, wine and, 250–51
 herbed, 49
 lemon-flecked, 46, *48*
 puttanesca, spaghetti with, 153
 storing, 47
 the winemaker's chicken with
  artichokes and, *230,* 231–32
Olive trees, utensils made from
 wood of, *33*
Onion(s), *102*
 caraway bread tart, *190, 191*
 garlic family soup, 103
 leaving skin on, for stock, 321

Parmesan gratin, 128–29
quiche, crustless, 34–35
red, braised, *106,* 130
Orange:
  liqueur, homemade ("44"), *336,*
    337
  zest, in Provençal penne, 161
Oregano, dried vs. fresh, 51
Osteria dell'Unione (Tresio), 241,
  331
Oven-roasted:
  leg of lamb (*gigot Provençal*), *266,*
    267–68
  tomatoes (pure tomato confit),
    118, 119
Oyster casserole, Walter's Thanksgiving, 219–20

Pacaud, Bernard, 124
Pancetta-wrapped cod, seared, 211
Pantry, 311–38
  aïoli (garlic mayonnaise), *83,* 314
  Chantal's bachelor's confiture,
    332, 333
  chicken stock, 322–23
  classic sugar syrup, 335
  double vinegar vinaigrette, 318
  "44" (homemade orange
    liqueur), *336, 337*
  fresh cherry wine, *334,* 335
  fresh herb sauce for meats, poul-
    try, fish, and vegetables, 317
  grapes in eau-de-vie, 338
  harissa (spicy red pepper sauce),
    320
  the mason's brine-cured black
    olives, *48,* 328–29
  mostarda (fig and prune chut-
    ney), 331
  pili pili (spicy herb oil), *312, 313*
  pistou (olive oil, basil, and garlic
    sauce), 316
  potager stock, 321
  preserved lemons, 319
  ras al hanout, 324
  raspberries in eau-de-vie, 338
  rouille (garlic, saffron, and red
    pepper mayonnaise), 315
  salt-cured anchovies, 330
  salt-cured black olives, 326–27
  tomato sauce, 325
Parchment:
  cooking with, 205
  sea bass in, with warm pistou,
    202, 203–4
Parmesan (Parmigiano-Reggiano):
  artichoke, and black truffle soup,
    94–95

and arugula salad, *58,* 59
braised and gratinéed fennel,
  122–23
celery gratin, 131
celery root lasagne, 124–25
and celery salad, 67
Chanteduc winter salad, 56
creamy semolina with bay leaf
  and, 243
Monsieur Henny's eggplant
  gratin, 120–21
onion gratin, 128–29
pepper loaf, golden, 175
potato and olive oil puree,
  creamy, 141
sliced artichoke and prosciutto
  salad, 76
Parsley, 55, 272
Parsnips, in winter pistou, 97
Passard, Alain, 54, 128, 143, 197, 320
Pasta, 145–63
  with artichoke and basil ragout,
    110
  Catalan fried noodles, 155
  Checchino dal 1887's spaghetti
    alla carbonara, 160
  fettucine with Roquefort, lemon
    zest, and rosemary, 147
  fusili with sausage, fennel, and
    red wine, *148,* 148–49
  Hervé's truffle butter, 158–59
  individual zucchini lasagne with
    spicy pizza sauce, 154
  Monday night spaghetti, 152
  Patricia's spaghetti with clams,
    162–63
  with Patricia's speedy ratatouille,
    116
  penne "risotto," 150–51
  Provençal penne, 161
  spaghetti with green olive put-
    tanesca, 153
  spicy red pepper spaghetti,
    156–57
  with tuna tapenade, 43
  water drained from, as source of
    starch, 157
Pastry:
  almond crust, 281, 282
  JR's shrimp with basil, 26–27
  lemon, shell, 296
Patricia's spaghetti with clams,
  162–63
Patricia's speedy ratatouille, 116
Pea(s):
  chilled cream of, soup, 93
  June vegetable ragout with herb
    garden pistou, 115

Peach(es), 309
  ice cream, chunky, 309
Pear(s), 303, *303*
  determining ripeness of, 303
  French café salad, 71
  gingered confit of apples and,
    302
  and watercress salad, 66
Pear trees, 303
Pecorino, in Checchino dal 1887's
  spaghetti alla carbonara, 160
Penne:
  Provençal, 161
  "risotto," 150–51
Pepper, red, *III*
  garlic, and saffron mayonnaise
    (rouille), 315
  sauce, spicy (*harissa*), 320
  spaghetti, spicy, 156–57
Pepper(corns), 272
  Parmesan loaf, golden, 175
Petite friture (fried baby fish),
  209–10, *210*
Picnic fare:
  poulet aux fines herbes (butter-
    roasted herbed chicken), *222,*
    222–24
  yogurt green bean salad, 65
Picodon de Dieulefit, 24
Pile ou Face (Paris), 300
Pili pili (spicy herb oil), *312, 313*
Pina's braised rabbit, 241–42
Pine nut(s):
  fresh cheese with honey and,
    306
  rolls, 169
Pistou (olive oil, basil, and garlic
  sauce), 316
  herb garden, June vegetable
    ragout with, 115
  warm, sea bass in parchment
    with, *202,* 203–4
Pistou (soup):
  summer, *84,* 85–87, *86*
  winter, 97
Pizza:
  braised red onions as topping for,
    106, 130
  bread dough for, 185
  meaty grilled mushrooms as top-
    ping for, 108–9
  sauce, spicy, individual zucchini
    lasagne with, 154
La Poissonnerie des Voconces (Vaison-la-Romaine), 209
Polenta, 179
  caraway corn-rye bread, 188–89
  and wheat bread, crusty, 178–79

Pompe à l'huile (Provençal olive oil brioche), *166,* 167–68
Poquet, Christine, *307*
Pork:
    brine-cured, spit-roasted, 269–71, *270*
    prosciutto and sliced artichoke salad, 76
Poron, Hervé, 158–59
Porquerolles Island toasted almonds, 30
Potage:
    Maggie's vegetable, 100
    origin and meaning of word, 101
Potager stock, 321
Potato(es):
    boiling vs. steaming, 141
    fake *frites,* 137
    garlic family soup, 103
    gratin dauphinois, *138,* 139
    JR's gratin dauphinois, 140
    leftover, tossed in dressing, 136
    leg of lamb on bed of artichokes, herbs and, 264–65
    Maggie's vegetable potage, 100
    pairing herbs with, 55
    Parmesan, and olive oil puree, creamy, 141
    roasted in sea salt, 135
    smashed, 136
    types of, 137
    winter pistou, 97
Pots de crème, lemon, 297
Poulet aux fines herbes (butter-roasted herbed chicken), *222,* 222–24
Poultry, 221–35
    duck with lime and honey, 233–35
    French country guinea hen and cabbage, 225
    fresh herb sauce for, 317
    herb roasting rack for, 227
    trimmings, making sauce with, 235
    trussing, 235
    the winemaker's duck with olives and artichokes, *230,* 231–32
    see also Chicken
Preserved lemons, *48,* 319
    Chanteduc rabbit with garlic and, *244,* 245–46
Prosciutto and sliced artichoke salad, 76
Proust, Marcel, 305
Provençal cuisine:
    aïoli (garlic mayonnaise), *83,* 314
    apricot-honey-almond tart, *280,* 281–82

la broufade (beef and white wine daube from Arles), 256–57
cachat (cheese spread), 41
carrots, 132
croquettes (honey-almond cookies), 284–85
gigot (oven-roasted leg of lamb), *266,* 267–68
Maggie's vegetable potage, 100
the mason's brine-cured black olives, *48,* 328–29
monkfish bouillabaisse with aïoli, *80,* 81–82
Monsieur Henny's three-beef daube, *252,* 253–54
penne, 161
pistou (olive oil, basil, and garlic sauce), 316
pompe à l'huile (olive oil brioche), *166,* 167–68
roast tomatoes, *112,* 113
rouille (garlic, saffron, and red pepper mayonnaise), 315
salt-cured black olives, 326–27
summer pistou, *84,* 85–87, *86*
winter pistou, 97
Prune and fig chutney, 331
Purees:
    basil, 26
    creamy olive oil and Parmesan potato, 141
    turnip and cumin, 117
Pure tomato confit (oven-roasted tomatoes), *118,* 119
Puttanesca, green olive, spaghetti with, 153

Quail, cumin-rubbed grilled, 236–37
Quiche, crustless onion, 34–35

Rabbit:
    bouillabaisse, Monsieur Henny's, 239–40
    braised, Pina's, 241–42
    cooking tip for, 240
    cutting up, 242
    with garlic and preserved lemons, Chanteduc, *244,* 245–46
Radishes, *108*
Ragouts:
    artichoke and basil, 110
    June vegetable, with herb garden pistou, 115
    origin and use of word, 111
Raisin, fig, apricot, and walnut rye, *182,* 183–84
Ras al hanout, 324

Raspberry(ies):
    in eau-de-vie, 338
    tart, *280,* 282
Ratatouille, Patricia's speedy, 116
Red and green salad, 62–63
Red snapper, 205
Red wine, fusili with sausage, fennel and, *148,* 148–49
Red wine vinegar, spicy herb, 313
Reynaud, Yves, 13, 245
Rice:
    basmati, 273
    brown, from the Camargue, 272
    storing, 272
Richardson, Rosamond, 209
Rita's rye, 186–87
Roast(ed):
    butter-, herbed chicken (*poulet aux fines herbes*), *222,* 222–24
    city steak, 255
    leg of lamb on bed of artichokes, potatoes, and herbs, 264–65
    meat, tips for, 251
    oven-, leg of lamb (*gigot Provençal*), *266,* 267–69
    oven-, tomatoes (pure tomato confit), *118,* 119
    potatoes, in sea salt, 135
    shallots, tender, 133
    spit-, brine-cured pork, 269–71, *270*
    tomatoes, Provençal, *112,* 113
    tomato soup with fresh herbs, 88
    whole fish in crust of sea salt, *212,* 213–14, *214*
Robuchon, Joël, 15, 26, 29, 57, 89, 109, 140, 222, 320
Rolls:
    bread dough for, 185
    pine nut, 169
Root-vegetable tops, in the true salad fan's salad, 57
Roquefort, 39
    dip, 39
    fettucine with lemon zest, rosemary and, 147
    French café salad, 71
    salad of walnuts, Belgian endive, lamb's lettuce and, *68,* 69
Rosemary, *102,* 272
    fettucine with Roquefort, lemon zest and, 147
Rouille (garlic, saffron, and red pepper mayonnaise), 315
Rue de Lévis "caviar," 44
Ruskin, John, 250

Rye:
    corn bread, caraway, 188–89
    fig, apricot, walnut, and raisin, *182, 183–84*
    Rita's, 186–87
    walnut, and currant loaf, 180–81

Saffron, garlic, and red pepper mayonnaise (rouille), 315
Sage, 55
Saint-Hubert (Entrechaux), 279
St. Marcellin cow's milk cheese, in truffle "sandwich," *158*
Salad dressings, 62
    see also Vinaigrettes
Salads, 53–77
    all-star herb, 54
    arugula and Parmesan, *58, 59*
    Chanteduc winter, 56
    cheesemaker's, 75
    Daniel's chickpea, 72–73
    French café, 71
    grated beet, 61
    minted crabmeat, 207
    Parmesan and celery, 67
    pear and watercress, 66
    plates for, 56
    proper tools for tossing, 57
    red and green, 62–63
    of Roquefort, walnuts, Belgian endive, and lamb's lettuce, *68, 69*
    Saturday beef, 74
    sliced artichoke and prosciutto, 76
    tarragon green bean, 64
    Toutoune's winter, 70
    the true salad fan's, 57
    yogurt green bean, 65
Salmon, 205
    steamed, with warm lemon vinaigrette, 206
Salt:
    -cured anchovies, 330
    -cured black olives, 326–27
    sea, 263
    sea, potatoes roasted in, 135
    sea, whole fish roasted in crust of, *212, 213–14, 214*
Saturday beef salad, 74
Sauces:
    aïoli (garlic mayonnaise), *83,* 314
    basil puree, 26
    fresh herb, for meats, poultry, fish, and vegetables, 317
    olive oil, basil, and garlic (pistou), 316
    with poultry trimmings, 235

rouille (garlic, saffron, and red pepper mayonnaise), 315
    spicy red pepper (*harissa*), 320
    tomato, 325
    see also Vinaigrettes
Sauce verte (fresh herb sauce for meats, poultry, fish, and vegetables), 317
Sausage(s), *44*
    fusili with fennel, red wine and, *148,* 148–49
Savory, 73
Scallop seviche, ginger and lime, 215
Schaum torte (meringues for month of May), *298,* 298–99
Scrubbed toast, 31
Sea bass, 205
    in parchment with warm pistou, *202,* 203–4
The Seafood Restaurant (Padstow, Cornwall), 175
Seared pancetta-wrapped cod, 211
Sea salt, 263
    potatoes roasted in, 135
    whole fish roasted in crust of, *212, 213–14, 214*
Sel gris de Guérande, 263
Semolina, 179
    creamy, with bay leaf and Parmesan, 243
Sesame, flax and sunflower seed bread, 176–77
Seviche, 215
    ginger and lime scallop, 215
Shallots, 37, *102*
    chicken with lemon, thyme and, 228–29
    garlic family soup, 103
    tender roasted, 133
Shapiro, Maggie, 100, 132
Sheep's milk cheese, 24
    Lou Canestéou's cheese chips, 25
Sheila and Julian's quick foie gras, 32–33
Shellfish, 195
    ginger and lime scallop seviche, 215
    JR's shrimp with basil, 26–27
    Maria's ginger shrimp, 196
    minted crabmeat salad, 207
    Patricia's spaghetti with clams, 162–63
    sherry and ginger lobster, *197,* 197–99
    Walter's Thanksgiving oyster casserole, 219–20

Sherry and ginger lobster, *197,* 197–99
Sherry vinegar, chicken with tarragon and, 226–27
Shrimp, 199
    with basil, JR's, 26–27
    Maria's ginger, 196
    removing vein from, 199
Side dishes:
    all-star herb salad, 54
    artichoke and basil ragout, 110
    Barcelona grilled artichokes, *106,* 107
    basmati rice, 273
    braised and gratinéed fennel, 122–23
    braised asparagus, *142,* 143
    braised red onions, *106,* 130
    brown rice from the Camargue, 272
    Catalan fried noodles, 155
    celery-Parmesan gratin, 131
    couscous my way, 247
    creamy olive oil and Parmesan potato puree, 141
    creamy semolina with bay leaf and Parmesan, 243
    Daniel's chickpea salad, 72–73
    fake *frites,* 137
    fresh beans with garlic and herbs, 127
    grated beet salad, 61
    gratin dauphinois, *138,* 139
    JR's gratin dauphinois, 140
    Monsieur Henny's eggplant gratin, 120–21
    onion-Parmesan gratin, 128–29
    Patricia's speedy ratatouille, 116
    potatoes roasted in sea salt, 135
    Provençal roast tomatoes, *112,* 113
    red and green salad, 62–63
    smashed potatoes, 136
    tarragon green been salad, 64
    tender roasted shallots, 133
    the true salad fan's salad, 57
    turnip and cumin puree, 117
    Walter's Thanksgiving oyster casserole, 219–20
    yogurt green bean salad, 65
Skate, 205
Skimmers, keeping food from sticking to, 27
Sliced artichoke and prosciutto salad, 76
Smashed potatoes, 136
Smoked trout tartare, 22

Snacks:
  cachat (Provençal cheese spread), 41
  Porquerolles Island toasted almonds, 30
  scrubbed toast, 31
Sole, 205
Sorrel soup, amazing, *90, 91*
Soups, 79–103
  amazing sorrel, *90, 91*
  artichoke, Parmesan, and black truffle, 94–95
  caramelized fennel, 98
  chilled cream of pea, 93
  cold tomato, with basil, 92
  curried cauliflower, 89
  garlic family, 103
  Maggie's vegetable potage, 100
  monkfish bouillabaisse with aïoli, *80,* 81–82
  origin and meaning of word, 101
  quick chicken-lemon, 99
  roasted tomato, with fresh herbs, 88
  summer pistou, *84, 85–87, 86*
  winter pistou, 97
Spaghetti:
  alla carbonara, Checchino dal 1887's, 160
  with clams, Patricia's, 162–63
  with green olive puttanesca, 153
  Monday night, 152
  spicy red pepper, 156–57
Spanish cuisine:
  Barcelona grilled artichokes, *106,* 107
  see also Catalan cuisine
Spices:
  bouquet garni, 272
  ras al hanout, 324
Spicy:
  herb oil (*pili pili*), *312, 313*
  lamb curry with yogurt and apples, 260–61
  red pepper sauce (*harissa*), 320
  red pepper spaghetti, 156–57
Spit-roasted brine-cured pork, 269–71, *270*
Spreads:
  herb cheese Lyonnais, 36
  Marie-Claude's Armagnac chèvre, 40
  Provençal cheese (*cachat*), 41
  Rue de Lévis "caviar," 44
  tuna tapenade, 43
Squash:
  winter, in winter pistou, 97
  see also Zucchini

Starch, water drained from pasta as source of, 157
Steak, city, 255
Steamed salmon with warm lemon vinaigrette, 206
Stein, Richard, 175
Stews:
  braises vs., 259
  monkfish bouillabaisse with aïoli, *80,* 81–82
  Monsieur Henny's rabbit bouillabaisse, 239–40
  see also Daubes
Stocks:
  blanching chicken for, 323
  chicken, 322–23
  leaving skin on onions for, 321
  potager, 321
  straining, 323
  tips for, 323
Strawberries, in *schaum torte* (meringues for month of May), *298,* 298–99
Sugar:
  substituting honey for, 285
  syrup, classic, 333
Summer pistou, *84, 85–87, 86*
Sunflower seed, sesame, and flax bread, 176–77
Swiss cheese, *see* Gruyère
Syrup, classic sugar, 335

Tapenades, *42*
  tuna, 43
Tarragon, 55
  chicken with sherry vinegar and, 226–27
  green bean salad, 64
Tarts:
  almond crust for, 281, 282
  apricot-honey-almond, *280,* 281–82
  bread, onion caraway, *190,* 191
  bread dough for, 185
  cherry-almond, *286,* 287–88
  fig, 281, *282*
  lemon lover's, 295
  lemon pastry shell for, 296
  raspberry, *280, 282*
Tender roasted shallots, 133
Thanksgiving oyster casserole, Walter's, 219–20
Three-beef daube, Monsieur Henny's, *252,* 253–54
Thyme, *102,* 229, 272
  chicken with shallots, lemon and, 228–29
  lemon lamb chops, 262–63

Till, Antonia, 297
Toasted almonds, Porquerolles Island, 30
Toasts:
  anchovy-garlic crisps, 45
  scrubbed, 31
Tomato(es), *111*
  clafoutis, 38
  confit, pure (oven-roasted tomatoes), *118,* 119
  June vegetable ragout with herb garden pistou, 115
  pairing herbs with, 55
  Patricia's speedy ratatouille, 116
  peeling, 119
  red and green salad, 62–63
  roast, Provençal, *112,* 113
  roasted, soup with fresh herbs, 88
  sauce, 325
  scrubbed toast, 31
  soup with basil, cold, 92
Toutoune's winter salad, 70
Trattoria Checchino dal 1887 (Rome), 160
Tricart, Colette, 328
Tricart, Jean-Claude, 14, 328
Troisgros, Jean and Pierre, 117
Trout, smoked, tartare, 22
The true salad fan's salad, 57
Truffle(s):
  black, *95*
  black, artichoke, and Parmesan soup, 94–95
  butter pasta, Hervé's, 158–59
  infusing eggs with essence of, 159, *159*
  "sandwich," *158*
Trussing, 235
Tuna, 205
  daube, Catalan, 216–17
  fresh, casserole, the Vaison fishmonger's, 218
  tapenade, 43
Turbot, 205
Turnip(s):
  and cumin puree, 117
  Maggie's vegetable potage, 100
  winter pistou, 97

Udron, Claude, 300

Les Vaccarès (Arles), 256
The Vaison fishmonger's fresh tuna casserole, 218
Vaison-la-Romaine, market in, *42, 109, 111, 187, 193, 194, 201, 307*
Vanilla-bean ice cream with fresh cherries, 289

Veal, daube of wine, green olives and, 250–51
Vegetable(s), 105–43
    artichoke and basil ragout, 110
    Barcelona grilled artichokes, *106*, 107
    braised and gratinéed fennel, 122–23
    braised asparagus, *142*, 143
    braised red onions, *106*, 130
    braised whole garlic, *106*, 130
    carrots Provençal, 132
    celery-Parmesan gratin, 131
    celery root lasagne, 124–25
    creamy olive oil and Parmesan potato puree, 141
    fake *frites*, 137
    fresh beans with garlic and herbs, 127
    fresh herb sauce for, 317
    gratin dauphinois, *138*, 139
    JR's gratin dauphinois, 140
    June, ragout with herb garden pistou, 115
    meaty grilled mushrooms, 108–9
    Monsieur Henny's eggplant gratin, 120–21
    onion-Parmesan gratin, 128–29
    pairing herbs with, 55
    Patricia's speedy ratatouille, 116
    potage, Maggie's, 100
    potatoes roasted in sea salt, 135
    Provençal roast tomatoes, *112*, 113
    pure tomato confit (oven-roasted tomatoes), *118*, 119
    smashed potatoes, 136
    summer pistou, *84*, 85–87, *86*
    tender roasted shallots, 133
    turnip and cumin puree, 117
    winter pistou, 97
Verbena, *see* Lemon verbena
Vinaigrettes, 61, 72, 73
    double vinegar, 318
    ratios for, 318
    temporary nature of emulsion in, 318
    warm lemon, steamed salmon with, 206
Vinegar:
    double, vinaigrette, 318
    red wine, spicy herb, 313
    sherry, chicken with tarragon and, 226–27
Viviani, Jean-Claude, 13

Walnut(s):
    fig, apricot, and raisin rye, *182*, 183–84
    French café salad, 71
    rye, and currant loaf, 180–81
    salad of Roquefort, Belgian endive, lamb's lettuce and, *68*, 69
Walter's Thanksgiving oyster casserole, 219–20
Warner, Charles Dudley, 34
Watercress and pear salad, 66
Waugh, Evelyn, 170
Wheat and polenta bread, crusty, 178–79
White wine:
    baked fruit and honey with Beaumes de Venise, 308
    and beef daube from Arles (*la broufade*), 256–57
    beef daube with mustard, herbs and, 258–59
    daube of veal, green olives and, 250–51
Wilde, Oscar, 241
Wine:
    fresh cherry, *334*, 335
    red, fusili with sausage, fennel and, *148*, 148–49
    see also White wine
The winemaker's duck with olives and artichokes, *230*, 231–32
Winemaker's grape cake, 277–78
Winkler, Heinz, 147
Winter:
    pistou, 97
    salad, Chanteduc, 56
    salad, Toutoune's, 70
Wolfe, Thomas, 262

Xenophanes, 183

Yogurt:
    green bean salad, 65
    spicy lamb curry with apples and, 260–61

Zabar, Eli, 304
Zucchini, *111*
    lasagne with spicy pizza sauce, individual, 154
    Maggie's vegetable potage, 100
    Patricia's speedy ratatouille, 116
    summer pistou, *84*, 85–87, *86*
Zucchini blossoms, curried, *28*, 28–29

ABOUT THE AUTHOR

PATRICIA WELLS began her journalistic career at the *Washington Post* in the 1970s, where she worked as a copy editor and art critic. She moved to the *New York Times* in 1976, where she became a food reporter on the newly created "Living Section." In 1980, she moved to Paris with her journalist husband, Walter, for what they thought would be a two-year stint at the *International Herald Tribune.* Their love of France grew, and soon they knew they had come to the point of no return. Patricia went to Paris without a word of French but a hope of writing the sort of food guide that did not exist. After years of trying to convince publishers that the idea would sell, her *Food Lover's Guide to Paris* was published to rave reviews in 1984. Soon Patricia was packing her bags for points north, south, east, and west, exploring the food, vineyards, markets, artisans, and restaurateurs of France. When *The Food Lover's Guide to France* was published in 1987, the French decided to call Patricia their own, and made her restaurant critic of the newsweekly *L'Express.* She became the only female and only foreigner to have ever held that post. Recipes gathered on her tour de France became the inspiration for the classic *Bistro Cooking,* published in 1989 and translated into seven languages. The same year, the French government honored her for contributions to French culture, awarding her the coveted Chevalier de l'Ordre des Arts et des Lettres. Her respect and admiration for French chef Joël Robuchon turned into a four-year project, out of which came *Simply French,* a book that is still among France's top-selling cookbooks. An assignment in Italy and a series of inspirational meals at casual eateries led to a two-year quest for the best of modern-day Italian trattoria fare, and became her bestselling *Patricia Wells' Trattoria,* published in 1993 and now available in six languages. During all this, Patricia nurtured another passion—Chanteduc—the farmhouse in Provence she and Walter acquired in 1984. Chanteduc soon became a refuge, a haven for the couple and their friends, as well as a dream to be pampered. Year in and year out, they have restored, rebuilt, and refurbished the old farmhouse, bringing in their own winemaker and establishing their own vineyard. *Patricia Wells at Home in Provence* is the culmination of more than a decade of life in Provence, where neighbors, merchants, friends, and family have inspired a cuisine that is rich with the textures, flavors, color, and aroma of their adopted land.

ABOUT THE PHOTOGRAPHER

After receiving his Master's degree in photography from a Swiss university in 1948, Robert Fréson emigrated from his native Belgium to the United States. For the next thirteen years, he worked with Irving Penn, and in 1962 Fréson launched himself as a photojournalist, freelancing for magazines in the United States and Europe including *Vogue, Esquire, National Geographic,* and more than twenty-five years for the London *Sunday Times Magazine.* A series of photographic articles on the regional gastronomy of France, first published over several weeks in *Marie-Claire* and later in the London *Sunday Times Magazine,* culminated in the publication of his first book, *The Taste of France.* With more than 150,000 copies in print, the book is still available in the United States and all over the world, and has won several awards, including the Glenfiddich Award and the Prix Littéraire des Relais Gourmands. Fréson has found both success and joy in food photography, illuminating the wonder of other people's work by recording it in its natural surroundings where their talent and the beauty of their creations are most clearly revealed.